THE NEW WEALTH WAY

UNLOCK THE POWER OF COMPOUNDING

PETE WARGENT

Published by:
Wilkinson Publishing Pty Ltd
ACN 006 042 173
Level 4, 2 Collins Street
Melbourne, Vic 3000
Ph: 03 9654 5446
www.wilkinsonpublishing.com.au

National Library of Australia Cataloguing-in-Publication entry

Creator: Wargent, Peter, author.

Title: The new wealth way : Unlock the power of Compounding / Pete Wargent.

ISBN: 9781923259126 (paperback)

Subjects: Finance, Personal--Australia.
        Saving and investment--Australia.
        Wealth--Australia.
        Success.
        Self-realization.

Design by Spike Creative Pty Ltd
Ph: (03) 9427 9500
spikecreative.com.au

DONATION

10 per cent of the author's proceeds will be donated to the McGrath Foundation in aid of furthering breast cancer research and support.

ABOUT THE AUTHOR

Pete Wargent is a finance and investment expert and one of Australia's most highly respected financial and housing market analysts with regular appearances on Australian and International television, radio, online, and in print media.

He is founder of **Next Level Wealth Coaching** where he runs a 1to1 coaching program for investors enabling them to maximise their financial potential, and also the co-founder of boutique real estate buyer's agent **AllenWargent Property Buyers**.

Pete trained as a chartered accountant in London and has worked for top accounting institutions and listed companies. He also holds a range of other financial qualifications, including diplomas in Financial Planning and Applied Corporate Governance.

Pete quit his full-time job at the age of 33, having achieved financial freedom through investing in shares, index funds, and investment properties. He is a keen blogger and posts his thoughts on finance, investment, the markets and more daily at petewargent.blogspot.com, which has over three million hits to date.

Pete is also the co-host of *The Australian Property Podcast*, Australia's most trusted property podcast, and is the author of seven previous books on personal finance, investing, and property, including *Get a Financial Grip: A simple plan for financial freedom*, which was rated in the Top 10 Finance books of 2012 by *Money* magazine and Dymocks.

An avid traveller & cricket tragic, Pete and his family split their time between living on Australia's Sunshine Coast and rural England.

Find out more at **petewargent.com**.

Also by Pete Wargent

Get a Financial Grip: A simple plan for financial freedom (Big Sky Publishing, Sydney, 2012). Rated in the Top 10 Finance books of 2012 by Money magazine and Dymocks.

Four Green Houses and a Red Hotel: New strategies for creating wealth through property (Big Sky Publishing, Sydney, 2013)

Take a Financial Leap: The 3 golden rules for financial and life success (Big Sky Publishing, Sydney, 2015)

The Wealth Way: Unlock the power of compounding (Wilkinson Publishing, Melbourne 2017)

Wealth Ways for the Young: What the rich are teaching their kids about money today (Wilkinson Publishing, Melbourne, 2019)

Low Rates High Returns: Timeless investment principles the low-risk way with Stephen Moriarty (Wilkinson Publishing, Melbourne, 2020).

The Buy Right Approach to Property Investing with Cate Bakos (Major Street Publishing, Melbourne, 2024).

This is a sensible, down-to-earth, well-written book about building wealth. Pete's ideas are not only easy to understand, they have the added advantage of being right: there's no doubt that the best and safest way to build wealth is to save, invest patiently, and let the power of compounding do the work.

Perhaps the most surprising thing is how hard that is to do, which is why books like this are so important.

Alan Kohler, ABC News and ABC Inside Business, and former editor-in-chief of Business Spectator and Eureka Report

Pete Wargent shines with his sensible, measured and insightful research which stands out amid the grandstanding and sensationalist rhetoric that is an ever-growing part of mainstream economic commentary.

At a time when markets are volatile and property markets fickle, Pete provides analysis to help all investors – big and small. His analysis of the housing market is a highlight and is a must read for all.

Stephen Koukoulas, leading global economist, Managing Director of Market Economics, and former Senior Economic Advisor to Prime Minister Gillard

In his latest book The Wealth Way, Pete Wargent explains why it is never too late to ta ke control of your personal finances by providing a road map to help readers get the wealth they want. If you want to get ahead financially you can't afford not to know the information in these pages.

After working with many successful business people, entrepreneurs and investors I've isolated one common factor – they all have mentors. I recommend you read this book and let Pete be your financial mentor.

Michael Yardney, number one best-selling author and once again voted Australia's leading expert wealth creation through property

There is no shortage of people willing to give advice on investing, however Pete Wargent is one of the best, cutting through the noise and providing sensible and valuable advice. While many base their advice purely on their own experiences, Pete uses both his background, as well as his careful analysis of data, providing a unique perspective on the best way to maximise your income.

Personally, I follow Pete's commentary closely and enjoy his take on economic, financial and political events in Australia and overseas.

Nerida Conisbee, Chief Economist, REA Group

CONTENTS

QUITTING CORPORATE LIFE

I'll never forget it. Having quit our corporate jobs, in 2011 my wife Heather and I set off from sunny Sydney in our campervan to spend a year driving the 'Big Lap' of Australia, then another couple of months doing a round-the-world voyage on a cruise ship from Sydney to Southampton. We'd originally started investing in property and shares as a route out of the rat race, as we had been working very long hours in well-paid but equally stressful financial services management roles.

While Heather is better at switching off, I tend to get restless quite easily, and pretty much by the time we'd reached Ettalong Beach I had decided I needed a new project, aside from trading shares (which was quite annoying for Heather, as I always wanted to be online between 10am and 4pm, while she understandably wanted to visit Australia's amazing natural parks, beaches, and other sights).

"I'm going to write a book" I said, brandishing my tiny Netbook laptop. "So many of the finance books out there are rubbish, I can easily do better!" I confidently exclaimed. Heather's reaction was unsurprisingly lukewarm. After all, how many people *say* they're going to author a book but then give up after a week or two? It must be an awful lot.

I wasn't as confident about the project as it may sound. Although we'd experienced success as investors and I knew I could write well, like many British-born types, I suffered from a reticence to put my name out there, I wasn't at all great at self-promotion, and worried about what my friends, family, and former work colleagues might say. I needn't have bothered as many of them had their say anyway!

Heather's smart advice was to draft the book first and worry about all that later. And so, I started writing, aiming to knock over 3,000 to 5,000 words per day with a gallon of coffee to hand, until eventually I had a 100,000-word manuscript. Then I spent the next few months editing it, re-editing it, and touching it up, to make sure I got just the right balance of humour, self-deprecation (I don't do this quite so much these days), and all the genuinely valuable information I had learned from my years in finance and as an investor. I'd read hundreds of books on investing over the years, but most of them were more focused on the US or UK rather than Australia, and thus were sometimes a little less useful than they might otherwise have been. I wanted to put this right based upon my own experience as an investor in Australia.

Eventually, Heather couldn't take all my editing and tweaking any longer and implored me to find a publisher. I was less keen, fearing secretly everything from rejection to ridicule, but eventually I sent the manuscript off to twelve publishers. Eventually I signed up with a publisher in Sydney, and by 2012, the book I had envisaged was on the shelves, and now I have written and published no fewer than eight books.

LIFE DELIVERS INEVITABLE SETBACKS, AND YET...

Here's one of the most remarkable statistics I have ever heard. One of the world's greatest ever investors, Warren Buffett of Berkshire Hathaway, had a net worth at around US$3 billion at the traditional retirement date of 65. Even though that's obviously a huge sum of money, if he'd quit investing then you'd quite likely never have heard of him. As I sit here and type today, Buffett is 93 years of age and has a net worth of around US$138 billion, a figure which will quite likely have compounded away to a much higher figure by the time you read this paragraph.

Here is the essence of *The Wealth Way* in a single anecdote. It's about compound growth and unlocking its incredible power to multiply your results over time. Over the long run, the investment conglomerate Berkshire Hathaway has generated returns of around 20 per cent per annum, but as the size of the funds invested have swelled dramatically, in recent decades Buffett has 'only' been increasing his net worth by around 13 per cent per annum. Still, look at what that's done to his net worth. One of his biggest secrets to success has been generating consistently strong returns for around 8 decades. He just keeps going, and going, and going! Note how the biggest results come later in the journey. In fact, around an incredible 98 per cent of Buffett's net worth has been generated after the traditional retirement date. What an arresting thought! Can you potentially harness similar powers? Guess what? You can!

Looking back over the 13 years since I wrote my first book, mine and Heather's net worth has increased fivefold. OK, so it's not quite the

50-times increase that Buffett's seen, but it's still a hell of a great result considering we've spent much time over the past dozen years travelling around Australia, south-east Asia, Europe, and more lately America. We still work hard on our businesses, but in more symbiotic balance with living and experiencing life and enjoying the journey.

If this comes across as arrogant or as though the journey was all plain sailing for us, rest assured that it most certainly hasn't been! Variously we've had to deal with family funerals, a distressingly complicated pregnancy, the joyous birth of two children, several business ideas and ventures which have completely flopped, and a decade-long struggle to get planning permission to build on one of our blocks of land. Have you ever seen that British TV show called *Grand Designs*, where years and years into a project the participants are asked about how things are going, and they're lamenting whether they should ever have started with the wretched project in the first place? Yep, that's been a bit like our experience of the UK planning approvals system too! There have been plenty of difficulties over the past decade, and no doubt the next decade will bring some challenges too. That's just the way it goes. But you can keep compounding the results all the while regardless.

Charlie Munger, Warren Buffett's sidekick and legendary billionaire investor of Berkshire Hathaway, recently passed, once said that it's iron-clad law of life that all of us will incur setbacks. And Munger should know, having experienced a personal family tragedy along the way. Despite everything the world threw at him, Munger remained rational about his finances to the very end, generating billions in wealth, through investments in just a handful of successful businesses.

The biggest change in mine and Heather's lives over the past decade has been having kids. Anyone who's a parent will know exactly what I mean by that! It's been hectic at times, variously juggling home-schooling, long-haul travel, and living in two countries. A few years ago, I authored a book called *Wealth Ways for the Young* to discuss what the wealthy are teaching their kids today, and now the challenge is for us to instil these principles ourselves. As I write this, we're just allocating some of our self-managed superannuation fund for our kids to help invest for us. Let's hope they remember what I've taught them!

WHAT'S CHANGED... AND WHAT HASN'T CHANGED?

What's changed and what hasn't changed since I wrote my first book? In some ways, the principles of how to build wealth successfully never change. If you watch a few YouTube videos of Jim Rohn, American entrepreneur and author, from decades ago you'll discover so many nuggets of truth and wisdom. "Work harder on yourself than you do on your job" was one nugget I have always tried to adhere to.

When I wrote my first book in 2011, the engineering construction phase of Australia's massive mining boom was in full swing. Then within a year or two we were coming down the other side and the economy and mining sector slowed. More recently, we've had an echo-boom in the resources sector, with enormous global demand for commodities sending Australia's terms of trade soaring again. Investments in the mining sector since 2009 have performed very well, but it's been a rollercoaster journey at times, that's for sure!

It wasn't so clear in 2011, but as interest rates fell and investors from the Chinese mainland began to look for ways to get capital out of China, there was a huge and unprecedented boom in high-rise apartment construction in Sydney, inner-city Melbourne, and inner-city Brisbane, as well as in parts of Perth, the Gold Coast, and elsewhere. There'd never been anything quite like it before in Australia and the overbuilding saw unit prices and rents decline temporarily. Moving onto 2024, post-pandemic, and Australia now has the lowest rental vacancies rate on record, and a chronic shortage of properties, sending unit prices in south-east Queensland rocketing higher. While it might seem highly unlikely now, it wouldn't at all surprise me if in 5 years from now we're talking about another construction boom and supply overhang. These are the market cycles, but as construction wages, materials prices, land prices, and the Aussie city populations increase, the long-term results continue to be strong for investors.

After 2011, interest rates were on a long, slow march to zero, and they did eventually get there during the pandemic, lockdowns, and international border closures of 2020. This unsurprisingly teed off an orgy of speculation as investors desperately sought a return on their capital and a way to hedge against soaring inflation. The subsequent spike in inflation and interest rates came unexpectedly, but as I've always said, you need to expect the unexpected. If you're going to follow Buffett's path of compounding your wealth for decades, you'll see almost everything eventually High interest rates, low interest rates, high inflation, low inflation or deflation, booms, busts, recessions, pandemics, Black Swan events, and more!

When I wrote my first book in 2011, exchange-traded funds (ETFs) in the stock market were becoming popular, but since then their popularity has absolutely exploded!

4 TYPES OF WEALTH

What is wealth, you might justifiably ask? History is littered with the names of billionaires and wildly wealthy individuals that suffered from sadness, personal tragedy, illness, or depression. While it may be hard for most of us to empathize with the super-wealthy, this alone is compelling evidence that success and happiness should be measured in more than solely financial terms. The extreme level of competition for high achievers can become intensely pressurised and wearying, while the constant comparisons with others can be anxiety-inducing. And, of course, total dedication to a career or running a business can leave precious little time for the simpler things in life…or indeed anything else!

In other words, wealth is a state of mind, not just a bank balance. We tend to associate wealth with financial abundance, and this is one obvious measure of the term. But another form of wealth is social status, or a sense of standing. We all like to have a role for ourselves in life, and having a sense of purpose is important to us (at the extreme end of this spectrum some will even become martyrs for their cause).

Less carefully considered is that in the hectic modern world time freedom is an increasingly precious commodity. And, as we are often reminded each time we're feeling indisposed or ill, all the monetary wealth in the world is of limited use if we don't have our health, both physically and mentally.

4 TYPES OF WEALTH

1. Financial	**2. Social**
3. Time	**4. Physical**

There's a potential trap here, then, being that an excessive focus on a career, occupation, or business that bestows you the first two types of wealth – financial and social standing – might also rob you of your time and even your physical wellbeing. Aside from being mindful of our time and physical health, what else can we do? Here are three key thoughts:

(i) Understand wealth – the famous author on success Napoleon Hill suggested that you need to understand that there are these multiple forms wealth before you can truly achieve it;

(ii) Know your values – Spiritual values outweigh financial wealth, with many of the happiest, purposeful, or most influential characters in history not being rich in the traditional sense of the word; and

(iii) Be optimistic & hopeful – the world can sure be a snarky and sceptical place these days! Yet a positive mental outlook is one of the most valuable forms of wealth there is. Getting on with people harmoniously tends to help.

As the motivational speaker Denis Waitley said: 'Time and health are two precious assets we don't recognise and appreciate until they're depleted.'

WHAT WORKS FOR YOU...

One of the interesting things about my journey as an author has been the varying feedback and reviews. My first book was ranked into the best finance books of the year by the bookstore Dymocks and Money Magazine, and it received many stunning 5-star reviews, with some readers even saying it was life-changing and the best book on finance and success they'd ever read! So, it clearly resonated with some people. Yet, trust me when I say that I've had more than my share of blowback on social media over the years as well, variously being labelled arrogant, obnoxious, and sometimes far worse things besides.

Have a think about the best book you've ever read, or one that's changed your life meaningfully. Now go to Amazon reviews and see how many 1-star reviews that book has received. Interesting, hey? To me, this confirms that there's not necessarily a right or a wrong way to go about your career, investing, and life, only a right way for you personally.

In other books, I've written about the Enneagram assessment, which broadly holds that there are nine different personality types. I won't repeat here what I've written elsewhere previously, except to note that it's worth spending a bit of time thinking about your personality type, motivations, and values. Some people, like me, value experiences, travel, and freedom, and these days I would avoid taking an office or factory job at any cost! But other people are more goals-oriented and driven by status and will keep working hard in their career or business deep into their 50s, 60s, or even into their seventies! Some people are far more introverted, conservative, risk-averse, and analytical, while others are extroverted, more social, and more willing to take risks.

There's no one size fits all, and this book talks about a framework around which you can build a life and a career or business which suits you best. I used to look at other people and wonder how they stuck at the same job or career for 25 years or more, while I could barely muster 18 months in a role without getting bored out of my mind. Reading about the Enneagram and the nine personality types helped me to understand better how people can be so different, and yet each can be happy in their own way.

HEY PETE, BUT WHAT ABOUT CRYPTO?

I've never invested in cryptocurrencies or indeed related projects, and as you go through the book, you'll discover why that's the case. It's not that I'm inherently against the idea, and I like to adopt innovative ideas and technologies too. In the end does it really matter how you make your wealth? – though I do worry about the reputational risk of getting involved in an area which has naturally attracted more than its fair share of grifters and fraudsters. It's more because everything I have learned about compounding has revolved around finding proven strategies and employing them for as long as possible, hopefully for decades and decades into the future. Could the price of Bitcoin go to $1 million or beyond? I honestly have no idea, and for all I know it might well do. But once you understand the concepts of leverage and compounding growth, you'll realise that it doesn't really matter that much, if you find a method which works for you.

There's often a sense of fear of missing out or 'FOMO' when it comes to asset price booms. But as the great man Charlie Munger once said 'someone is always getting richer faster than you. This is not a tragedy."

I've had clients and friends who've made millions from timing their run in crypto, a couple of whom have parlayed their gains into unencumbered home ownership. And good for them! For the purposes of balance, I've also had dozens of clients sitting on worthless investments they variously bought along the way, with the prices having fallen so low they can only pray for a return from here. It's a zero-sum game in that regard. The wins can only come from someone else's losses, in the manner of a pyramid scheme. So, if crypto is your thing, that's great, but it's not what this book is about! Instead, it's about following tried and tested principles that have worked for the past one hundred years or more.

CHAPTER 1
RUNNING YOUR OWN RACE

A BETTER WAY

Since the global financial crisis there has grown an increasing mistrust of the financial services industry, which is perhaps understandable. After all, unscrupulous lenders and industry participants were at the very root of the financial meltdown, while many fund managers who had promised outperforming returns remained heavily invested in the stock markets as they tanked, yet continued to charge their hefty management fees as they did so. It is little wonder that so many have lost faith in the system.

More challenging still, around the developed world interest rates were for a time dropped to exceptionally low levels that were considered almost unthinkable until comparatively recently. While this may have made life comparatively easy in terms of mortgage repayments – for a while, and for those fortunate enough to remain employed and owning a home at least – the dynamic also created a whole new range of headaches for retirees who had previously sought to live on the interest payments from deposits.

Indeed, personal finances have become a challenging prospect for most people today. There is more information available than ever before. Some people – at least temporarily – take an interest in creating financial abundance and try all manner of trading programs, get rich quick ideas, or gamble on the direction of share markets. But it is very hard to make money from trading markets these days. It always has been, in fact, but this is even more so the case today where high frequency trading (HFT) takes place at something approximating to the speed of light, a game that individuals sitting at home on a clunky laptop don't have a prayer of competing in. It is true that some lucky folks do make a good living from expensive trading programs and packages, but here's a hint: it's not the people that are buying them!

With markets seemingly rigged against us by robots and market professionals, and fund managers reportedly bleeding us dry in our pension accounts, is it any surprise that so many people have all but given up on the idea of growing their wealth successfully? Some try to earn their way to financial freedom, but unless you can command an enormous salary, generally this simply doesn't work (the taxman takes close to half of your earnings and living expenses seem to increase the higher your salary becomes).

We all need to take a healthy step back from the nonsense and holler of day to day market news and financial headlines. The internet and financial television channels overwhelm us with information, speculating upon what might happen in the next few days or weeks, encouraging us to buy, sell, buy, sell, buy, sell. Unsurprisingly most average investors who follow the advice to move their money around frequently – buy, sell, buy, sell, buy, sell – achieve very little except for generating untold transaction costs and losing out to the professionals.

That's the last of the bad news!

But there is no need to be glum, and I now have nothing but good news for you in this book! The good news is that there is a simple way to win the game more passively by using time as your friend and accepting that most people won't beat the market. For the average investor, building a solid financial plan to achieve financial freedom should not and does not have to be this hard.

This book is here to help you by providing a very simple but equally very effective plan to build your wealth from the ground up. And remember, I have only good news for you in this book! The answers lie in simple, sometimes even old-fashioned, but tremendously powerful principles, and I will explain them clearly and succinctly in this book, and without the needless financial jargon which seemingly plagues most financial literature these days. In short, we are going to begin by building you a spending plan (not a budget!), setting aside as much money as you can reasonably afford to invest passively in assets which can go out to earn money for you every day, for the rest of your life. It's a plan which is straightforward, efficient, and very effective. And it can be followed by anyone.

Better still, by building solid financial foundations you can do what you enjoy. The plan discussed in this book is not just about trying to retire as young as you can and spending your life at the beach. Instead, by building yourself a solid financial base, you can spend some time thinking about what you want to do with your life, perhaps building a business based on what you are truly passionate about.

CONCENTRATING ON YOUR OWN GAME

It's one of the most famous photographs in sporting history, taken at the men's 100 metres final at the Seoul Olympics in 1988. Nobody can recall what had happened to the poor ailing fellow in lane two, but with arm outstretched, Canada's Ben Johnson raised his finger aloft to the heavens to signify that he is just about to complete the fastest 100 metres of all time at a blistering 9.79 seconds. To Johnson's left in the centre-right of shot, also in red, Carl Lewis, the poster boy for the United States of America, could only look on in dismay. Despite coasting to what should have been the fastest 100 metre time ever at well under 10 seconds, Lewis had to accept that he wasn't anywhere near the fastest in the field on that fateful day.

If you play back the video on the internet of this infamous event, Carl Lewis was interviewed almost immediately after the finish of the race. After expressing confusion and disbelief at Johnson's flying start, Lewis noted unconvincingly that he was 'happy with my race', while in truth looking anything but happy. Athletes are trained to concentrate on their own performance, rather than that of their opponents, or to 'control the controllables' in psychologist-speak. It is almost impossible to do so completely, of course, as Lewis neatly betrayed in his post-race laments.

Two days later it transpired that the race had not been held on a level playing field when Ben Johnson was disqualified after testing positive for drugs. The gold medal was thus awarded to Carl Lewis, and Linford Christie of Great Britain was in turn awarded the silver. Yet subsequent events and revelations led the race to be labelled with the moniker 'the dirtiest race in history', with no fewer than six of the eight participants being linked to or implicated in drug scandals.[1] Arguably the true gold medal could or should belong to the sprinter all the way over in lane one, Robson da Silva, who ran 10.11 seconds on the day and was never in any way linked to drugs throughout his career.[2] Da Silva once said, 'I chose not to do drugs, but I sleep well at night'.

The playing field may not be level.

In life, we should all concentrate on our own progress rather than comparing ourselves too readily with others. After all, we may never know the full story, and life is rarely held on an equal footing. There are some valuable lessons to be learned here for the way we invest, and indeed the way we approach and live our lives in general. While it is human nature to compare ourselves all too often with our peers, it is not necessarily always helpful for us to do so. For all we know, the playing field may not even be remotely level, and trying to 'keep up with the Joneses' is a game that ultimately can't be won.

I'm not insinuating here that your friends and peers may be cheats, by the way! Rather that all of us have different backgrounds, skills, goals, wants, needs and desires, strengths and weaknesses. Some of us start out in life with absolutely nothing in financial terms, while others inherit incredible wealth. Some are destined to be great business leaders; others have an entirely different skill set and work better alone. Each of us will suffer different setbacks, yet encounter random strokes of good fortune too. All of us have different risk profiles, goals and ideal portfolios, so what might represent perfect common sense for one investor might be disastrously risky for another. Comparing our own journey too frequently to that of our peers can correspondingly be fraught with danger.

Run your own race. Win your own race!

One of the challenges facing us today in developed countries is that we have become conditioned to contrast our lives with those of our peer group, and often with people who have more than we do. It's not necessarily all our fault, we are increasingly groomed to do so by slick advertising. Think about this for a moment. We wake up, flick on a television screen, which practically attacks us with advertisements while we eat our breakfast. We read iPhone screens on the way to work, and then stare at computer screens while at work. After the working day is over we go to work out on gym contraptions which for some reason are deliberately set up to face more screens, and then we get home just in time for something to eat and another couple of hours in front of a television screen. This is hardly accidental. The modern world revolves around advertisers trying to get as many eyeballs in front of screens and their products as possible.

Having been privileged enough to live in both developed and developing countries it is strikingly obvious to me that today's world is fraught with traps for those of us lucky enough to live in the wealthier countries. Instead of looking at those less fortunate than ourselves and being thankful for what we have, we are encouraged to look at those with 'more' than us and feel envious for what we don't have. To repeat myself, momentarily: this is a fruitless game that cannot be won! Whatever you have, someone else will always have more – a better car, a bigger house, a flashier watch, or any number of other 'doodads'. The 'secret' to financial success – and to some extent life satisfaction – is to focus on your own race by executing a simple and efficient plan to snowball your wealth and the quality of your life steadily but surely, for every year that you live.

By way of a personal example of how the journey is different for all of us, a University friend of mine went into business at the age of 20 and after a few false starts now has a business which generates a turnover that is on a par with the GDP of a small nation. He still has money headaches, but not the kind of problems that most people have – rather they are related to how big his tax bill is, where he should invest his surplus cash, and how best to protect his burgeoning wealth. The truth is that most people will never be able to generate such a level of passive wealth, but this doesn't matter! There is plenty in the world to go around, so if you have friends who are wealthier than you are, be happy for them and wish them luck!

You should aim to think abundance not scarcity. Simply because someone else achieves success does not mean that there is less to go around for everyone else. By using time as your ally and compounding your wealth you can achieve surprisingly powerful results over time – results that will amaze you as your returns begin to multiply – but it is vitally important that you focus on your own game and not anyone else's.

CHANGING YOUR THINKING

The aim of this book is to change the way you think about money – to turn it completely on its head. Instead of seeing money as something to be earned and then promptly spent, I want you to consider how you can find a way to send your money out to work for you. That is, spending less than you earn, and getting every dollar you save to go out to work for you, every day, for so long as you live. In this book, I will show you the strategies and the assets that can achieve this for you.

A simple illustrative example: Warren Buffett had a net worth of US$3 billion when he was 65, but since he's continued investing throughout his lifetime, his net worth at the time of writing is above US$138 billion; meaning that he's made more than 98 per cent of his net worth after the traditional retirement date. Sure, he's the greatest investor of our time, but the returns made by Buffett over the past 20 years haven't been much different from the returns you could've made investing passively. The real secret has been time! He's been an investor for 8 decades, continuing to compound his wealth.

This is the reason I tend to stick to the traditional asset classes of property and shares. We have over a century of data to prove their long-term effectiveness for growing your income and wealth. Of course, there are other new asset classes such as cryptocurrencies and digital assets, but it's much harder to know where things will be 20, 30, or 40 years from now for asset classes which haven't been around for so long.

How can you go about compounding your wealth for the long term? This will likely mean making some changes to your spending profile. If you cannot face that – although I am going to try to convince you that you should at least try – then it will mean finding ways to earn more dollars. Either approach can work, or a combination of both can be more effective still. And then it will involve finding quality, income-producing and appreciating investments which you can hold on to forever.

What are your ultimate goals? Or, what is your life's motto? We all have different aims, and these are not straightforward questions to answer. In this book, I'm going to discuss how you can win your own financial race. Once you have passive income which flows to you and is greater than your monthly expenses you will be financially free. Better still, once your portfolio of investments reaches a critical mass it can continue to snowball or compound, creating greater wealth throughout your life. Don't get me wrong, this is not an easy goal to achieve, and it will require some sacrifice – at least initially – and it does of course take time to get the power of compound growth working for you. But it can be done.

As humans, we are ingrained with a 'present bias', which causes us to focus on today at the expense of what might happen tomorrow. This is an important part of our make-up and a key survival mechanism, but it is not necessarily the ideal way to approach your personal finances. If you are wondering whether it is worth making sacrifices today for a wealthier tomorrow, note that I achieved my goal of financial freedom at the age of 33, from a standing start as a young adult. The sacrifices you make today can pay off for many years into the future, but you do have to make some sacrifices in the first instance. Sure, it took a lot of focus, some significant short term cutbacks to lifestyle and – truthfully – a certain level of luck, but the power of compounding or snowballing growth means that my financial results have kept getting better and better, repaying my sacrifice many times over.

Perhaps the biggest payback of all is the gift of time. Freed from the shackles of full-time employment as a Chartered Accountant, I have had more precious time to spend with my family, to do things that I love doing such as writing articles, blogs and books, and simply to enjoy life more than before. These were all luxuries that I simply did not have when I was working in my professional career where the hours were frequently long and the work often onerous. It doesn't matter if you are young, old, a high-income earner, or earning a basic salary, the savings can be made and the dollars you save can be sent out to work for you in perpetuity ... forever! The one thing you must be able to commit to, however, is thinking differently from the herd, because most sheep invariably end up in the wrong paddock!

THE MONTE CARLO FALLACY

When I was younger – quite a lot younger, I should say! – a few friends of mine got into the idea of playing cards and roulette at the casino, for a bit of fun. Like most young people going to the casino, we won a little bit, drank some beer, and promptly lost quite a bit more. That tends to go with the territory, for the odds are naturally skewed in favour of the house –particularly so for roulette. One salutary lesson which always stuck with me was that if you start off on a losing streak on any visit to the casino, it is nearly always better to quit while you are not ahead, rather than trying to recover your losses through ramping up your stake. This is a lesson which almost every gambler must learn the hard way!

Don't try to play catch up; slow and steady wins the race.

Indeed, anyone who has been to a casino to play roulette will be familiar with the concept of the Monte Carlo fallacy (if not the term, then at least the concept). Humans mistakenly believe that we can project accurately what will happen in the future based upon what has occurred in the recent past. Yet simply because on the last three occasions the roulette wheel came up red does not mean that black is more likely to come up next time around. In case you're doubtful on this point, trust me when I say that I have watched people looking on in horror while seeing 20 and then 25 or 30 reds come up in a row!

Years of working in, investing in and observing financial markets have taught me that predicting the future with any significant level of accuracy is not possible, so we must work with probabilities, and taking a longer-term outlook can help us to deal with the inherent uncertainties. Casino gamblers will be all too familiar with the fact that once you begin trying to recover losses or make up ground through gambling with bigger stakes, things can rapidly turn from bad to worse, or to outright disaster. This is precisely why trying to play 'catch up' with other members of your peer group is nearly always an ill-advised venture. Slow and steady wins the race in investment and – so often – in life. Resolve to win your own race!

If I am successful in making you radically change the way you think about money, your career and investing, then by the end of this book you should have a clear vision of your financial future which brings you security and success without worrying what your peers, friends and family are up to.

'DUMB MONEY': PASSIVE INVESTING

A key premise of this book is that if you can find the way to save up to 20 per cent of your income using the strategies I discuss in a later chapter and invest this money regularly in assets such as property and shares – in particular, certain types of quality investments that you never need to sell – then slowly but surely you can snowball your wealth until it reaches a critical mass which takes on a life of its own.

I said that I wouldn't fill this book with jargon, but it is important to define a few terms here at the outset. Firstly, active investing is the strategy of attempting to beat or outperform the stock market by trading, buying and selling investments. This is what fund managers do typically in a vain attempt to beat the market each year (so that people will choose to invest with them instead of the next guy). While this is understandable enough behaviour, in aggregate it achieves very little. In fact, often all this myopic trading achieves is endless transaction costs and inefficiencies, and indeed in aggregate fund managers underperform the stock market after their fees are subtracted.

This is to say that, on average, you would do better to simply buy a low-cost index fund and to hold it for the long term. An index fund aims to mirror or track the performance of a stock market index by holding all the significant component parts thereof, and thus provides the investor with broad diversification and exposure to the market. It has very low turnover aiming to hold investments rather than endlessly buying and selling them, and unlike an actively managed fund, does not incur the hefty fees for the investor. It is an efficient form of investment.

The polar-opposite of active investing, passive investing entails long term holding of investments such as property and/or shares in a low maintenance fashion to benefit from steadily growing income streams and long term market appreciation. The strategy of passive investing accepts that there will be market downturns as well as booms, but doesn't waste too much precious time trying to predict when they will come or what will cause each cycle to occur.

This is not to say that you might not choose to invest a bit more heavily when share markets or property markets are cheap, but you won't need to lose so much sleep worrying about when the market downturns will come. Accepting that there will be winter and summer seasons through each market cycle, you can sleep soundly at night with a long-term plan in place. One of the greatest investors to have ever lived, Warren Buffett, once famously observed that:

'Once dumb money recognises its limitations, paradoxically it ceases to be dumb.'

What Buffett was referring to here is that while there are a few experts – including himself – who can consistently beat the market by analysing in great depth and then selecting superior investments, most average investors cannot or will not manage to do this consistently. And, for that matter, even most fund managers don't manage it either over time, particularly after costs. But importantly, there is a way to win the game passively, by investing regular amounts in a cross-section of all industries. I also discuss in this book how a property portfolio can help you to achieve your financial dreams.

'The best way is just buy a low-cost index fund and keep buying it regularly over time, because you'll be buying into a wonderful industry, which in effect is all of American industry. People ought to sit back and relax and keep accumulating over time.'
– Warren Buffett.

Simple and honest advice from the mouth of one of the most intelligent investment minds ever. In recent decades, a whole new industry has sprouted up, whereby talking heads hyperventilate over equities markets, making daily or even hourly predictions over what prices will do next, acting as though they have any real clue. And it's not only shares or equities markets – it is also oil or iron ore prices, it is real estate, it is interest rate futures. In short, it's everything! A truly vast amount of time and energy is wasted on short term crystal ball gazing, but the great bulk of it is little better than guesswork. Today's financial industry is also crammed full of often meaningless jargon, at times deliberately to make individual investors feel inadequate and that they need professionals to manage their money for them.

This is a book about passive investing, and how to build your own personal cash machine by gradually building up a solid portfolio of sufficient size or critical mass that your passive income – which flows to you without you having to work for it – exceeds your monthly living expenses. That, in short, is financial freedom. To get there sooner you will probably need to cut some expenditure and make a few key tweaks here and there, but the challenge is to see this not as a sacrifice, but as a thrilling gift to yourself. The beautiful thing about saving money from consumer goods expenditure is it is totally risk free and only good things can come from it! We are going to look at how you can cut back on wasteful spending, and how you can automate your savings and your investment plan.

TIME ON YOUR SIDE

One of the key themes of this book is the importance of time, and why you should aim to become a master it. So often today, time seems to be people's enemy. 'I don't have time' is an all-too-common lament. But is this true? Or is that people don't always prioritise their time optimally?

'You have the same number of hours per day that were given to Helen Keller, Pasteur, Michelangelo, Mother Teresa, Leonardo da Vinci, Thomas Jefferson, and Albert Einstein. Don't say you don't have time.' – H. Jackson Brown Jr.

The legendary entrepreneur and motivational speaker Jim Rohn once said that time is more valuable than money, because while you can get more money you can't get more time. And how right he was! A key secret to success in personal finance is to embrace time as your greatest friend rather than viewing time as an enemy. When money is invested in the right way – in quality investments for the long term, the longer the period that you can hold the investment for, the greater the returns. Because of the snowballing or compounding effect of returns from quality investments, this can turn a simple investment into a very powerful tool for achieving your goals.

Once you understand the simple rule of compounding you can learn to make your money work harder for you so that you don't have to. In other words, you will no longer be compelled to trade your time for money in order to get by or to survive from month to month. You will be buying your life back, or buying yourself more time to focus on the things which are most important to you – whether that be friends, family, travel, setting up a business in a field that you are passionate about, or committing to another pastime. What could that be worth to you?

BECOMING A MARKET INSIDER

In this book, I will also debunk some myths about investing, exposing the reasons why most people can never seem to get ahead. I will then go on to detail the strategies used by market insiders in shares and property in order that you too can invest like 'the 1 per cent'. Everyone seemingly has advice when it comes to money, personal finance and investing. Yet, have the people dishing out the advice achieved their goals? Sometimes, yes, but most often they have not, or their situation might not be directly comparable with yours and therefore much of the personal finance advice you receive from friends, family or the media may be of questionable value.

Lest any of us need reminding that the financial crisis brought disillusionment to so many households. The pension system appears to be failing them and as an industry fund managers failed to protect their downside. Understandably more people want to take control of their own finances, but they aren't sure how best to do so. My premise is clear: don't try to compete with rigged markets by trading them for short term gains now that the low-hanging fruit – or cheap bargains – after the financial crisis have been plucked. Instead focus on achieving long term success by investing passively.

I understand that personal finance and investing can seem overwhelming today, with all the conflicting advice out there. In some ways, the financial industry likes it to be just that way, to make it sound as though investing is simply too complex for the average person to understand – that way you must pay fund managers to do the job for you. As I will show you in this book, fund managers are creaming off billions of dollars in fees yet in aggregate they do not even beat the wider market.

The good news is that to achieve your financial goals you don't necessarily need to earn a high income and become a master of all markets in your spare time, because you can simply choose to own the whole market, or at least a broad cross-section of it. Being active is not necessarily smarter, and often all it achieves is generating transaction costs and taxes, even if you get the timing right, which most people don't. When there is nothing to do, as the adage goes, it is best to do nothing.

Some compensating good news is that in many ways the investment game has become easier today. Information is far more freely available than it was even 20 years ago, let alone 50 years ago. You can find a copy of a company's annual report at the click of a mouse instead of having to become a shareholder and order one through the mail. With the advent of online broking you never need to speak to a stockbroker in your life if you don't want to (and who could blame you for that?). Now is the time for a better plan where you get to keep all your returns and your fund manager doesn't get his grubby mitts on any of it! It is time to show you the insider strategies you can use to achieve the financial freedom you deserve.

INVESTMENT MENTOR

During my work as a property buyer and investment mentor one thing that I have consistently found to be the case is the importance of time. What is remarkable as an investor is how the small but satisfying gains which you generate in the early days can grow and compound when reinvested until the gains become larger than you had ever anticipated or even dared to dream when you started out.

'The most powerful force in the Universe is compound interest.'
– Albert Einstein.

This snowballing effect can help you to make huge strides as your life progresses, exceeding what you believed was possible at the beginning of your journey. The gains you make later in life can total more than the sum of your preceding results combined. Your second million will be considerably easier to make than your first, and your third million easier again. Better still, a commitment to consistent and never-ending improvements can also start a chain reaction of positivity into other areas of your life.

Transitioning away from reliance on a pay cheque is challenging but achievable with patience, time and discipline.

What has become clear to me through my mentoring sessions is that so many everyday people have the same (or at least very similar) questions about how to get started and how to be successful in investment. While the specifics of each question always differ, similar themes crop up repeatedly. The years of mentoring my clients has given me a deeper understanding of the most common challenges and hurdles that people face and how they can overcome them. I therefore set out to present to you in this book how to first design and then live the life you dream of, using simple principles to invest passively in the share markets and in real estate.

TRUE WEALTH

It is important to recognise that happiness and success are rarely derived solely from material possessions or personal financial wealth. While it may be something of a cliché, something I nevertheless learned from living in a developing country, material wealth and possessions are not in themselves what cause people to be happy or otherwise.

The American industrialist John Paul Getty was once named as the richest living American yet famously said that he would gladly give away his millions for one lasting marital success (and being married five times, he had plenty of attempts!). Human relationships are important to us. In fact, true wealth comes in many different guises. This is one of those things that you hear people say regularly, but is surely true! To be happy, we need our health, meaningful human relationships, and a true purpose and meaning to our lives (which is why I suggest that setting up a business in a field you are passionate about is ultimately worthy of your consideration).

Thus, while this book in part shows you specifically how to build financial wealth its true scope is wider than that. As well as snowballing or compounding your wealth, I want to inspire you to compound your education, your quality of life, to widen your horizons and to find a real meaning for your life, and a means of contribution. If you can learn to use time as your friend in terms of growing your investment returns, then you can effectively buy back the time to spend doing what is important to you.

WHAT WE WILL COVER IN THIS BOOK

I've been studying finance in one way, shape or form for more than two decades now, almost my entire adult life. My goal in writing this book was to compress everything useful that I know about personal finance into one bite-sized read as a simple guide to building wealth passively and efficiently. For that reason, the book does not go into exhaustive detail, getting bogged down in tedious academic theories concerning why certain strategies work and others do not, and it certainly isn't intended to cover everything there is to know about personal finance. Instead it is written to be an easy to follow guide that anyone can use to their advantage to ensure that they radically improve their financial health. I challenge you to take the information and use it to the very best of your ability!

And so, to summarise briefly what we will cover. In Chapter 2 we will look at how globally the economic and financial outlook has changed, and why in today's world simply waiting to draw your pension and living off fixed interest rate investments or annuities in retirement isn't likely to be good enough for most people. Instead of aiming just to 'get by' and spending the last dollar on the day you die, we are instead going to construct a plan to continue building your wealth in perpetuity, for so long as you live! We will identify the scripts or stories you tell yourself about money, replace them with more empowering beliefs, and resolve to use the power of compound growth to get your financial plan rolling.

In Chapter 3 we will make a list of your financial bad debts – those pesky liabilities that cost you money every month – and put together a coherent plan to get them cleared as quickly as possible. I then look at how you can recognise true assets and liabilities so that in future you only acquire assets which will continue to move you closer to your financial goals. I will also help you to draw up a budget or a spending plan (but not in a boring way, I promise!) to help you get started on your journey to financial success.

In Chapter 4 we will look at in a little more detail at understanding exactly what your personal wealth creation plan will be, and why. I will summarise the most important aspects of the psychology of wealth creation, why we act in the way we do when it comes to money and personal finances, and detail why a longer-term outlook is so important for the average investor.

In Chapter 5 we will set some more specific financial targets, partly because if you don't know where you're headed it's impossible to know how best to get there, but equally important because if you have potent, exciting and inspiring goals, then these can become a devastatingly effective motivational tool for you. I will explain why simply buying and holding quality investments can be the most efficient way to create wealth, in part because this allows you to compound your wealth in a tax-deferred manner.

Chapter 6 will help you design your ultimate bucket list, in this context meaning exactly where you are going to invest those dollars saved to earn passive income for you for the rest of your life. The good news is that you don't necessarily need to become an expert in all things financial to win your own personal finance race. By accepting consistently solid average returns and investing in well diversified and low cost products which do not attract crippling management fees and costs, you can begin to move ahead and snowball your wealth.

Chapter 7 covers the nuts and bolts of passive investing in more detail, looking at what you can invest in and how, so that you can invest with peace of mind and without fear of the markets. I look at how time in the market can over time trump even successful timing of the market, and by investing small amounts in the market regularly you can help to spread your risk.

In Chapter 8 we will focus on real estate and consider profitable property investment and how this can fit in as part of your plan to achieve your financial goals. While the principles of investing in quality assets to compound your wealth are like those of the share markets, real estate is unique as an investment and consumption asset. This chapter clarifies how you can grow your wealth safely and sustainably in the property market by showing you what types of property to buy and where – and exactly how you can build a very substantial property portfolio in practice.

In Chapter 9 we will cover 'controlling the controllables' – by focussing on the things that you can control rather than constantly wondering or second-guessing what other people, the economy or financial markets are up to, you can run and then win your own race. Through finding a higher purpose for your financial goals you can make your success more sustainable, and by investing in your human capital you can focus on being the best you that you can be. By now you will have the basics in place, and will understand the myths of the market.

Of course, as you become inspired to reach your financial goals, you will be impatient to get there sooner! Therefore, Chapter 10 narrows in even further on your financial plan and shows you how you can accelerate your results so that you can get to your goals as quickly and efficiently as possible.

As you grow your portfolio of investments I hope to inspire you to choose to gradually move away from employment and towards self-employment or running your own business in the field or area which interests and excites you most. This isn't a route for everyone, but it may be for some of you! In Chapter 11, then, I look at how you can go about generating an income from self-employment or a business in the field of your life's passion.

Hand on heart I can tell you that there are few things better in life than waking up on a Monday morning raring to go, following a career or business that you are passionate about. I've been on the other side of that equation too, working in boring, stressful or miserable jobs and to be blunt, it sucks! Life is too short to spend it doing things that don't inspire you! This chapter looks at how gradually over time you can transition towards self-employment or a business that puts you in control. Imagine getting out of bed each day and being in control of how you spend it. Doesn't that sound great?

In Chapter 12 we will discuss how and why an unencumbered home should ultimately feature as part of your financial plan. Renting where you live can be a smart move when you are younger, and can even help to accelerate your investment plan, since renting a place to live is often cheaper than being an owner from a monthly cash flow perspective. However, ultimately owning a home which you can live in with no mortgage is a great place to get to, so I look at how you can achieve this as part of your plan. This represents rather a lot of ground to cover in a limited amount of space, so let's get cracking!

Chapter 1 Summary

- Focusing on the results achieved by others and events which are beyond our control is a potential path to misery!
- True wealth is about more than just money, but financial freedom when combined with a higher purpose is a worthy goal.
- You need to make time your greatest ally and friend, not an enemy.
- Dare to be different from the crowd – it's a prerequisite for achieving better than average results.
- Financial freedom is defined as receiving passive income from your investments exceeding your expenses. You may then work because you want to (and not because you must).
- Resolve to run your own race … and win it!
- Set specific financial targets and then set about building a plan to help you reach those targets over time.
- Can the 'end game' for you be setting up a business in the field of your life's passion?

CHAPTER 2
FINANCIAL FITNESS

FINANCIAL FITNESS FOR LIFE

Henceforth, we are now going to set about knocking your financial fitness into shape for life! What we are not going to look at are silly get rich quick ideas, which people typically gravitate towards, pushing too hard and then quickly running out of puff. The power of compounding growth means that over the medium term you can achieve fabulous results without the need to take great risks investing in the schemes and scams that are plastered all over the internet these days. Remember the adage: if it sounds too good to be true, then it almost certainly is!

The only thing that sounds too good to be true in finance but is for real is compound growth, where you multiply your money year after year. In fact, compound growth seems to defy logic as the results keep getting better and better.

Most employees remain far too reliant on their salary throughout their careers and don't plan their race. Instead we are going to be more thoughtful and plan accordingly, and importantly you will concentrate on becoming financially fit and winning your own race. Together we will work on a plan upon which you can build steadily, and you are not going to run out of puff! Better still, we are going to accelerate to the finish by formulating a plan which multiplies your results and becomes self-sustaining. In short, we will put together a strategy whereby every dollar you save can be sent out to work harder for you for as long as you live. Forever. Your money can go out to work harder and harder for you each year so that you don't have to.

CHANGING TIMES

When my Dad started his career, he undertook three years of working in a hostel for young offenders, which is where I spent my formative years. Working in the hostel formed part of his training as a probation officer, a role for which he qualified when he was 23. Some 42 years later the old man retired from his career in the probation service and began to draw his hard-earned pension (a defined benefit pension, meaning that he will receive it guaranteed for so long as he lives). Strangely enough, within a couple of years of retirement he was working again, although this time in an unpaid capacity!

To say that the nature of the workforce and careers have changed over the past few decades would be one heck of an understatement. What's more, the game of money has completely changed too. No, more than that, it has been completely turned on its head! Back in my Dad's day folk typically worked in the same job or career for a long period. There was no email, no internet and no social media. Many employees such as my father worked in one line of work for their entire careers. Job stability was considered important, and pension schemes were often a key incentive to remain in the same employment for a long period. People fretted hard and often about rocketing inflation destroying the value of their money, double digit rates of unemployment, periodically sky-high interest rates, and how they would afford the mortgage.

Life expectancies have increased and in many developed countries are continuing to increase, and therefore today we have the potential for longer retirements. In fact, if you live to the traditional retirement age today there is every chance that you could live for several decades into retirement, which is potentially a great thing! One of the biggest challenges facing those in the workforce today is that the old defined benefit pension schemes of our parents' generation are largely a relic of a bygone era, and almost certainly a thing of the past for most employees of today. Thus, not only are we responsible for building our own pension balance, we might potentially live for decades into retirement. Happily, there is a solution. You need to think differently about building wealth, by building a portfolio of a critical mass which continues to grow in value and pay you income for life. And here is the first step ...

FROM CONSUMER TO STAKEHOLDER

If we were to chart how most people progress through life today in terms of their wealth or net worth, the result would likely look something like the graphic below. I deliberately haven't included numbers or ages on the chart because we all tend to earn different salaries; some people start out with inherited money (though many of us don't!) and some will live much longer than others. The principle is the important thing to take note of here.

What tends to happen is that in our early adult lives we can build up some debt from funding higher education, travel, or for buying our first car (or, in some cases, all the above!). Then as we transition into the workforce we can steadily begin to get this debt cleared until we are in a break-even position, with a net worth or personal wealth of somewhere close to zero. Then as we progress through our career we begin to earn a higher salary and we build up a level of wealth in our homes, in our pensions, and for some, in other investments. This is the accumulation stage of our financial lives.

Figure 2.1 – Life cycle consumption theory

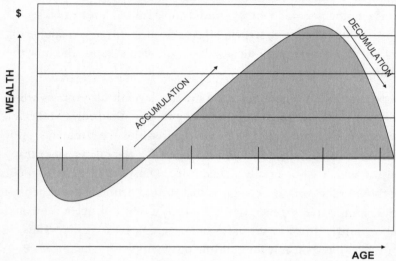

Of course, the dollar values tend to be different for each of us, but remember that it is the principle that is important here. When people reach somewhere around the traditional retirement age they often elect to withdraw their pension as a lump sum, perhaps buying an annuity, and begin to run down their wealth for the remainder of their lives. As you can see on the graphic above, this is known as the 'decumulation phase'. Hopefully the individual in question won't outlive the balance of money they have accumulated! Sadly, most people today still have at least some level of reliance on the state pension.

The chart will rarely be as smooth as this for most employees today. After all, more people take career breaks to travel, and there may be periods of illness or unemployment. Certainly, more people will get divorced than was formerly the case, another significant change from only one generation ago (and if like me you grew up in a broken family you will be all too familiar with how a divorce can devastate personal finances).

I noted in the first chapter that in this book I am going to recommend that you consider thinking a little differently. Instead of seeing your wealth creation plan as something which builds up steadily through your working lifetime, and then dives towards zero at an unnerving speed once you retire, why not aim to think a little more positively? Instead of planning to build up a net worth which will hopefully last for the duration of your retirement, why not instead consider how you can build a portfolio of assets which you can hold on to in perpetuity? That means forever!

Once you have built a portfolio of a sufficiently critical mass it will throw off more than enough income for you to live on comfortably, while you can also continue to re-invest some of the profits into more investments. Therefore, what I am suggesting is that instead of making a goal to build a retirement portfolio which might just about see you through your later years, perhaps with the help of the state pension, try to envisage a bigger picture. Aim to build a legacy with your net worth continuing to increase throughout your entire lifetime, and even beyond your own lifetime. That's the kind of bigger picture I'm talking about!

Figure 2.2 – New life cycle consumption theory

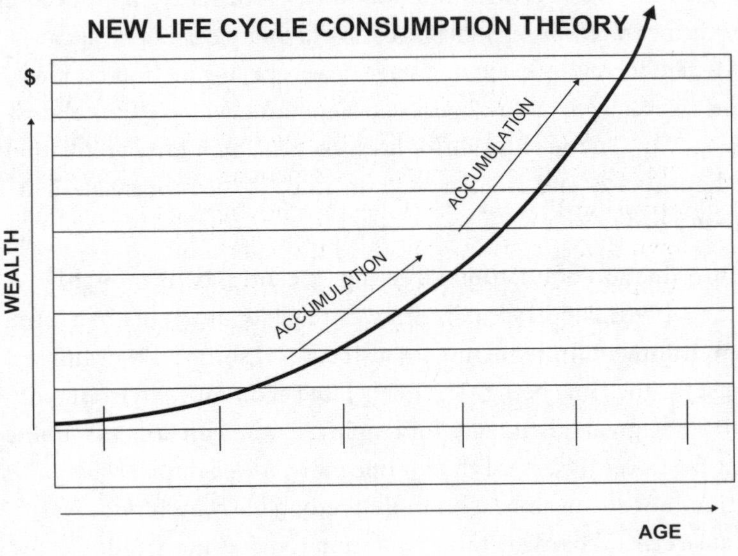

The good news is that this can certainly be achieved, but to kick-start such a plan the first thing you will need to do is stop being a part of the consumer economy, and instead become an owner or stakeholder in the economy. And the way to do that is buying collecting assets.

Of course, this is easy to say, but harder to actually do! Now, don't get me wrong, you don't have to live like a monk or survive on lentils and water or anything like that, and I'm certainly not saying that you cannot ever have luxuries or buy nice things. However, if you want to follow my plan to financial freedom some of those nice things may have to come later, after you have built your wealth or net worth to the critical mass from which it will begin to snowball for you effectively, as I will demonstrate in the chapters ahead. If you can get the value of your assets and investments up to a certain level the gains can begin to take on a life of their own. This is what you will come to know as compounding growth.

ARE WE IN AN ERA OF LOWER INTEREST RATES?

The generation known as the Baby Boomers, being those born approximately in the two decades following the end of the last World War in 1945, lived through periods of high inflation and high interest rates. I can remember coming home from school one day when interest rates had been hiked from 10 per cent to 12 per cent in a single day and the government vowing to hike them to 15 per cent in due course. That was not a particularly happy evening around the dinner table for my mortgaged-to-the-hilt parents as you can imagine! My father recalls that at one stage he was paying an interest rate on the home mortgage of up to 17 per cent, something which seems almost unthinkable today. On the plus side for homeowners, high rates of inflation pushed up house prices and inflated away the value of their mortgage debt, so it wasn't always bad news.

With the introduction of inflation targeting by central banks roughly from the early 1990s and beyond, today we are generally living in a lower inflation environment, in tandem with a structural shift to lower interest rates, at least for the time being. The new global economic environment comes with some great advantages for employees and consumers – home loan debt is far easier to service than it once was, for example. Most of the time inflation now seems to be a bit more predictable than it once was, partly because central bankers target inflation today. And paradoxically, as households load up on cheaper debt, this may even serve in some cases to keep downward pressure on interest rates, keeping them on average much lower than was the case in decades gone by. So, that's the good news.

For retirees and net savers, however, structurally low interest rates also bring tremendous challenges. The problems presented by low interest rates might even be the reason that you picked up this book. Term deposits, which could once be relied upon to pay healthy rates of interest (if not capital growth) are, in today's lower interest rate environment, often providing cripplingly low returns. For retirees that are uncomfortable with the risks associated with volatile share markets this has often led to excruciatingly weak levels of income that had not been anticipated in the lead up to their retirement. This must often seem like scant reward for decades spent in the workforce.

In some other ways, the game of money has improved. Today there is more information freely available. You can access share markets via inexpensive brokerage websites, without the need to call a broker to help you. Company Annual Reports and stock exchange data is generally available on request. When I worked as a Financial Controller for listed companies I would often be required to post by hand copies of those glossy Annual Reports I'd written to shareholders, for the few shareholders who asked for them. And I'm not even that old! These days they are freely available to anyone at the click of a button.

To achieve your financial goals, you will need to be an investor in the economy – an owner or a stakeholder, and not only a consumer. Many folks choose to work until they are older these days, even if they are financially secure, particularly since more than three quarters of employment is in the services sector of the economy rather than more labour-intensive positions. But if you want to achieve financial freedom, you will need to own assets.

It's time to shatter a few myths about what money is, what money means to you, the keys to successful and safe investment, and the markets, so you can invest like 'the 1 per cent'. And then in time you may even be able to join the 1 per cent.

WHAT IS MONEY?

Just as if you were preparing for a running race, you need to get yourself mentally prepared for a financial race, and making the required changes all starts with the mind. Let's start with the basics.

What is money these days? If you go back through history, money was largely represented by something tangible, such as gold or silver. Over time paper notes took precedence, and with today's fiat currencies even the paper in our pocket often doesn't hold its value very well as inflation dilutes its spending power over time.

Today money often isn't even paper, for most of us it is a number on a bank statement – or even just on a computer or cash machine screen – which denotes your worth, at least in dollar or monetary terms. But when we talk about wanting and having more money, we aren't talking about having more notes and coins in our pocket. What we want are the emotions and the feelings associated with wealth. To be freed from the anxieties of worrying about money. Imagine having enough money at your disposal that you never need to worry about money again. Can you picture for a moment what a wonderful feeling that would be?

To my friend Bill, having more money would give him the freedom to tell his boss where he could stick his job (into an uncomfortable place, I sensed from Bill's tone of voice!). To one of my clients, Sarah, more money would represent security, freedom from the worry of paying for school fees and holidays, and the ability to make more compelling choices. The truth is that money and happiness mean different things to different people. For some people, more money represents more choice, such as where to live, work, or play. For others money equals excitement, toys, or adventure! For others, more money is an opportunity for contribution or to help others, such as friends, family, or their favourite charity.

Have a think about this! What does money mean to you? Is your main goal financial security, a certainty that your retirement will be secure? Or are you looking for variety, personal growth and experiences? Or is your main goal achieving status or significance, or even finding love? Spend a little time considering these questions. As we will see in the next section of the book, this is important because what money means to you will form an important part of how you think of your personal finances unconsciously. Find your meaning. For now, perhaps, just aim to be mindful of it.

To achieve your ultimate financial goals, it is likely that you need to change the way you think about money to a greater or lesser extent, and the very first step in the process is to acknowledge what your existing money beliefs or scripts are. You may not even consciously have many thoughts about money, but unconsciously you surely have a code of beliefs. How do I know that? Because we all do!

MONEY MANTRAS!

We all hold internal dialogues: we tell ourselves stories, and we do so about all manner of things. For example, some people tell themselves stories about why they cannot succeed at school ('I just can't do exams', or 'I am simply not meant for the classroom'). There may be some underlying truths in these internalised statements, but they are rarely empowering beliefs or mantras because they do not provide any solutions. Others tell themselves stories about why they can't lose weight ('I have a slow metabolism' or 'there is no point in dieting, it does not work'). Again, these internal statements may or may not be true for the person engaging with them, but they are still not empowering beliefs, and they provide no cues or solutions for how to tackle the issue at hand.

What is certain is that all of us tell ourselves stories about our relationship with money. These internal dialogues or mantras are like life scripts which we follow, as if we are acting out our own play or drama. The interesting thing is that these dialogues are not necessarily true or false, rather they merely represent stories which we have mentally written for ourselves based upon our experiences to date and our unconscious beliefs.

What stories do you tell yourself about money?

Take the example of the mantra: 'I always buy the best of everything', which is the mantra often adopted by higher income earners or even people in middle management roles in modern times. Sometimes buying the best may indeed be the smart thing to do. For example, if you are keen walker, then buying a quality pair of hiking boots may represent a wise purchase. You will get great use out of the boots because you are an eager walker, and a quality pair of boots that is well manufactured has the potential to improve your experience dramatically over a period of years.

On the other hand, what about buying the best white goods? Well, this might make sense some of the time, but today there are new-fangled products which do all kinds of whacky things with features that you would never use in a month of Sundays! Take the example of some of the top-of-the range dishwashers or other domestic goods, which may look flash, but (if you're anything like me, at least) deep down you know that you probably won't use many of the features.

The reverse may also hold true. Having a mantra which maintains that 'I always buy the cheapest choice of everything' might not be the smartest move either. For example, it is possible to buy incredibly cheap socks, but if the manufacturing quality is so poor that the socks only last one wearing then this may prove to be a false economy. This is where the phrase 'spend to save' comes from.

Now these are only a few trivial examples of money mantras. What I want you to recognise here is that you and I inevitably have a sweeping range of unconscious thoughts and beliefs when it comes to money. It is close to a certainty that some of your unconscious beliefs are holding you back from reaching your full potential, simply because this is true for almost all of us. Here are just a handful of examples of money mantras which people carry around with them:

- Money doesn't grow on trees!
- There's not enough money … don't go spending it all
- Our family cannot afford to have nice things
- I shouldn't have my share unless others have had their share first
- Taking risks is nearly always a bad idea
- I don't trust anyone when it comes to money; it's best to do it all yourself
- Having more is better
- My money is running out!
- If you want more money, then you must work hard for it
- Money isn't all that important to me
- If you're rich, then you must be greedy
- He's not smart enough to have money
- Most rich people have inherited their wealth
- I don't deserve to inherit money because …
- If you come into money, it's best not to tell anyone about it
- There is only so much money to go around the in the world

- There is plenty to go around, and enough money in the world for everyone!
- … and many, many more!

On and on goes the list. It is worth having a think here for a moment about your unconscious money mantras, and which of them are holding you back. In my case, I know that for some years I didn't feel worthy of maximising my potential, almost a fear of being 'found out'. Another thing I struggled with for some years was worrying too much about what others thought of me. This is a personality trait which often intends to come from a good place as a generally caring person, yet over-thinking the views of other people (something over which you have little control) can be detrimental to your progress. I think when I was growing up (in a hostel or 'half way house' remember, in an area where there was a good deal of poverty) although our family was clearly very much middle class there was nevertheless an unspoken rule that being wealthy was a generally unseemly thing.

Your beliefs determine your 'wealth thermostat' and ultimately the level of your personal wealth.

Why is all of this so important? To be blunt, because the level of your wealth is directly related to your beliefs about money! You may not believe that to be true, and I appreciate what you may be thinking: 'No, that's not right – the reason I don't have more money is because of …' And there will always be a reason. You have come from a family which is not well off, or you had some bad luck which incurred unforeseen expenditure. You invested in something which didn't pay off, or you took some bad advice. Sure, these may all be inputs or factors in your current financial situation, but they are not the prime determinants of where you are today. Your beliefs or mantras about money are. This is a challenging concept and a hard thing to accept, and it took me years to come around to believing it myself. But I can assure you that ultimately it is true.

Some people who inherit large sums of money manage to rid themselves of it in a remarkably short period. The same is true of lottery winners, who often panic upon seeing their rapidly diminishing pile of cash, which leads them to spend the bulk of the loot on a house and two cars for fear of the money vanishing completely within a few short years. It should be no surprise that this happens, for if you have no context for investing money, then eventually it tends to get spent. When you start to delve into this subject a little further, you will begin to realise that we have money mantras which cover a huge range of related topics, such as:

- Investing
- The poor …
- … and the rich!
- Higher education expenses
- Insurance
- Budgeting
- Financial planners and advisors
- Marriage
- Relatives
- Saving …
- … and spending
- Investing
- Wills and inheritances
- Giving
- Receiving
- Children
- Happiness
- Spirituality
- … and much, much more!

And this is only the tip of the iceberg. Now, isn't this food for thought? Allow me to give you a few brief examples of my money mantras from when I was 21 years of age, if for no other reason than the person I am most familiar with is obviously myself. When I was 21 I believed that there were essentially two ways to become wealthy: either through somehow winning a massive windfall of cash, or secondly through landing a very highly paid job. If I'd thought harder I should have added marrying into wealth, but I was 21 and I didn't want to get married. Here is a list of a few of the money mantras I had at that time:

- The most likely way to become rich is through landing a high-paying position of employment
- You could give me almost any sum of money and I could find a way to spend it!
- A flash sports car (or perhaps a yacht) is a symbol of success
- Wealthy people are often snobbish, uncaring, aloof, disrespectful, or distasteful
- Going into business is a risky proposition

Remember that money mantras may carry a level of truth for the person who holds them, since they can become self-fulfilling. For example, it is probably true that I could have found a way to spend almost any sum of cash when I was 21. That's because I knew very little about the merits of investing for returns and therefore had no context for retaining large sums of money. And secondly, because I had a wish list of 'things' I wanted to own that was as long as my arm. Perhaps I associated an importance to material possessions, a trait which stemmed from a lack of self-confidence. It probably would also have been a risk for me to start a business at the age of 21, because I had very little worldly experience and I had no portfolio of investments behind me, so I would have been entirely reliant upon achieving early success in business to sustain myself.

Perhaps most importantly, having hailed from a large family in an ordinary city in the north of England, I held a view that wealthy people from London or elsewhere were not particularly nice people. If ever there was a way to ensure that you won't maximise your potential, it is to believe that where you ideally want to get to is a bad place! I note briefly here that there is little value in looking back at previous mistakes or failings with sadness, shame, or regret. All we need to do is accept that we have all made errors, and to resolve to learn from them as we move forward. Indeed, this is a personality trait of successful people – treating mistakes as lessons to be learned from rather than a reason to give up or accept mediocre results in the future.

In fact, if you look back at your past relationship with money and feel a little guilty about some of your past purchases or investment decisions, this is likely to be a good thing, for it says that you are going to be better in the future than you were in the past! We have already partially taken the first step, which is to acknowledge that whether we like it or not these dialogues do exist and do take place. We are now going to delete your old money mantras and replace them with a long-term plan for success. It is important to be mindful of these belief systems, for ultimately they will drive the full cycle of your financial existence.

Figure 2.3 – Financial consciousness

FINANCIAL CONSCIOUSNESS

THOUGHTS
(Money Mantras)

EMOTIONS
(Feelings)

BEHAVIOUR
(Actions)

PHYSIOLOGY
(Body /Sensations)

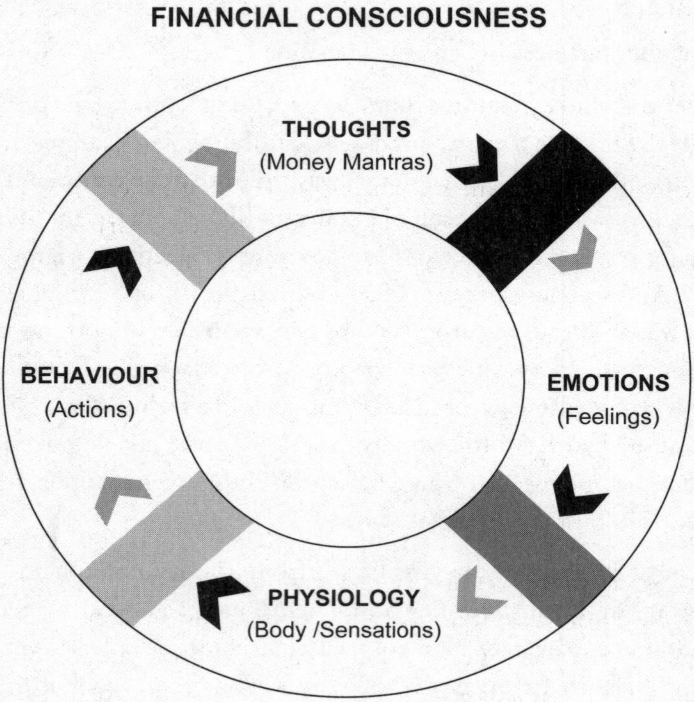

While we are in the process of growing up our learned money mantras or internal dialogues tend to serve us reasonably well. For those of us lucky enough to have parents who lent a hand with pocket money or allowances, we found that Mum and Dad could cover the financial shortfalls we inevitably had as teenagers. I had a job washing pots and dishes in the kitchen of the local pub from the age of 14, with my parents generously adding a contribution in the form of a monthly allowance. Life was good.

Unfortunately, one day things change – disaster! We grow up and are forced to enter the real world! And one day our parents change too, and they say that they won't cover our shortfall any more. And it hurts! I can remember the conversation reasonably clearly, so it must have stuck with me. 'You are 17 now, Peter. You are old enough to earn your own spending money now, like an adult.' (I was always known as Peter and not Pete when I was on the receiving end of a stern talking to, of course.)

By that time in my life I'd already been working in the kitchens of the local pub for a few years, and I earned a few quid per hour from that, plus the tips for the pub meals we served were sometimes reasonably good. But I was a young man with a thirst and a few quid per hour was never going to be enough! When we are hurt in this way, many of us tend to self-medicate to numb the pain, with the response being either behavioural (such as retail therapy) or chemical (such as smoking or drinking). Being a young Englishman at that time, I was sure to opt for the latter pursuits, and so I did! The problem with these responses is that it becomes hard to change behaviours positively while we are numbing our emotions. Blame doesn't help either, although we usually try that too, and so we continue this cycle of financial unconsciousness.

As we become adults our old money mantras or internal dialogues become obsolete and don't work for us any longer, and so we must learn to replace them with more empowering beliefs. But since typically we know almost nothing about personal finances other than what our schooling, parents, or friends have already taught us, we persist with or perpetuate money mantras or dialogues which may not be appropriate for today's new financial era, perhaps learning a little by trial and error as we go. Remember, the financial plan which worked for people like my Dad isn't likely to be good enough in the new financial environment. For one thing, a job for life is often not a reality for most people these days, while the generous defined benefit pension schemes have largely gone the way of the dodo.

Of course, you may try to aim for a big windfall or get rich quick ideas which almost never work. You can gamble on horses, buy lottery tickets, speculate on cheap penny stocks, go to the casino, enter competitions … there are any number of ways in which you can fail to achieve financial success! They don't work and even on the very rare occasions that such strategies do result in a surprise cash windfall the recipient still often has little or no context for investing the money safely, and eventually it gets spent. Some people are drawn to trading contracts for difference (CFDs) and they usually do OK while the market is going up – as you would – and then promptly get totally wiped out the first time the market crashes. Regardless of what your friends and work colleagues may be up to, you and I both need to remember that wealth is best to be built steadily and surely over time, like the building of a wall that cannot be knocked down. Brick by brick.

It's no coincidence to my mind that most people only have two successful investments, being their home and their pension. The reason for this is that most people don't sell their home (because they need to live in it) or their pension (because they cannot redeem it before the retirement date), and therefore understand that they must be long term investments. The values of these investments can continue to grow and compound. In the case of the home the value can grow and compound unhindered by taxes and transaction costs, which is why over the long term the family home often proves to be the most successful financial investment most people ever make.

We have looked briefly in this section at the important step of moving towards financial consciousness, and recognising and understanding your flawed money dialogues, of which you are sure to have at least some. Resolve to use any financial pain you have experienced in the past as a powerful tool for change. Pain can be a great teacher, particularly when that pain is trying to tell you an important message.

DELETING YOUR OLD MONEY MANTRAS

It's now time to replace your old money mantras with a new set of empowering beliefs. However, we cannot do that in just one paragraph or section of the book, because a genuine belief needs to be supported by some form of foundation or evidence-based information. The very first idea you can install into your financial 'operating system' right now, however, is that you will make no more excuses! All the information is available today to improve your financial future, and as I will show you, it doesn't need to be that complicated. The buck stops with you. Now let's move on to building your new empowering beliefs about money.

YOUR FIRST NEW MONEY MANTRA: THE SNOWBALL

The most important rule of personal finance is this: the awesome power of compound growth! Compounding is the dynamic of growth upon growth, where gains can increase and multiply over time, like a snowball gathering pace and mass as it rolls down a mountainside. Take a glance at the following table, in which the 'Rule of 72' shows how if you can invest in asset which increases in value by one per cent per annum, over 72 years it will have doubled in value.

Intuitively you might expect this investment to take 100 years to double in value, but because each year the increases in value get a little bit bigger, this gradual snowballing or compounding effect means that it takes 72 years. Of course, 72 years is still a very long time, but look at what happens if you can increase the rate of return on an investment to, say, 6 per cent. The time it takes the asset to double in value is cut to 12 years, which you can easily calculate yourself using the rule of 72 (72/6 = 12 years). And if you can ratchet up the returns higher then you can double your dollars more quickly still, so if you can invest in an asset which grows at 10 per cent per annum, it doubles in value in only 7.2 years (72/10 = 7.2 years).

Figure 2.4 – The rule of 72

Annual Growth Rate (%)	Years to Double in Value
1	72
2	36
3	24
4	18
5	14.4
6	12
7	10.3
8	9
9	8
10	7.2
11	6.5
12	6
13	5.5
14	5.1
15	4.8
16	4.5
17	4.2
18	4.0
19	3.8
20	3.6

At a growth rate of 20 per cent, an asset doubles in value in just 3.6 years. The reason this happens is compound interest, or growth upon growth. The numbers in the above table may not seem to mean a lot in themselves, but trust me when I say that this is the single most important principle in investment and personal finance in general.

And we are going to need to install it as the basis or foundation of your new money mantras.

Money mantra #1: I will make compound growth work for me and not against me!

Unfortunately, interest income from a bank account is usually taxed and inflation tends to eat away at the purchasing power of the balance, so leaving money in the bank is rarely an effective tool for compounding your wealth. At the time of writing interest rates are stuck at miserably low levels too, so it follows that you clearly need a better plan than simply trying to pile up money in the bank. This rarely works in any case, because if you have money sitting in the bank, sooner or later it is likely that you will find a way to spend it!

As you can glean from the short example above, it is the rate of return and the length of time over which your money remains invested that determines how much wealth you will accumulate. Crucially, note how if you can find investments whereby your unrealised gains are not taxed each year, the compounding interest in year two will be higher than that in year one – the returns are very gradually beginning to snowball.

The simplest way to calculate how compounding will impact an investment is to use the Rule of 72 – this essentially uses a very simple formula which divides the number 72 by the compounding annual rate of return to calculate how quickly an investment will double in value.

Remember: divide the number 72 by the annual growth rate and this tells you how quickly the asset will double in value. So, if you can get an annual return of 7 per cent, then it will take you around 10 years to double the value of your investment (72/7 = 10.3). And if you can turn up the heat to get a return of 10 per cent per annum it will take you just 7 years to double your money (72/10 = 7.2).

Whether you realise it or not, you essentially only have two choices in life when it comes to your personal finances. You can either choose to have compound interest working for you, or it will inevitably work against you, which particularly happens when you take on consumer or credit card debt. I'll just make that point more clearly just in case you missed it!

Compound interest either works for you or against you.

When people say that 'the rich get richer' or 'money goes to money', unfortunately this is almost invariably correct. Why is this so? At least partly this is because the wealthy understand the awesome power of compound growth. They therefore tend not to carry consumer debt, or debt on credit cards. In fact, in often owning an unencumbered home the wealthy rarely carry much debt at all, except for debt which is used to magnify their returns and wealth (known as leverage).

The wealthy very rarely spend more than they earn from their investments. What the wealthy do have is assets, which continue to pay them income, grow in value, snowball and compound, so that with every passing year they become wealthier still. That somehow doesn't seem fair, does it? And it's not, really. People with the luxury of having money at their disposal don't need to go into debt to pay for higher education, to buy a car, or to buy their first home. Instead they have excess wealth and they can use compounding growth in their favour to accumulate more wealth. The result is rising inequality.

Well, that's the bad news. Now here's the good news. Believe me when I say that it doesn't matter where you are starting from today, provided you dedicate yourself first to understanding compound growth and then putting a plan of action in place to make it work for you and not against you, for so long as possible.

There is better news still, and that is that people who are born into money will never be able to achieve the same sense of satisfaction that comes from building substantial wealth or financial freedom from scratch, or from a relatively mediocre starting position. Inheriting wealth is of course great if it happens to you. But for the rest of us who start out with no such help can come the true sense of satisfaction of mastering money and achieving financial freedom for yourself. You can enjoy the landmarks, the journey, and the pleasures of kicking your goals along the way. Here is another vitally important rule of personal finance:

Spend less than you earn and invest the difference.

Spend less than you earn because you can compound your wealth. The implications of this simple rule are so profound! Remember here that the size of the numbers that I use in these examples is not important, but the principles themselves are always vital to understand. Imagine that you receive a $10,000 cash bonus today. You can either reward yourself by spending it on a lavish break or short holiday, or you can invest it for your future. $10,000 itself may not seem like enough to make a huge difference to your financial future, so most people opt to spend their bonus.

Yet if you can invest $10,000 at an 8 per cent per annum return over the typical working lifetime of 45 years the amount can snowball or compound to be worth $319,204. That's not a typing error; it's nearly three hundred and twenty thousand dollars, although that amount of money will be worth less in the future. That's the power of compounding at work with the initial investment doubling five times in value (at 8 per cent per annum, the value of the investment doubles every 9 years).

One of the potentially infuriating facets of compounding growth is that once you fully understand it and begin to use it in your favour, you will inevitably begin to wish that you had started investing your money sooner! If you start investing in earnest when you are 50, then you will wish you had started at 45. Yet if you start when you are 30 years of age, then you will wonder why you did not begin at 25. Unfortunately, this is almost a given, but the inescapable conclusion of this is that the best time to act is today!

It is important to understand that by cutting back on consumer expenditure you stand to gain a great deal. If people feel that they are giving something up or making a painful sacrifice, they can probably manage to deny themselves for a while, but then eventually they tend to fail. But it is crucial to remember that by taking control of your personal finances, you aren't giving something up, you are gaining a wealthier and more financially secure future. Choose instead to get excited about that!

As humans, we are designed with an in-built survival instinct which causes us to value today over tomorrow. We make choices today that we probably wouldn't make in the future given the same information being available. This is known as present bias. In simple terms, we prefer one dollar today over three dollars of money tomorrow, even when this make little sense to do so.

Money mantra #2: I cannot earn my way to financial freedom from a salary!

The next new money mantra which you need to install in your code of beliefs is that you will not earn your way to wealth, for this is nigh on impossible to do. The taxman will take close to half, and in time you will probably spend most of the remainder. In developed countries, we can somehow continue to feel relatively poor even as we earn more, because someone always has more than us. We can forget relatively quickly what we do have and where we have come from. Most of us in developed countries also already live lives of comparative luxury compared to the rest of the world, yet we don't always feel this way, so as we earn more we tend to spend more.

Think of the endless list of celebrities who have earned millions and still ended up broke, of whom I will not name since this is a book about positive thinking (you can surely think of a few!). You cannot earn your way to financial freedom! What you can do is build a portfolio of assets that begins to compound your wealth substantially. Better still, it need not take you a lifetime to achieve this. With masses of dedication and, truthfully, a bit of luck, I managed to hit my target of financial freedom when I was 33. It doesn't matter how old you are or where you are starting out from today, the important thing is to get started and get the snowball rolling in your favour.

THE QUESTIONS YOU ASK YOURSELF

People who achieve success in life are often those who ask themselves the right questions. The co-founder of the London School of Economics and great Irish playwright George Bernard Shaw once observed:

'Some men see things as they are and say 'why?' Others dream of things that never were and ask 'why not?''

I believe that this is a very important analogy. Too often people are limited in what they can achieve in life because they ask themselves such disempowering questions, such as 'why does this always happen to me?' instead of asking 'how can I change this? How can I instead find ways in which to achieve everything that I have always wanted?' This is a subtle yet crucial distinction. Humans are naturally inquisitive creatures and we are designed to ask ourselves internal questions almost all the time. The process often happens unconsciously, yet we are continually posing questions to ourselves. Rarely is this more so the case than when it comes to personal finance and investing. Suppose you get an annual bonus. What is the first question which you ask yourself? Consider the following possibility:

- What can I spend this money on as a reward for my hard work? What can I treat myself to this year? Perhaps I would enjoy driving a new sports car, or a trip to Paris?

Alternatively, you could ask yourself the following empowering question:

- How I can best use this money to secure my long term financial future and to achieve my financial freedom? What investments can I buy with these funds which will bring me returns forever? How can I make sacrifices today so that my life tomorrow will be filled with abundance?

When it comes to personal finances and investment success, you will very often find that the difference between success and failure is determined by whether someone is prepared to make sacrifices today to secure their long-term future. The alternative approach of looking for short term pleasure or gratification practically guarantees suboptimal results. The same is true of some other areas of your life, hence the phrase 'no pain, no gain'. If you ask yourself the right questions, you can achieve outstanding results, and making sacrifices today can help you to achieve the goals you want.

WHO WANTS TO BE A MILLIONAIRE?

Legend has it that the initial proposal for the television game show Who Wants to Be a Millionaire? was just four short pages long. One of the killer aspects of the proposed format for the show was that for each question the contestant answered their potential prize money was doubled, up to a total of £1 million if the contestant could answer a series of fifteen questions correctly.

The game show proposal had a couple of other neat twists. For example, contestants could use 'lifelines' by phoning a friend or asking the audience for help, which certainly appealed to those of us with only an average general knowledge! Contestants would remain in play until they got a question wrong, and if the end of the show came around while they were still playing, their turn would carry over to the next day's show, a cliff hanger that was quite unique for a game show. It was very clever. Yet another part of the simple genius of the show was that the early questions for new contestants in the hot seat were relatively easy, giving viewers the sense that 'I could do that!", and because each question was in a multiple-choice format, well, you could always guess your way to becoming an instant millionaire! The game show was breath-taking in its simplicity and went on to be a smash hit success, being exported around the globe.

Interestingly, while it inevitably takes more than half an hour to achieve, this is exactly how investors become wealthy, by looking to double their wealth again and again using compounding growth. Precisely the same principles which apply to younger investors who are just starting out also apply to wealthier investors who command portfolios worth tens of millions of dollars. The small gains which are made when you start out gradually begin to grow and multiply until eventually you reach a critical mass when your own personal cash machine continues to make you wealthier passively.

Figure 2.5 – The ladder of wealth

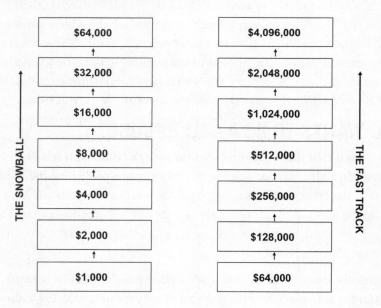

I will shortly look at a few of the few key strategies that can allow you as an average individual to achieve this goal passively, using a 'set and forget' approach to investing your savings in assets that you can hold forever.

PRACTICAL TIPS ON COMPOUNDING

Compounding! The most important rule of finance. From little things, big things can grow. To my mind there are few better examples of compound growth at work than the explosion in Australia's rabbit population. In the mid-19th century an Englishman by the name of Thomas Austin brought two dozen rabbits to Australia for a spot of shooting practice. The year was 1859. Unfortunately, a few of the rabbits got away, and because Australia did not have freezing winters as Britain did, the lucky bunnies bred throughout the year. With the number of rabbits multiplying by the year within a decade two million rabbits could be shot or trapped each year with no noticeable effect on the surviving population. It was the fastest recorded spread of any mammalian population anywhere in the history of the world, and a classic example of compound growth in action. Each pair of coupling rabbits could produce several more rabbits, and the growth upon growth continued to escalate wildly.

Compound growth outstrips linear growth, so it must only be used wisely and in your favour.

This demonstrates two things rather neatly. Firstly, where growth is compounding in nature (rather than linear or arithmetic) its reach and impact can be staggering. Secondly, while compounding growth can be an incredibly powerful force where it is used to your benefit, the unintended consequences from the misuse thereof or poor planning can also potentially be devastating. Despite the construction of three colossal rabbit-proof fences, those seemingly-innocent bunnies continue to destroy millions of dollars of crop value every year. The compounding effect has seemingly taken on a life of its own.

The key point to take away from this is that if you want to become wealthy you need to get your dollars breeding for you, a bit like the rabbits in the Australian outback. If you can resolve to invest your earnings rather than spending them on consumer goods, every dollar you earn and then save can be sent out to breed more dollars for you and keep bringing more money back to you, forever. You can achieve this if you learn to acquire the right assets.

Once you understand this simple point, it becomes easier to make the paradigm shift from an earn-and-spend mentality to an earn-save-and-invest lifestyle. Typically, for every 100 dollars you earn the taxman takes perhaps between a third and half, and most – if not all – of the rest gets spent on necessities and luxuries. What if you could find a way to invest your income before the taxman gets his hands on it? What if you could grow and compound every dollar you earn forever?

Most of us have heard of at least some examples of compound growth, with the snowballing or multiplying effect caused by growth upon growth. You probably know this kind of thing: if you put a grain of rice on the first square of a chess board, two grains on the second square, four on the third, and so on ... all the rice in India wouldn't be enough to cover the final square. Or if you could somehow manage to fold a piece of paper 42 times (which is impossible by the way, I tried it and the most number of times you can fold a piece of paper is seven times!) it would be thick enough to reach the moon.

These anecdotes tend to be mildly interesting but not particularly useful in a practical sense. The good news is that, unlike the folds in a piece of paper, there is almost no limit to the number of times you can double your investment portfolio. What this means is that time is very much the friend of the efficient buy-and-hold investment. $100,000 invested at the age of 25 at a rate of return 10 per cent per annum compounded is seen to be worth a staggering $5.5 million by the traditional retirement date – even without any extra funds invested. It is this simple concept which allowed folk like Warren Buffett to become a billionaire so many times over.

ILLOGICAL RULES ABOUT COMPOUNDING

There are a few things to note about compounding that don't appear at first glance to make any logical sense. One is that where you build a portfolio which doubles in value consistently, the increase in value of the portfolio at each interval totals more than all the previous gains. For example, in the example below where the portfolio doubles in value every seven years through recording gains of a shade over 10 per cent per annum, in the seven-year period between year 35 and year 42 the portfolio gain of $3.2 million exceeds the gains of all the previous 35 years ($3.1 million).

Figure 2.6 – Compounding in action

Year	Portfolio
0	$100,000
7	$200,000
14	$400,000
21	$800,000
28	$1,600,000
35	$3,200,000
42	$6,400,000

Watching how the gains can accelerate when left to grow unimpeded by capital gains taxes and transaction costs should draw you to two logical conclusions:

- (i) It's best to start investing now; and
- (ii) investing in quality assets which you never need to sell can be extremely appealing!

As we will explore in Chapter 6, examples of such assets might include:

- (i) A low-cost index fund or 'exchange-traded fund' (ETF); or
- (ii) a listed investment company (LIC) with a low management expense ratio (MER) which invests in more than 100 profitable and dividend-paying industrial companies; or
- (iii) a well-located property, in a capital city that has strong and sustainable population growth.

I'm not sure there is much value in adding another numerical example here, only to reiterate that time is such a powerful multiplier that often an investor who starts earlier achieves a far better result than one who starts later. Running simple numbers through a model invariably shows that even if the later starter invests more capital per annum, it becomes extremely difficult to 'play catch-up' simply because of the accelerating power of compounding growth. As you can see, building wealth is ultimately only reliant upon three things:

- (i) Having some initial capital to invest;
- (ii) the ability to command satisfactory returns consistently; and

- (iii) time to allow the value of your portfolio to compound.

It is this simple realisation that allows some apparently ordinary folk to build massive multi-million-dollar investment portfolios. Note that it is not necessarily down to exceptional asset selection – investments in a few low-cost products and well-located properties can easily do the trick. It is much more about patience, time and understanding how wealth is created through compounding returns.

FIVE PRACTICAL TIPS ON COMPOUNDING

Now we have established the theoretical importance of compounding growth, here are some practical ideas and tips on compounding your wealth:

1. Starting small is OK

If there's one thing that the above concepts tell us, it's that it is better to invest something rather than nothing! Investing small amounts regularly can still work wonders over time because of the compounding effect. However, if you are going to start small be aware of the impact of transaction costs, such as brokerage or fund management fees, and invest efficiently wherever possible. More on exactly how to do this later!

2. Forced saving is good

Have you ever heard anyone curse thus: 'Money in my pocket or in my bank account just seems to disappear'? I have. In fact, I've probably said it myself at one time or another! It is a truism of personal finance that simply attempting to pile money up in a bank account doesn't often work very effectively over the long term. Partly this is because you must pay tax on the interest, while inflation in the price of goods hungrily nibbles away at the value or purchasing power of the balance. Moreover, this is also because sooner or later that balance of money tends to get spent. How can you set up a means of forced saving? A standing order or a direct debit into a specified investment account?

3. You don't miss what you've never had

You don't miss what you've never had – another truism, and one which suggests that the more automated your system is for investing – such as a standing order from your pay cheque – the greater the likelihood of your success. This also leads to the logical conclusion that it can be a great idea to ...

4. Re-invest your gains!

Investing for the long term in quality assets which generate wealth-creating rates of return is a route to long term financial freedom, but it is the re-investment of gains which allows you to multiply your wealth. Sometimes you might hear the bean-counters (of which I am one myself) say that you shouldn't re-invest dividends because this can lead to an accounting headache when capital gains taxes fall due some time down the track. I've heard similar arguments in favour of not using a line of credit against your home to re-invest in further investments because the accounting entries can 'all get a bit tricky'. Don't worry if you don't know what a dividend is, by the way, I'll explain further and more clearly in Chapter 6 and beyond.

In fact, from a value investor's perspective there actually are some sound logical arguments in favour of not re-investing dividends at certain points in the share market cycle, particularly when share market indices are expensive or significantly over-valued. However, believe it or not, engaging a lazy professional who can't be bothered to run a simple spreadsheet to keep track of a few accounting entries is not a solid argument against re-investment!

As a rule, re-investment during the earlier growth phase of your investment portfolio can be an efficient way to grow and compound your wealth. Just as importantly, re-investment of your gains makes use of the underlying principles of the first three tips listed above: small amounts make a big difference, re-investment is another form of forced saving, and you don't miss what you've never had.

5. Most people just aren't very good at saving!

Unfortunate, but true. Most of us begrudgingly pay our electricity bills when they fall due, but equally, most people just aren't very good at saving dollars every month (at least, not over the long term). Many of us might be able to build up a decent balance over the course of a financial year through spending less than we earn, but sadly it is also deceptively easy to spend the balance on a car or a holiday when that time of year rolls around again. This is just another strong point in favour of setting up an automated investment strategy.

THE ROLE OF TAX

Finally, for this important chapter, here are a couple more important new money mantras for you:

Money mantra #3: I will not waste money needlessly on capital gains taxes!

The most efficient form of investing is generally to buy and hold quality assets which you can hold forever and never sell, because then you never need to pay tax on the profits. This is a simple point but it is also vital if you want to invest your money in the most efficient manner. Too many people invest in shares or property in the hope of making a fast gain, and if they are lucky enough to do so they immediately sell their asset which inevitably leads to transaction costs and capital gains tax liabilities. This leads us to a fourth new money mantra:

Money mantra #4: Buy and hold investing is more efficient than trading.

Most average investors stand a far better chance of achieving your financial goals if you can learn to invest in high quality assets which you never need to sell because then your gains can be allowed to compound or snowball in perpetuity without ever being impeded by tax. Thus, we occasionally read stories in the financial press about old ladies who have built great fortunes. Frequently it transpires that they have bought shares in a few companies – or often an index of companies – decades ago and simply never sold them, allowing the gains to grow and compound unimpeded by tax. Incidentally, it is no coincidence that it is so often ladies in these stories. Men tend to trade too often, forever wanting to act frenetically, take control, or just do something. Perhaps this desire to act and trade is just in our DNA, but typically this hurts our returns!

So many people today only have two successful investments, their home and their pension. Some people don't benefit from these choices either, and the only option that remains for many is the state pension. As I have already said, in my opinion it is no coincidence that these are the only two successful investments which so many people make, and this is simply because these are often the only two financial investments which people make with a long-term view in mind. In the case of the home, because people need somewhere to live, they buy, hold, and never sell. And the pension typically can't be accessed before the pension age.

Often the pension doesn't prove to be as good an investment as it should, and I will tackle why this is the case in Chapter 6 and specifically what you can do about it. Over time I have found that while both shares and property have their own respective merits, which are the right asset classes and investment types for you often boils down to which asset class you feel the most comfortable with. While I invest in both shares and property, the strongest returns for me have come from buying and holding prime location capital city property for the long term by never selling.

Indeed, neither my wife nor I have sold a single property across two decades of investing. On the other hand, I have friends who have achieved financial freedom through investing in shares only, and not holding any property at all outside of the ownership of their own home. Ultimately you can use either path, or ideally a combination of both. But for most people, I have found over time that they will have a natural inclination to one asset class or the other, and this inherent preference tends to form the basis of their portfolio.

So many folks think that their best chance of becoming rich is either by earning lots of money or through receiving a big windfall. This helps to explain the popularity of the UK National Lottery with people prepared to bet surprisingly large amounts of money each week in the hope of achieving an extremely unlikely outcome, the odds of a jackpot win being beyond remote! Incredibly Australians gamble more than $20 billion per annum, with most of that money going into poker machines.1 For such a small population this is a vast sum of money.

The average poker machine player loses $2500 every year.[2] Given that $2500 invested at 8 per cent over 45 years could be worth nearly $80,000 by the retirement age, just imagine what could be achieved if an extra $2500 could be set aside for retirement every year when invested wisely. The results could be staggering. What could it be worth to you if you saved this amount every year? In a nutshell, wasting or gambling such a sum of money every year could be the difference between achieving your financial freedom and not.

The problem seems to be that people want to chase a jackpot today and will do so at the expense of a practically guaranteed jackpot at the retirement date. In fact, if people could simply get their head around starting to compound their wealth today and to commit to doing so voraciously – to vow to never give up, like a dog with a bone – they could potentially achieve financial freedom far earlier than they can even imagine.

But as it stands, most never become wealthy. Worse still, even most lottery winners end up broke within a few years. Why is this so? Usually this is because they have no context for investing the money which they have won. They are neither familiar nor comfortable with the position of having money, and their wealth 'thermostat' is still dialled to a low position. The key to becoming wealthy in a sustainable manner is not hoping or praying for a big win or a windfall. The key to becoming wealthy is spending less than you earn and investing the difference in quality assets for the long term. You need to become a stakeholder that benefits from the growth in the economy – rather than just a mindless consumer, you need to become a mindful or conscious consumer, and perhaps then a business owner in your own right.

BUILD YOUR OWN CASH MACHINE

Earning a higher salary is a great benefit to those who have the discipline to save and invest, and this can certainly help to supercharge your wealth creation plan. However, it is highly unlikely that your salary alone will make you wealthy. Remember, firstly, this is because as your income increases so does your tax bill. And secondly, because if you are like most people then each pay rise is likely to be met with an equivalent increase in expenditure.

It's easy to believe otherwise and think that you will set aside money as your income grows. Yet think again of those big earners who have managed to spend every cent that they earned (and then some, in many cases!). The list is seemingly endless. So many high-income earners spend as if the good times will last forever, but unfortunately they never do! To achieve financial freedom, you need to build a portfolio of income-producing assets which generates a passive income that is greater than your expenses. It's that simple.

In this context, passive income refers to that which flows to you without you having to work for it – you need to build your own personal cash machine. There are different ways to go about this as I will look at in the coming chapters. Some people have a leaning towards property as an asset class which they feel familiar with. Others prefer the share markets and look to own shares in those wonderful companies which pay out dividends from their profits twice per year, every year. I believe that a portfolio should incorporate different asset types to diversify your risk, which we will cover in more detail when we look at asset allocation in Chapter 6.

Chapter 2 Summary

- Be mindful of your finances, and consider what your disempowering beliefs about money may be.

- Choose new and empowering 'money mantras'.

- Your retirement is your own responsibility, not that of your employer, Pension fund manager, financial planner, or anyone else.

- Aim to build wealth for so long as you live (not spending the last cent on your last day!).

- You cannot easily earn your way to financial freedom.

- The key to financial success is understanding and then using compounding growth.

- The most efficient form of investing is often simpley to buy and hold quality assets for the long term!

CHAPTER 3
LOSE THE FAT

MAKE YOUR PLAN STREAMLINED!

Personal finances and the game of money is a marathon not a sprint, and to win the game you need to have an efficient plan, not one which continually drags you back. One type of excess baggage that drags most people back is debt. It comes in different guises: a massive mortgage, credit card debt for consumer goods, car loans, student debts or higher education loans, or debt to friends and family. The problem with debt is that typically it incurs interest charges and this costs you. In fact, debt costs you in more ways than one. Firstly, there is the interest cost, but secondly there is the opportunity cost of what you could do with that money instead. As I said in the previous chapter, compound growth is either working for you or it is working against you.

Formulating an efficient plan for your money means lowering your expenses (at least initially), minimising the fees paid to people to manage your money such as fund managers, minimising the money you pay in tax, and as we will consider in this chapter, eradicating your bad debt. It may be possible that you can achieve financial success without taking these steps but the sums of money you potentially need to earn can quickly become vast. It is time to make your plan more streamlined.

GETTING STARTED IS WHAT COUNTS

In the modern age, it is quite common for our financial profiles to have a negative net worth in the earlier part of our adult life, meaning that we have more debts or liabilities than assets. This is partly because many of us must pay for our higher education, and partly because we are encouraged to get into consumer debt to buy cars and other depreciating assets.

'The secret to getting ahead is getting started.' – **Mark Twain**

If you are in the position whereby you have some debts right now, don't worry. We will address how to deal with those first so that you can get yourself into a stronger position to begin tackling your route to financial freedom. It doesn't matter where you are starting from today, but it does matter that you decide to get started.

MAKING A GENUINE DECISION

The first thing you must do if you want to escape from the rat race of dependence on a pay cheque and begin to live the life you truly want to lead is to make a genuine decision to do so. What does it mean to make a real decision? The word is derived from the Latin *decider,* meaning to cut off. To make a real decision means that you have literally chosen to cut off all other alternatives. And that is how it is when it comes to building wealth and designing the life you want to lead. You need to decide to cut yourself away from the choice of failure.

Deciding to achieve a goal means cutting off all other alternatives.

Why is this so vital? The reason is that in the life of every person there will be failures and setbacks. What separates the winners from the also-rans is a total and absolute commitment when things do not go as planned to resolve to get back on the horse and never give up. The goal of this book is to guide you on how to get from where you are today to where you want to be, but you will encounter obstacles to success whatever plans and strategies you implement. Only you can decide if you truly have the burning desire and commitment to overcome them.

GETTING OUT OF BAD DEBT

The first step is to acknowledge where you are starting from today. On a piece of paper make a list your bad debt – that is, debt which doesn't earn you an income or relate to your home, such as a mortgage – the amounts you owe, and to whom you owe them. If you know the interest rates that you must pay on that debt then make a list of those too.

The good news is that there is a proven method to get out of bad debt. Firstly, resolve to start by targeting the debt with the highest cost attached to it first. In purely financial terms, the debt with the highest cost attached to it means that which attracts the highest rate of interest or the greatest penalty charges. Alternatively, there may be debts which have the potential to damage your credit score, so you might deem these to be of the highest priority. However, there can be debts with an even higher cost of a different kind, such as debts to friends and family. Ultimately it is up to you which of your bad debts you prioritise for repayment.

Commit to saving as much money as you can each month, and use this amount to pay off the highest priority debt first. Go at it as hard as you can! When the first tranche of debt is paid off move on to the next highest priority debt, paying down the same amount as you were before, plus the amount of any interest you have now saved from the first debt which you no longer have. It may take some time, but the proven process is simply to repeat this strategy until all your bad debt is paid off. It should go without saying, of course, that you must resolve to not take any further bad debts for consumer liabilities and not to buy anything which you cannot afford!

Money mantra #5: I will eradicate all bad debt, permanently!

That is one proven way to get out of bad debt, but there are others. What I have described above may be the most efficient way to clear your debts from a purely financial perspective. However, what is most important here is that you get started and get motivated to clear your bad debts! Another alternative is simply to start by paying off your smallest debts first. While this may not technically be the most effective method of reducing your interest payments, what this can give you is the great satisfaction of clearing a debt. Since what is believable is also achievable, paying off one of your less intimidating debts can give you the confidence and self-belief to move on and tackle the next largest tranche of bad debt. It helps you to get motivated, pay off a small debt first and feel the sense of achievement. Then you can move on to the next debt and pay that off too.

Get your bad debts paid off as soon as you can and then you are on your way! You are now ready to be an investor and a stakeholder in the economy rather than a bystander or consumer. You can instead become a conscious consumer and begin to make things happen for you, rather than allowing them to happen to you.

GETTING YOUR FINANCIAL HOUSE IN ORDER

When accountants are drawing up the Annual Report or financials of a business there are two primary financial statements which they focus on. These are:

- The **Income Statement**, or what we used to call the 'profit and loss account' – this summarises all income and expenditure for a financial year or period; and
- The Statement of Financial Position, or what we more commonly refer to as a **Balance Sheet** – this summarises all the assets and liabilities of a business.

It is possible to prepare financial statements for individuals as well as businesses: an income statement summarising your income and outgoings for a year, and a balance sheet summarising all your assets (such as cash in the bank, your home and investments) and your liabilities (your mortgage, higher education loans, credit card balances and any other debts).

If you are feeling particularly sharp-witted today you may have noticed that the name Balance Sheet implies that the figures should, well, balance! If your assets are greater than your liabilities, then the balancing figure is known as your equity, which essentially represents your present level of wealth or net worth. Of course, if your liabilities are greater than your assets, which they may be when you are just starting out in your journey, then your equity or net worth will be negative.

Without getting too bogged down in terminology and financial jargon, accounting entries are governed by the principles of double entry book-keeping, meaning that for each transaction that takes place there is an equal and opposite entry. So, for example, if you buy a car then you have an asset (albeit a depreciating one!) which fits snugly into your asset column, but you also have less cash, so there is a deduction to be made from your cash assets. Although you have purchased an asset, you are no wealthier after the purchase, and in fact when the car gradually loses value you will become less well off.

If you also borrow money to make the purchase then instead of deducting cash from your assets today, the accounting entry instead creates an asset (the car) and a liability (being the car loan). Over time the loan will attract interest, so there will be additional expenses to pay as the loan is repaid. What this should tell you is that while borrowing money to buy assets which go up in value and pay you income may be a smart idea if done wisely, borrowing money to buy things which decline in value over time is generally a terrible idea which clobbers you twice – once in the form of interest repayments, and a second time as the value of your asset depreciates. Ouch!

If you were to look at your financial statements visually they might look something like the below graphic. In the first financial statement is a list of your annual income and expenditure. And in the second financial statement (the balance sheet) is a list of all your assets and their values, and all your liabilities and debts, too. Incidentally, the total of your assets less your liabilities is known as your net worth. It's what you are worth today, in financial terms at least.

Figure 3.1 – Your financial statements

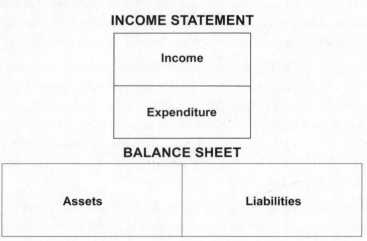

If you are between the ages of 20 and 35 and are like most people in your age group, you will be rather light on assets and you may well have some debt. If you are younger than 20 years of age today then I envy you because by reading this book you are getting access to invaluable information at a young age! The most important aspect of the concept of compounding growth is that the longer you can let its power work in your favour, the more devastatingly effective it can be. If you start investing in earnest at the age of 50, you will wish you had started five years earlier, of course. But the same also holds true if you start investing at 45, or 40, or 35, or indeed, at any age. The inescapable conclusion is that the time to take more action is always now, because this maximises the time you have available to build your wealth.

One of the great challenges today is that we are force-fed adverts which compel us to buy luxury items or things that we don't necessarily need. Most employees today are consumers, meaning that they earn money and promptly spend it again. They have financial statements which look something like the graphic below. Each month they have salary income which flows in to their income account, but they tend to have expenses that are at least as high as their income and therefore at the end of the month they are no better off than when they started it, despite working full time!

Consumers often have various forms of loans and debt, such as credit cards, store card loans, or car loans, but very few genuine income-producing assets. Since debt incurs interest this adds to the monthly expenses, making it even harder to save any money to invest. The enigma of compound interest is that if it isn't working for you, then it's effectively working against you. What happens to consumers is that while some money flows in from salaried employment, expenses and interest on the debt see the money flowing straight back out again in expenses.

Figure 3.2 – A consumer's financial statements

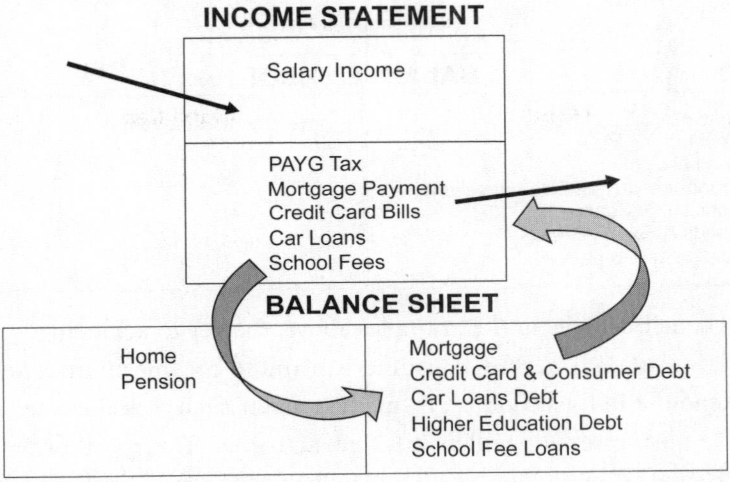

INCOME STATEMENT

Salary Income

PAYG Tax
Mortgage Payment
Credit Card Bills
Car Loans
School Fees

BALANCE SHEET

Home
Pension

Mortgage
Credit Card & Consumer Debt
Car Loans Debt
Higher Education Debt
School Fee Loans

The challenge I present to you here is to find ways to spend less than you earn so you can invest the difference, thereby loading up your personal balance sheet with income-producing assets, while at the same time shunning bad debt and consumer liabilities. Financial freedom is achieved when you have assets which generate a monthly income which is greater than your expenses. It is as simple as that!

Money mantra #6: I will acquire assets, not liabilities!

Of course, there are two variables which you can target here to move towards the goal of financial freedom. Firstly, you can reduce your monthly expenditure. And secondly you can increase the passive income from your investments, which means acquiring more assets. It is that straightforward! The financial statements of an investor might look something more like the below. Because the investor has loaded up their balance sheet with income-producing assets (and not liabilities which incur interest expenses) the income that continues to flow to them is greater than their expenses. They are financially free!

Figure 3.3 – An investor's financial statements

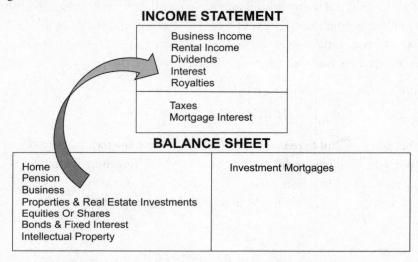

As you can clearly see in the examples above, the key to achieving financial freedom is to shun consumerism and to become an investor or stakeholder in the economy. By owning assets such as real estate and shares in businesses you will be just that: an owner. This must form a fundamental point of your new financial beliefs. Acquire quality assets and not liabilities, and hold on to them for the long term.

BUDGETING ... A SPENDING PLAN!

Yes, yes, I know what you're thinking. Budgeting is about as exciting as watching paint dry! In fact, it is probably less fun than watching paint dry, because at least watching paint dry is a passive activity. Look, I hear you on this point! Remember through my professional career I worked as a Chartered Accountant, and therefore trust me when I say that from painful experience I know better than most just how boring the idea of spreadsheets can be. Throughout my career as a CA every year without fail those wretched budgets would need preparing, and in the listed corporate world this tends to be an excruciating process of back and forth, amendments, reviews, more amendments, more reviews ... ad nauseam.

You can imagine, therefore, that the last thing I felt like doing when escaping the drudgery of the office for the weekend was drawing up a personal budget of my own finances. It would be like the proverbial busman's holiday, and not a very good one! So yes, I do get it when you say that you aren't going to spend hours going through every tiny morsel of money you spend each month with the proverbial fine toothcomb. I wouldn't do that either, and I'm certainly not going to ask you to do anything that I wouldn't do myself. This is one of the reasons why we will look specifically at setting exciting goals in Chapter 5. And in fact, we aren't even going to call it a budget. We are going to call it a spending plan, because we are using positive vocabulary!

What is important here is that you just need to get the basics down on paper, where you are today, and broadly speaking how much money you spend on living costs. How do you draw up a simple spending plan? Simple. Grab a sheet of paper and write three headings on it:

- Fixed essential costs
- Variable essential costs
- Luxury costs

Under the heading for fixed essential costs, make a brief list of those fixed costs which you incur each month. Typically, these would include your household expenses – such as your monthly rent or mortgage payments, insurance, and utilities – and repayments on car loans, student loans, or other such debt. Then under the heading for variable essential costs list the costs which you incur each month such as food, fuel, transport, repairs, phone and internet, doctor and dentist, school uniforms, and so on. And thirdly, draw up a list of discretionary, luxury and entertainment costs which you incur each month. Under this heading make a short list of your typical monthly costs over the year for travel, holidays, 'toys' and luxury items, clothes, eating out, cinema, birthdays, Christmas, and so forth.

Now if you want to become a stakeholder or owner in the economy, you will need to make one small but key adjustment to your spending plan. When you visualise your monthly financial expenses, I want you to imagine that you now have four buckets rather than three. Your fourth bucket will be for your investments which you will use to compound or snowball your way to wealth.

Your challenge will be to reduce the amount of money which drops into the first three buckets, because these are dollars which are leaking out of your life forever! Instead your goal must become to aim to drop as many dollars as you can into the investment bucket. In Chapter 7 and beyond I am going to show you specifically the types of investments you can put these dollars into so that they will go out to work for you in perpetuity. Every dollar you save and drop into this bucket can be sent out to work for you every day from now for the rest of your life. Cool, huh?

Figure 3.4 – A budget or 'spending plan'

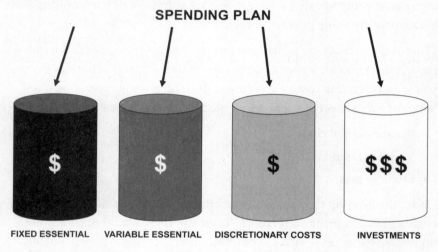

SPENDING PLAN

FIXED ESSENTIAL VARIABLE ESSENTIAL DISCRETIONARY COSTS INVESTMENTS

One of the reasons that most people never achieve true financial freedom is that they simply cannot get their head around this concept at all! They earn money and spend it, and that's that. They get a pay rise, a bonus or another financial windfall, so they spend some more. Very little ever gets invested outside of their home and their pension (and if they ever do invest, they trade too much and try to second guess what markets will do next, or gamble in the hope of an instant cash windfall). Instead, we are going to draw up a plan to maximise the amount that you can invest, and these dollars are going to be invested in quality income-producing assets which you will never have to sell. By re-investing the profits, you can begin to compound and snowball your wealth for so long as you live. If you can get your head around this simple shift in mind-set, then you are well and truly on your way.

LIFETIME EARNINGS (AND SPENDING LESS)

The amount you could potentially earn in your lifetime may be far greater than you imagine. Run some sums working on the assumption that you work through until you're 65 – even without pay increases and bonuses the figure can be surprisingly large. Taxes will account for some of your income of course, but the question is not so much whether you can make a million dollars, rather the question is whether you can keep a million dollars!

While folk often seen television adverts as a form of light entertainment, the truth is that advertisements are specifically designed and targeted at encouraging us to spend, spend, and spend some more. Now I certainly don't intend to insult your intelligence by listing all the ways in which you can save money. The simplest way to tackle this is just to look at the monthly expenses fleeing your bank account and to take note of where you spend your cash, and to think of as many ways as you can to reduce the expenditure. Where does money leak out of your life? How can you plug those gaps?

Let us consider a few of the big-ticket items, though. Today I must confess here that I am a multiple car owner, but for a while I wasn't. When I was in the earlier stages of my investing life I realised when I was living in the centre of a city that I was hardly driving at all, instead using buses or walking to most places. I worked out that for less than half of the cost of annual servicing, repairs, insurance and fuel I could hire a car whenever I wanted to use one. For a while I also used a car share service whereby it was possible to book cars online and then pick one up whenever required from specially allocated parking bays on the street. I'm not saying you should rush out and sell your car, of course. This is merely one personal example of how saving money can be achieved with a bit of thought. I already mentioned in my first book *Get a Financial Grip* the huge average cost of weddings these days, so I won't mention that again here!

Consider whether sometimes you can buy second hand goods instead of buying new. What about food? Buy in value supermarkets where you can, and look for home brands. Eating out and going out 'boozing' are two luxuries which you can go a long way to holding you back financially. Sure, we all enjoy a night out when we're younger. I can tell you for sure that I did! Yet consider that $5000 could be worth nearly $160,000 if invested for 45 years at an 8 per cent return. Try to think of the opportunity cost!

As I said, I certainly don't want to insult your intelligence by listing a thousand ways in which you can save, because I know you can manage this yourself, but let's at least get you started by brainstorming a few ideas. Remember, the savings are there somewhere, so it will be up to you to find them and make it happen. After all, saving is the foundation of your financial plan.

Before getting started, make sure that the money that you do save is in an account which doesn't incur unnecessary fees and pays you a fair rate of interest. A penny saved is two pennies earned, but it can be more if you earn a fair rate of return on that penny! Be as flexible as you can, but be realistic. Discipline brings rewards but you also want to build a plan which is sustainable, since acting obsessively or simply going cold turkey won't work over the longer term. Be well organised, manage and track your bank account online, and keep filed records of your wage slips and other financial records.

DON'T BUY WHAT YOU CAN'T AFFORD ...

The legendary comedian Steve Martin once acted out a characteristically hilarious sketch on Saturday Night Live called 'Don't buy stuff you can't afford'. You can find it on YouTube. It sounds so obvious, of course, but think back to the financial statements of most consumers that we looked at in Figure 3.2. Most people today do indeed buy stuff that they can't afford, and often they pay for it using credit. Simply put, if you do this regularly you will never be able to achieve financial freedom.

Money mantra #7: Think three times before spending money needlessly.

Try not to see shopping as a pastime or a leisure activity. Pay for consumer goods using cash because then the amount you spend will feel more real, which tends not to be the case if you pay using plastic. Don't buy the first thing you see, and aim to think three times before spending any money whilst out shopping. Do you need what you are about to buy? Can you get it cheaper elsewhere? Is there a way to get better value for your money? Why not ask for discounts? It's sometimes scary, I know, but what's the worst that can happen?

Cash flow is important. Just as businesses go bust because of a lack of cash flow, so it is for the individual consumer. Can you delay consumer purchases until a later date? Should you wait until the end of year financial sales? On the other hand, planning can also save you money when done wisely, such as buying your Christmas goods in January. Better still can you make some of your own Christmas gifts? One year I made jam, marmalade and preserves, despite being a terrible cook! It took me absolutely ages to make, to be honest, but I rather enjoyed it, and in the end the gifts were well received. Instead of buying trendy or branded goods, can you buy own brand, second hand or generic products? Here are a few more ideas:

- Shop at value supermarkets and find items that are on offer.
- Eat at home more often!
- Have movie nights at home instead of expensive trips out.
- Save water and power when you can.
- Think of your mobile phone, internet, and online expenses – track your costs, and cut down on the dear stuff. Look for cheap phone deals to save money on calls.
- Get in touch with the outdoors, because most of it is free – go hiking, take a swim at the beach, go surfing (I'm British by birth, and so naturally terrible at this, but hey, at least it costs nothing) or take up gardening.
- The best things in life are free sang The Beatles, so why not try some of them? (I think from memory this was from the song Money though, so perhaps not the best example quote).
- Try ordering goods, hotels and flights over the internet to save.
- Despite lower oil prices petrol is likely to become more expensive over time as it is a soft target for government tax grabs. How can you find ways to spend less on fuel? What are your main travel costs? Can you find ways to reduce them?
- Entertainment. Can you stop going out as much as you do? Do you spend as much as I used to on smoking and drinking? If so, you'll know what a terrible drain on finances these vices can be!
- Do you have expensive hobbies? How can you make them less dear?
- Designer clothes and accessories have the potential to be very costly. Can you find better value alternatives?

When it comes to savings, the little bits and pieces can add up. I once had a job as a Financial Controller in Sydney – generally an expensive city to live in at the best of times – for which I unerringly picked up a large Starbucks coffee while walking into the office from where I lived at Darling Harbour (this is an expensive part of town). The $4 for the coffee was expensive enough, but the trouble was that my job was so dull that by 10am my accounts assistant was dragging me out for another coffee! I was not hauled out kicking and screaming, it must be said, because I will always choose coffee over accountancy. Throw in the odd sweet snack here, the odd fizzy drink there, a newspaper, a burrito, a magazine, or a lotto ticket, and it can all add up to a surprising amount of money through the working week.

Whether you decide to send your children to a private school or drive a new car is of course none of my business. However, what I am saying here is that you should try to be mindful of your spending! Going cold turkey will probably not work over any kind of meaningful time scale, and your plan needs to be sustainable. It's not about austerity, you see, it is about taking control of your financial future! And it's not that you cannot have nice things, but remember that a sustainable spending plan which allows for delayed gratification will make for a far wealthier tomorrow.

BECOMING A TIME LORD!

Recall that the great Jim Rohn once said that time is more valuable than money, because while you can get more money, but you can't get more time. Such wise words! In this book, I aim to change the way you think about time in a few different ways. Too often today we hear people say that they are struggling for time, or they don't have the time to do the things they want to do. Instead of seeing time as your enemy, I want you to make time your ally, and for you to become a master of time.

'Time is the most valuable thing a man can spend.' – Theophrastus

Have you ever heard of the concept of opportunity cost? Here is an example of it. When companies calculate the cost of their capital, they do so in part because they understand that it would be nonsensical to undertake projects which return less than the cost of financing them. For example, a mining company might elect to invest one million dollars in a new piece of crushing equipment which could increase its throughput rates and increase annual profits by $50,000. Before it does so, however, the company will generally need to look at what else that money might be doing for them instead (the opportunity cost).

Opportunity cost can be intuitive.

Whether you realise it or not, opportunity cost applies to your own personal finances. Each time you spend your hard-earned dollars on a treat or a luxury, there is a twin cost attached to this. Firstly, once you spend your dollars, you do not have that money in your pocket or bank account any longer. And secondly, those dollars spent could have been invested in assets which might earn you many more dollars in the future.

What is perhaps slightly less obvious is that opportunity cost also applies to your time. It is amazing how often I hear people say that they do not have time to sort out their personal finances, get started in investing, or attempt to chase the life of their dreams. For some reason people feel unable to commit even an hour a week to thinking about their personal finances, while spending up to 50 hours a week in an office. Madness! The fact is that you have 24 hours in a day and 7 days in a week, just the same as I do. What is more, Mark Zuckerberg and Bill Gates have the same number of hours in a day that we have!

It does not make sense to say that we don't have the time to do something, for we all have the same amount of time in a week as each other. What we are talking about is how we prioritise our time. This is not something to become stressed about. In fact, whether we realise it or not, we all weigh up opportunity cost almost every time we decide to do anything. Each time you elect to work overtime instead of going to the pub, go to the football or go shopping, or choose a slice of cake instead of going to the gym, you are intuitively weighing up the costs and benefits of each decision.

Opportunity cost can impact careers too.

Over recent years, for example, an increasingly tough choice has faced many youngsters. With the introduction of expensive university tuition fees, students must balance up the benefits of a university education which may see them incur considerable debt against the long-term benefits of attaining a degree or higher education qualification. By the time a student has graduated with a debt burden, his or her school friend that shunned higher education may have worked for several years and saved a significant amount towards buying their first house. A graduate might typically earn a higher salary but they probably need to do so to pay off their student debts! This can be a very tough decision to make at such a young age.

My simple aim here is to subtly change the way you think about time. Firstly, I want you to realise that time is the greatest friend of a quality investment, because the more time that you own it for, the more time compound growth can work its magic. Warren Buffett said that time is the friend of the wonderful investment, but the enemy of the mediocre, because over time the gap in the respective performance of the investment becomes a gulf. Secondly, consider that by spending less than you earn you can send your dollars out to work harder for you so that ultimately you will not have to. You will in effect be buying your life back. Once your investments reach a critical mass you will be able to choose whether to continue trading your valuable time for money. You may of course continue to do so, or you might choose to set up a business in the field of your passion. Time can become your friend, instead of an enemy.

LIVE IN A CHEAPER PLACE?

One more radical idea that you can use to make your lifestyle less costly, is simply to live in a cheaper place, or even a cheaper part of the world. I did this myself on a couple of occasions throughout my professional career, living in a developing country where the tax rate was only a fraction of what I would have paid in London or Sydney. It's not the reason I decided to work overseas – I did that because I love travel and experiences – but it was impossible not to notice the difference paying less tax makes to net monthly income.

In today's more fluid corporate world I have a great many friends who have made the journey to work in countries with lower income tax rates such as Singapore and Hong Kong. Some are almost in economic exile being a position where their after-tax income is perhaps double what it would be in their home country! Not everyone wants to live or work overseas, I understand that, and there can also be foreign exchange and tax domicile implications to take account of. But it's worth at least considering. Another action you can take is simply to live somewhere cheaper in your own country – either in a cheaper part of the country by moving interstate, or simply by opting to move to an inexpensive neighbourhood.

Presented here are merely a handful of ideas. The real point is to get creative and think of ways you can reduce your expenditure to ramp up the amount you can invest each month or quarter. Where can you make savings? How can you kick start your plan?

RENTING WHERE YOU LIVE

If you are young and have not yet bought a place to live as a home – or even if you are older and have not yet done so for that matter – it is worth considering whether you might be better off renting anyway. The problem with buying a home is that most often people buy the most expensive home they can afford which can all but cripple them financially, at least from a monthly cash flow perspective. While this strategy of stretching yourself to buy a home tends to work reasonably well over the long term, provided you decide to stay in the same house for a reasonable period, it can also make it extremely difficult to have any money left over at all each month to invest in income-producing assets.

One of the reasons that renting can be an effective strategy is that it is typically cheaper to rent where you live in terms of the monthly cash flow. Better still you don't have those annoying sundry costs that harass homeowners such as repairs, maintenance, and, in some circumstances, body corporate fees and property taxes. Don't get me wrong, owning your own home is still something to aspire to, and a successful retirement plan should involve the ownership of an unencumbered home. But in today's more fluid world where employees can change jobs and even careers so frequently, you may wish to consider buying later when you have made more headway financially, and have more certainty about where you wish to settle.

YOUR GOLDEN NUMBER!

How much of your net income after tax will you save per month? Can you save as much as 20 per cent of your after-tax income? For most people, the immediate or instinctive answer to that question is something like: 'Absolutely not! You don't understand, I have high expenses that I have to pay, there's no way I can save that much!' If that sounds familiar, then there is no need to panic. Even if you can't get there immediately, you can get there in time as we will discover in the coming chapters.

Money mantra #8: I will eventually find a way to save at least 20 per cent of my income!

If you want to improve your finances dramatically, you absolutely must find a way to save at least 10 per cent of your income, but ideally it should be 20 per cent, or even more if you can manage that. Choose your number (did I already say I think it should be 20 per cent? Go for 20 per cent!). Make it another new money mantra. Next we will look at the ways in which you can get there. The answer, of course, is the same way in which most goals can be achieved: one step at a time!

Chapter 3 Summary

- Aim to clear your bad debt first, and resolve to eradicate bad debt from your life permanently.
- To achieve financial freedom, you must move from being consumer to being a stakeholder or investor.
- Draw up a high-level budget or spending plan.
- Find ways to reduce needless expenditure …
- … and then get radical … find even more ways to save!
- Resolve to save 20 per cent of your income, either from today or as soon as you reasonably can!
- Acquire appreciating and income-producing assets, not liabilities.

CHAPTER 4
WARMING
UP

WARMING UP

A key part of the preparation for any race is to make a few mental preparations and to get appropriately warmed up – through doing so you can reduce the risk of starting too enthusiastically but running out of steam quickly. It is important to build a plan which incorporates the whole race, whereby you can build and progress from the ground up, right the way through to the end.

YOUR PAST DOES NOT EQUAL YOUR FUTURE

It is all too easy to believe that because in the past you have not necessarily fulfilled your potential then it must always necessarily be so. Nothing could be further from the truth! The past need not in any way equal the future, not for you or anyone else. Look at the lives of the most successful people in their fields and you will very often find that before they began to achieve great success they also ground down many of the same challenges that face lesser mortals. Indeed, there may be no more important lesson life has than this – persistence pays.

Persistence pays off.

Famously the great author J. K. Rowling saw her initial Harry Potter manuscripts rejected by a dozen publishers before finding a publishing house executive who was wise enough to let her nine-year-old daughter proof-read the draft manuscripts for her, thus allowing the true magic of her work to be discovered. And as the popular media never tires of reminding us, Rowling had previously battled personal traumas. Yet J.K. Rowling went on to produce one the most popular book series ever written, at the same time amassing personal fortune of well over half a billion pounds. Today, she is recognised as one of the most prolific charitable givers in British history. Of course, there would be a stream of folk who came forward to tell us how unremarkable J.K. Rowling was before she found fame and success – if anything, this simply underscores the fact that persistence pays off! The take-away point here is that your past need not equal your future. This has been proven time and time again.

'There's a very fine line between pleasure and pain. They are two sides of the same coin, one not existing without the other.' – E.L. James.

The Beatles were infamously turned down by Decca Records, which is another oft-quoted example of an early rejection. In fact, you could produce a very long list of wildly successful famous people who once experienced rejections or sackings, from Thomas Edison to Andy Warhol, Steven Spielberg, Walt Disney, Oprah Winfrey, U2 and Madonna. Persistence pays! You will encounter setbacks on your journey. How do I know that? Because we all do. What determines whether you succeed or not is how you respond to the setbacks and failures.

NOT RANDOM CREATURES

Here is my key question to you: what will it take for you to get started and keep going? The reason I ask this is that while many people start out with the best of intentions when it comes to knocking their personal finances into shape, after a period they lose interest. Why does this happen? Often because they feel as though they are quitting treating themselves or giving something up. In my experience if you feel as though you have to deny yourself the pleasure of something – be it spending, eating chocolate, smoking, or whatever else takes your fancy – then sheer willpower only tends to get you so far. Instead, you need to believe that you are gaining something, and you will be over the longer term, which will be the great feeling of never having to worry about money again. However, this does take short term sacrifice.

The Pleasure-Pain Principle holds that what we associate pleasure and pain in life to determines our behaviours. Humans will often go to greater lengths to avoid pain than we will to achieve the ultimate pleasure. This is an important principle because it can help you to understand human behaviour and therefore how to be more successful in everything that you do. Thus, while the behaviour of individuals may at times appear to be quite random, it is not so. Importantly, if you can understand the Pleasure-Pain Principle you can also begin to comprehend why you are achieving satisfactory results in some parts of your life, but poor results in others. More excitingly, you can use the Pleasure-Pain Principle as a tool to dramatically change the results that you are getting in life.

It is vital for all of us to realise and then understand that we as humans are not random beings. Everything we do, every choice we make and each action we take happens for a reason. We may not always be conscious or aware of the reasons for our actions of course and oftentimes we just seem to do stuff without thinking about it. But whether it is conscious or unconscious, there is always an underlying driver for our behaviours.

What stops you from saving your income, from starting a business, from building a portfolio of investments for the future, or from aiming for the goals and life of your dreams? What stops you from following your passion? Usually procrastination or a failure to get started ultimately comes back to an inherent imbalance between pleasure and pain. Often the pain of uncertainty seems to outweigh the potential pleasure of achieving our goals through taking what may appear to be great risks.

Think about the following question for one moment. What do all of us want to achieve in life? Is it not to change the way that we feel about life? I believe so. It is true for everyone through history, from the most bullishly aggressive of businessmen to the most caring of people. As diverse as these apparently contradictory character traits may appear to be, just like all of us they have focused on what brings the most pleasure to their lives, such as doing large business deals and helping less fortunate people. Strange though these examples may seem, these people are also driven to avoid pain. Megalomaniac business types cannot stand coming second at anything in life, seeing life a race to be won – to them people who sleep for more than four hours a day are wasting their time. Caring personalities cannot stand the pain in seeing others suffer, and so devote their lives to ensuring as few people as possible continue to do so.

We all ultimately reach pain thresholds.

In many areas of our lives, we can all ultimately reach pain thresholds where we finally decide that change is necessary. How long will it be before you hit the pain threshold and decide to change? In a job? In a relationship? In your personal finances? At some point the pain of not changing begins to exceed the short-term relief and apparent comfort of maintaining the status quo.

Perhaps the most interesting and important aspects of the Pleasure-Pain Principle is that we will most often do more to avoid pain than we will to do whatever it takes to achieve the ultimate pleasure of sustained success. We frequently take short term measures to dodge relatively small individual instances of pain, but this approach rarely works to our long-term advantage. Damaging behaviours and addictions are often caused by the pain of withdrawal, which keeps people coming back again and again to avoid it. This is only one simple analogy but similar patterns are repeated throughout our existence on this planet.

'Numbing the pain for a while will make it worse when you finally feel it.' – J.K. Rowling, Harry Potter and the Goblet of Fire

Indelibly linked to the Pleasure-Pain Principle is the fact that far too often people adopt a short-term approach to life instead of focussing on long term results, and thus they drift through life with no firm plan, as if carried on a river with strong flow. Anthony Robbins, a leader in the science of peak performance, coined the phrase Niagara Syndrome to describe this phenomenon.[1] People, argues Robbins, are so often carried along by a current through life with no real plan of where they are trying to get to. Instead they focus on avoiding the next rock and keeping their head above water, until eventually they are dragged close to the edge of the waterfall.[2] At this stage they may try to swim against the tide, but it is often too late and they are destined for a big fall, be it emotional, financial, a relationship crash or another type of fall.[3]

It does not have to be that way, but you do need to seize control of your future by setting some inspiring goals and then putting together a specific plan to reach those targets. The alternative is to allow your life to be carried along in a haphazard manner which will lead, at best, to haphazard results.

WHY THIS PRINCIPLE IS SO IMPORTANT

The reason that this is important is because it is perfectly possible for us to train ourselves to link pain and pleasure to the key issues facing us in our lives. If, for example, you have a problem with smoking, overeating, or consuming too much junk food, it is entirely achievable that you can correct your behaviour patterns over the short term through sheer willpower or abstinence. However, it is less likely that you will achieve long term success until you can link enough pain to the old pattern and enough equivalent pleasure to a stimulating or empowering new alternative. The same applies to quitting gambling, consuming too much alcohol, indulging in retail therapy, compulsive spending, and all manner of other damaging behaviour patterns.

The Pleasure-Pain Principle can be used scientifically to achieve your ultimate goals.

How exactly, then, can we utilise this knowledge to change our behaviours to achieve success? Firstly, you need to write down what it is you truly want to achieve, whether it be to achieve financial freedom, own a yacht, quit working full time, become a multi-millionaire, to run your own business, or whatever else your ultimate goals may include. Then you must list the limiting behaviour patterns which have prevented you from achieving your goals in the past and what this will cost you if you fail to make the required changes. Remember that pain can be a greater driver of change than the pursuit pleasure. Next, you must list next to those limiting behaviour patterns a new list of empowering alternatives which will allow you to achieve your goals.

Once you have made your list you then need to consciously associate massive pain to the old behaviour patterns until the point that they become utterly unthinkable for you to continue indulging in. At the same time, you need to be able to associate huge and overwhelming pleasure to new and empowering behaviour patterns. This all sounds great in theory, of course, but how might it work in practice? We will take a look in the sections that follow.

In my case when I did this exercise I came to realise that I spent far too much time worrying what other people think about me. While this emotion might come from a good place – after all, I do want to be known as an honest, trustworthy person, and an inspiring person! – it was holding me back because I was continually reticent to promote myself, my books and my business for fear of what friends and family might say about me. I still haven't conquered this drag on my success, but I'm working on it.

SHORT TERM VERSUS LONG TERM GOALS

This all sounds straightforward, so why then do we so often link pleasure and pain to the wrong things? The reason is that we as humans tend to draw immediate associations between pleasure and how we are feeling at that given point in time. Reaching for a bar of chocolate can be a great comfort, and the sweet taste and sugar hit can result in a pleasurable feeling. And I say that as someone who loves chocolate, albeit the dairy-free stuff! The fact of the matter is, however, that few of our problems are likely to be solved by eating confectionery, and if we keep eating sugary products too regularly, the longer-term outcome could indeed be painful, perhaps for your health or even to your hip pocket if a costly trip to the dentist is needed.

Anything which is worth having in life rarely comes easily, and long term pleasure usually requires short term sacrifice.

The trouble is that too many people get this completely back to front by taking short term pleasure for relief which results in longer term pain. Willpower might only get you so far, so what you need to be able to do is set an inspiring alternative goal which you can work towards and link pleasure to that. Now you understand the principle, the true challenge is to use this to your lasting advantage.

PLEASURE AND PAIN IN INVESTING

The Pleasure-Pain Principle has great relevance when it comes to how you approach your personal finances and investing. One of the greatest problems I see with my clients and mentees today is that people are focussing on shorter and shorter timeframes, so when investors see markets moving down they feel pain. Too many folks are forever focussed on trying to avoid the next rock, but meanwhile they are drifting downstream towards the waterfall. What exactly do I mean by this? By way of an example, look at the online coverage of financial markets:

- 'Stocks crash by 1 per cent.'
- 'Share markets rebound as bargain hunters take charge.'
- 'Market could correct this week.'
- 'Analyst recommends rotating from retail into healthcare stocks.'
- 'Short covering sees weekly trend reversal.'

And so forth, ad nauseam. The jargon that has been invented to describe what is essentially a share price or index moving up or down has expanded beyond belief. An entire industry has sprung up to hyperventilate over equities markets and what prices are doing on a daily or even an hourly basis. So much time and energy is wasted on guessing what the stock markets and other financial markets are going to do next. And make no mistake, the great majority of it is guesswork. Ask a dozen different talking heads and you will get a dozen different opinions or guesses on what the markets will do next. Switch the daily market news and gloom off!

Unfortunately, what this short-term approach to investing – if you can even call it investing – means is that almost half of the time investors are associating investing for their future with pain and not pleasure. Yet a cursory glance at the long-term direction of share markets and property markets should tell you most of what you need to know. That is, you should buy shares in a basket of quality profit-making, dividend-paying companies and hold them for the long term to benefit from income and capital gains. The same holds true for property markets – buy quality assets and hold on to them for as long as possible. Don't listen to short term noise and the endless media doom and gloom.

TIME AS YOUR GREATEST ALLY ... NOT AN ENEMY

I often hear people say that they do not have the time or money to invest, but is this true? Sometimes, perhaps, but often people who say they cannot afford to invest simply do not want to experience any short-term pain in cutting back on what they consider to be necessities such as long overseas holidays or expensive cars. That may be fine, but it is not the same thing as being unable to invest, merely a different priority.

Ultimately the pleasure of long term success in investing can be achieved by anyone, but in life very little that is worth having comes easily. It is likely that you will need to make short term sacrifices to achieve long term goals and take pleasure in achieving them. The way in which this becomes possible is to link pain directly to frivolous expenditure and pleasure towards thrift in the knowledge that the quality investments you will buy instead can continue to work for you forever. While your peers will need to work harder and harder just to keep up, you can take pleasure in your investments working harder and harder for you. You will need to make some time to dedicate to investing, and it is also time that can be your greatest ally as an investor. The longer you hold a quality investment for, the more it can grow, compound and create wealth for you.

PSYCHOLOGY OF WEALTH CREATION – SIX RULES

In my book *Take a Financial Leap* I wrote about the six key rules of the psychology of wealth creation.[4] You see, when I was younger I felt that 'the mind-set of wealth creation' was just some sort of psycho-babble. Essentially I believed that if you worked harder you would be better off and if you didn't, then you wouldn't. Simple! Now, I'm a little older, and a little wiser, I know that this is not the case. Understanding and then using the psychology of wealth creation is of real importance in achieving success. In fact, it's vital. Our internal beliefs concerning money and wealth were ingrained into our subconscious without us ever having realised it. As we have already seen in Chapter 2, we developed what I call 'money mantras'. Consider what happened to us when we were young. What did our parents teach us about money? Get a good job? Work hard? Rich people are to be mistrusted?

'Money doesn't grow on trees, you know! We'll never be able to afford that!'

These can be powerful messages being programmed into our subconscious. It is important to remove your limiting beliefs about money if you want to build wealth. Here are just six key points to explain of the psychology of wealth creation which should be followed if wealth for the long term is your goal:

1. Increasing your self-esteem

Why is self-esteem relevant to wealth creation? The reason is because if your self-esteem is low and you then achieve a level of success that exceeds what you believe you are worth, you will unconsciously sabotage your success. Consider the analogy of a thermostat: each of us has a financial thermostat that is programmed to a certain level. The temperature may fluctuate a little from time to time, but eventually we return to the level at which our thermostat is set. Why is it that some people have difficulty with the concept of charging anything at all for their time, while a top consultant or specialist is comfortable with charging handsomely? Put simply, because people have different beliefs about what their time is worth. It wouldn't be possible or sustainable to value your time at a higher level without a commensurate level of self-esteem.

Share trading author and doyen Dr Alexander Elder once said that 'failure is a curable disease'.[5] He believes that if we can understand and recognise our own potential to self-sabotage then we can re-train our brains to think more positively. We can be cured of our propensity to make suboptimal decisions, he argues.[6] Further, Elder states, we will never be successful until we can remove this subconscious need to sabotage any outperformance of our expectations.[7] Important points, and uncannily accurate, in my experience!

2. It pays to invest for the long term

Too many of us devise plans to make ourselves a little better off in the short term, but have no cogent plan for building wealth over the long term. True wealth and fortunes are built slowly but surely. One oft-quoted example is that of the American Indians having sold the island of Manhattan to the Dutch leader Peter Minuit in 1626 for beads and trinkets worth just $24. Historians naturally noted that the American Indians were dealt a raw deal.

Yet controversially, revisionists mischievously argued that had the $24 from the beads and trinkets been invested safely at a rate of return of 8 per cent per annum, the unhindered compound growth would have ensured that the trinkets could today buy back Manhattan in its entirety, with its prime-location real estate, leaving a few hundred million dollars over as walking around money, which is food for thought, and another example of the potentially awesome power of compound growth. Following the principle and power of compound growth is the key to building wealth. If you can add some leverage – the use of other people's time and other people's money – you can join the ranks of the super-wealthy over time.

3. Study and counsel with wise men

If you want to be successful, learn from successful people! Find someone who has achieved what you want to achieve. Study and follow their methods. You may even be able to learn from some of their mistakes and reach your goals even more quickly and completely than they did themselves. This is a powerful tool known as 'modelling'. I consciously use it every day.

4. Pay yourself first

What do most of us do? Pay our mortgage, pay our bills, pay our credit cards, and pay for other essentials. Then we look to see what is left over at the end of the month. We need to see things another way. Invest a decent sum safely away first and then worry about the other payments thereafter. It sounds arrogant but it works!

5. Controlling expenditure

Financial freedom is about having passive income – which flows to you regardless of whether you work – that is greater than your outgoings. There are two variables in that equation that can be adjusted to achieve the goal. One is to increase the passive income figure (through investment). The other is reducing the outgoings (through thrift). Where are the holes in your financial foundations? Where do you tend to spend big? Holidays? Nights out? Shopping? How can you plug the biggest leaks?

6. Action

It's all well and good studying the first steps, but what counts is taking massive and consistent action and simply never giving up. What is holding you back from starting today? A fear of failure? A fear of losing money? You're 'doing OK' without investing? When will you start to act? Next month, next year, next decade? You need to dare to be different to achieve wealth. Procrastination is the killer of all opportunity. Act today!

THE 5 STEPS TO FINANCIAL WEALTH

Too often people over-complicate what building wealth is all about. While there are ways in which you can accelerate your plan, which we will look at in Chapter 10, building wealth safely is fundamentally a simple concept which involves the following five simple steps.

Step 1 – Spending less than you earn

Firstly, you need to set up your spending plan, as discussed briefly in Chapter 3. Find the big-ticket items and think of ways in which you can stop money from leaking out of your spending plan.

Think three times before spending your money.

Aiming to deny yourself treats from now until forever is unlikely to work. Instead you will need to aim to link pleasure to saving by considering what your savings could be worth when invested over the long term. At the same time, you will need to link pain to frivolous or wasteful spending. Aim to save pay increases and bonuses so that over time the amount you can save and invest each month increases.

Step 2 – Investing the difference

The second step is to ensure that you invest the difference in quality assets that you can hold onto forever. In Chapter 6 we will look at which assets fit these requirements. Importantly we will consider investments where crippling fund management fees will not eat away at your returns year in and year out!

Step 3 – Don't put all your eggs in one basket

Diversification is important and it is wise to follow the adage that says you shouldn't put all your eggs in one basket. The reason for this is that no matter what your favourite asset class is – be it shares, property or another asset – there will be times when the market is moving against you. In these periods, it can help your peace of mind if you have a nice spread of assets.

There are different ways in which it is possible to diversify. Firstly, you can diversify across securities (different types of shares), which is one of the main purposes of an index fund or a low-cost listed investment company (LIC). If you invest in a heavily diversified index which holds the top hundred or more companies of a country by market capitalisation and liquidity then it doesn't matter so much if one or two of those companies falls upon hard times (and despite what you may think, all businesses have a life-cycle). Indeed, periodically companies will fall upon hard times, and this is inevitable. The good news is that when this happens the index will be rebalanced to reflect the new top companies, with new and growing companies taking the place of those which are shrinking.

So, for example if you want to get exposure to the proven resilience of the United States economy, you might opt to buy a product which tracks the S&P 500 index. Investing in an index fund as a strategy openly accepts that companies will underperform or fail from time to time and doesn't try to pick the winners. One of the great things about an index fund which can give you great peace of mind is that you don't need to worry too much about trying to find the next Apple or Microsoft. When a thriving company becomes big enough it will make its way into the index and you will own a share of it. On the flip-side it equally matters not when the next high profile corporate insolvency comes around. While such events are rarely good for market confidence (and can see the share prices of all companies in an index take a hit to some extent) one company sliding out of the index will not hurt your account too much.

That's one way in which it is possible to diversify relatively easily. Instead of buying shares in one to two companies and hoping or praying that you have picked a winner which might go up in value, you can instead own a huge bucket of companies, effectively representing all the major industries of a country, such as the S&P 500 in the US.

A second way in which it is possible to spread risk is to diversify over time. There are two ways to invest in share markets. You can either invest all your money in a lump sum, or spread your investments over time by dripping your money into the market. In fact, as a net buyer of shares, future corrections in share markets can serve to improve long term returns because the averaging or smoothing effect of buying shares regularly means that you effectively buy more units when the share markets are cheap. Since the last financial crisis share markets rebounded strongly and returns have been very solid.

Investing smaller amounts regularly spreads risk.

The third way to diversify is across asset classes. For example, in my portfolio I always hold shares, property (residential and other types) and cash. There are other asset classes too including fixed interest investments such as bonds, or precious metals including gold and silver. Although a long-term investment strategy in any asset class may succeed, provided you have a sensible investment plan, a level of diversification across asset classes can help you to sleep more soundly at night.

A fundamental idea behind a diversified portfolio holds that when one asset class is struggling another might be doing well for you. For example, when share markets are struggling, bonds may be performing more strongly as interest rates fall. It is impossible to include in this book the perfect asset allocation, although some template portfolios do exist, because what is right for one person at a time in their life may not be right for another. In the broadest terms, it is generally the case that the nearer one gets to retirement and the greater the investment portfolio, the tolerance for risk declines.

There are several ways in which you can attain diversification: across securities, across time, across asset classes and across markets. And it can make sense to use all these options. Index funds are one very useful low cost product which you can use as a form of instant diversification. Another good choice in Australia might be a low cost listed investment company

(LIC) which can perform a similar function to an index fund.

I will look at this in a little more detail in Chapter 7, and I will also consider how investing safely in property can form an important part of your plan.

Step 4 – Re-invest your profits

The fourth step is to re-invest your profits. Investing in quality assets that you can hold onto for the long term is a powerful strategy which you can use to snowball or compound your wealth. However, the way in which it becomes possible to supercharge and multiply your wealth is by re-investing the gains from your investments.

Step 5 – Protect your wealth

In Chapter 10 I will look at how you can accelerate your results once the initial four steps are in place. We should remember that there is no point in building your net worth to the point where you have achieved your goals if you subsequently lose your wealth. Because so many people are trained to have a wealth 'thermostat' which is set at a relatively low level, some can become uncomfortable with achieving success and therefore unconsciously sabotage their results. The means through which results are sabotaged varies – some take greater and greater risks with their investments, other get divorced, others begin to feel uncomfortable with achieving a certain level of success and all but give their money away (of course, charitable giving can be a great thing, and immensely satisfying). I note that buy-and-hold investing in quality assets affords investors fewer opportunities to take undue risks!

There are ways in which it is possible to protect your wealth. Firstly, you can hold different types of insurance against adverse outcomes. Secondly, you can protect your wealth through using appropriate structures to hold your wealth such as companies or trusts. If this is something which interests you then I recommend you speak to a financial advisor, since ownership structures must be tailored personally to suit your own needs, and as such are outside the scope of this book.

Another important way to minimise the risk of losing your wealth is to effectively automate the investment process and make fewer decisions rather than more. By choosing to invest in assets for the long term, which you never need to sell, you can greatly minimise the odds of making a rash decision or taking undue risks. Compare this with the share trader who might choose to risk a significant portion of his or her net worth on any given trade – the risk of loss remains ever-present, particularly for someone who has not yet fully developed the mind-set of a wealthy person.

Finally for this chapter, if you are interested in exploring passive investment in index funds in more detail, here are some tremendous resources which can help you to do exactly that

www.passiveinvestingaustralia.com/

www.strongmoneyaustralia.com/

Chapter 4 Summary

- There is a proven path to financial freedom … you can choose to follow it!
- Don't put all your eggs in one basket.
- Diversify your investments across securities, asset classes, time, and markets.
- Use time as your friend, not an enemy.
- Snowball or compound your wealth safely over time.
- We are not random creatures – what we do, we do for a reason, and the results surely follow.

CHAPTER 5
ON YOUR
MARKS

FINANCIAL SECURITY TO FINANCIAL FREEDOM

Deep down, most of us probably know that saving and investing is a good thing, so why doesn't everyone do it? There are a range of reasons, but I believe that one key factor is that people simply don't believe that saving and investing will make that much difference to their lives. Perhaps they tried saving once, but then a key item of expenditure came along. Or they bought some shares on a tip from a friend, which went down in value and hurt them financially and emotionally.

What determines why one person decides to take massive and consistent action towards achieving their goals, while another does nothing at all? People are neither inherently lazy nor industrious, but some do have impotent goals, while others have goals that are so exciting and inspiring to them that they decide to act consistently. Having exciting goals is therefore a huge part of this equation! But there is more than this too – to be achievable goals also need to be believable. It's all well and good to have a pipe dream goal of being a zillionaire, but if you don't believe you can achieve the goal then you will never begin in earnest, you will not act in the manner befitting the status you seek. And, inevitably, you will never achieve the goal. To be a true driving force for your life, your goals must be:

- defined
- believable
- desired
- planned
- vividly imagined!

The key to winning is often simply to get started rather than deferring action until a later date. From the first step, bigger things grow. For this reason, I am going to ask you to set two separate financial goals, rather than just one. The first goal will be your target figure for financial freedom: the dollar figure at which the monthly income you can earn from your money exceeds all your expenses. That is, if you don't want to work ever again, you do not have to, because your passive income exceeds your expenses.

The second target I will ask you to set will be a greater figure, being the dollar value you need to buy everything you want and to fulfil all your financial dreams! There is a key reason why I am ask you to set these two different goals.

The reason for the first target, which is lower, is because if a goal is not believable to you then you are unlikely to commit to taking the massive action needed and therefore you will likely fail, or at least fail to optimise your results. The intention of the second target is to show you that achieving all your financial goals and dreams need not be as expensive as you first think.

People often overestimate what they can achieve safely in a year which leads them to gamble, or take risks, or chase fast returns. But more significantly, people tend to massively underestimate what they can achieve over a few decades by sticking to a few basic rules of personal finance. The reason for this is that our brains tend to think in a linear fashion, but your wealth can snowball, compound, multiply, and grow exponentially – particularly if you determine to follow the rules I am laying down for you in this book. Remember that a dollar saved is effectively the same as two dollars earned, because when you earn money you generally must pay tax on it. Looked at another way, every time you spend a dollar, you must go and earn two dollars to make that dollar back! And then, there's the opportunity cost of the returns that you could have achieved instead.

To recap, firstly you will set a goal for financial freedom, the point at which your passive income can exceed your expenses if you so choose. And secondly you will compile a bucket list of everything that you want to live the life of your dreams, and we will attach a dollar figure to that goal too, which may be surprisingly lower than you intuitively think. Now, don't worry, nobody needs to see your bucket list goals except for you, so you can be as honest with yourself as you like!

FINANCIAL GOAL 1: FINANCIAL FREEDOM

To calculate your first financial goal, assess your annual living costs for a comfortable lifestyle. Now since I know that if you're anything like me you won't do exercises in books, I've deliberately made this very easy for you! There is no need to go into detail (not least because goals generally change over time, particularly with the inflation in living costs), but the idea here is to set yourself an approximate target. Of course, the numbers will be dramatically different for different people. Some of us have expensive living costs, in part because of where we choose to live, others have lower outgoings. What matters here are the numbers that are relevant to you.

Write in the box below the approximate amount of money you need each month to be financially free, to not work if that is what you choose.

Rent or mortgage per month	$
Food and other essential costs per month	$
Lifestyle and discretionary costs per month	$
Buffer per month	$
Total per month	$

As noted above, there is no real need to go into too much detail here, because living costs and expectations change over time as our circumstances change. The important thing here is to have an idea of approximately how much income per month you would need to no longer be reliant on any salary or business income, because once you have a number you can consciously think about, the goal becomes real, and therefore achievable!

Now annualise this number by multiplying it by twelve. To get an approximate idea of how much equity or net worth you will need to achieve the goal of financial freedom multiply this figure by 25. In other words, if we use an assumption that you can safely earn a very conservative 4 per cent income return on your capital, then you will need equity of around 25 times your annual expenses to achieve the goal of financial freedom. So, if you have annual expenses of $100,000, for example, your target for equity or net worth is $2.5 million ($100,000 x 2.5 = $2.5 million).

Of course, if you are just starting out in your financial journey the numbers may look daunting – perhaps even depressing! – unfortunately that is the nature of the beast. But take heart, because using the rules I will show you in this book, through using some leverage and multiplying your wealth you may be able to get to your goal more quickly than you might think. I achieved financial freedom at the age of 33 from scratch, and I'm not particularly smart, I just became highly motivated through using exercises exactly like the ones I am explaining here!

You may or may not get to your goal as quickly as I did – or you may achieve the goal even sooner still! – the thing to know is that you can get there over time. Interestingly if you are reading this book some years after it was written these numbers tend to begin to look comparatively smaller due to the nature of inflation. For this reason, it's important that you have an inflation-busting financial and investment plan that allows you to keep moving ahead regardless of the economic climate.

FINANCIAL GOAL 2: YOUR BUCKET LIST!

Now that you have your first financial freedom goal written down, it's time to think a bit bigger. For your second financial goal, I want you to consider what amount of money you would need to buy everything you want. Perhaps this would include a house, two cars, a holiday home, 'toys', charitable donations, an elaborate round-the-world-trip, and anything else you want in your bucket list. There is an important reason for doing this, and that is to help you understand that the total figure need not be as high as you might think.

You may discover that the number of dollars you need might not be quite as large as you believe.

For example, it is possible to rent luxury houses and sports cars for a fraction of the cost of owning them. Take the example of driving a Ferrari (I don't know why this choice comes up so often, but it does – a lot of people seem to want to drive a Ferrari!). Guess what? You can rent a Ferrari and it doesn't cost anywhere near as much as owning one, together with the ancillary costs of ownership. Of course, I'm not saying that driving a Ferrari should be on your bucket list. What I am saying is that it may be possible to achieve many of the same experiences as those enjoyed by the super-wealthy for a considerably lower cost than is generally believed. And, generally, you don't go on holiday every week of the year, so these costs need not be as extravagant as you think either.

I recall when my Dad retired he said he was amazed at how much cheaper his living costs were. Why? Firstly, he no longer needed to live within easy commuting distance of London, so he could sell his small flat and move to a more spacious house located a few hours away from the city. Secondly, there are things associated with employment, such as travel, lunches out in the city, nights out in the city, and social events. Thirdly, when you are not working in full time employment you will find that you have a great deal more time to be discerning with your money. Note that I said discerning, not tight-fisted! It's about getting value for your money no matter what you do.

Make a list of some approximate numbers for what your ultimate bucket list might cost you on average for a month.

House per month	$
Cars per month	$
Essential expenditure	$
Holiday home per month	$
Toys cost per month	$
Lifestyle costs per month	$
Buffer per month	$
Total per month	**$**

Of course, this figure is likely to be quite high – this is a bucket list after all! Yet if you are discerning in your choices you may find that you can live out most of your dreams for much less than you might have thought. Take these figures as an example.

House per month	$4,000
Car per month	$1,000
Essential expenditure	$2,000
Holiday home per month	$1,000
Toys cost per month	$2,000
Lifestyle costs per month	$2,000
Buffer per month	$500
Total per month	**$12,500**

OK, so to earn $12,500 per month at a conservative 4 per cent return, you will need equity of $3,000,000, which is an achievable goal over a reasonable period. Of course, I'm not suggesting that you need to limit your goals at all, and remember that the principle here is more important than the actual numbers, since each of us has different earning potential and goals. And in fact, once you understand the multiplying power of compounding growth, you are unlikely to ever stop using this massively

effectively tool in your favour. But remember that believable goals
are achievable goals, so this exercise can help you to visualise why it's
important to get started today, and to start that snowball rolling.

WHERE ARE YOU TODAY? HONESTLY!

Now that we have set your two financial goals, it is important to take stock
of where you are at today. Please note that it doesn't necessarily matter
where you are starting from, if it is from a very low base or even from
scratch. The most important thing is that you have decided to follow a new
plan. To achieve financial freedom, you will need your personal finances
to be organised, streamlined and transparent. Take an inventory of where
you are today by summarising your income, expenditure, assets, and
liabilities. Then you will need to resolve to minimise your bad debts and
other liabilities and maximise your assets, which ultimately will form your
own personal cash machine.

From this point forth it becomes a case of saving and investing and making
small tweaks and adjustments to your plan as you go. A boxer with a big fight
ahead will weigh themselves every day in anticipation of the main event. If
they are on track to be overweight, then they will train a little harder to make
the necessary downward adjustment. If on the other hand their weight looks
to be on the low side, they will take on more fuel. To get yourself started on
the route to financial freedom, consider the following:

*To speed up your route to financial freedom, you may need to commit
to saving 20 per cent of income for investment in assets.*

Now, yes, I know what you may be thinking: '20 per cent? I can't even
make it to the end of the month without running out of money!' Look, I
was a youngster myself not so many years ago, and yes I do know what you
mean! Here's the rub: if you want it badly enough you can save 20 per cent
of your income by making the requisite changes. However, I recognise that
it may very well be the case that you cannot save that much of your income
immediately. I do acknowledge that. If, for example, you have bad debts to
pay off then these will need attending to first.

If saving 20 per cent of your income seems like an impossibility, rather
than giving up before you have even started, consider instead how you can
plan to save 20 per cent of your income as soon as practicable. One of the

most effective methods of doing so is to continue to make savings to the extent that is possible, and then save all future pay increases and bonuses. Of course, most people fall into the trap of adjusting their expenditure higher each time they receive a pay rise! This is easily done, naturally, particularly if the members of your peer group are doing the same thing. Remember, though, that you are going to resolve to win your own race. Let others worry about what their strategies are and resolve solely to focus on your own!

Figure 5.1 – Saving more

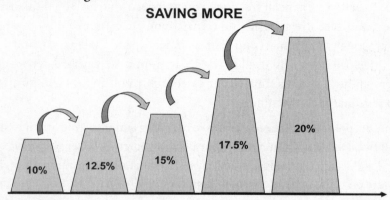

SAVING MORE

Granted, this may be a difficult adjustment to make. Achieving financial security means that you will have enough capital at your disposal to retire at the traditional retirement date, which is what most employees are aiming for. The aim of this book is to gently guide you towards higher goals! Financial freedom is defined as the point at which you have income that flows to you passively that is greater than your expenses. At this point you will be working only because you choose to, not because you must! The only way that this can become possible for most employees is to spend less than you earn.

RETURNS ON YOUR CAPITAL

How will you generate the strongest and most efficient returns over time on your capital? The best asset classes for achieving this goal are generally shares and property, because these assets pay you an increasing income in the form of dividends and rent, as well as providing the opportunity for capital growth.

I am going to use an assumption through this book that during the growth phase of your investment life you can learn the skills to attain returns of 6 to 8 per cent from your investments. In the share markets, historically it has been possible at times to attain average returns of a significantly higher figure than this, and it may be possible that you can continue to do so into the future. Indeed, over long periods of time it has been possible to generate returns at double digit levels in percentage terms.

However, we have likely transitioned into an era of lower inflation, lower economic growth and lower gross returns, so to be somewhat conservative I will assume that an investment in a well-diversified equities product can generate returns of around 8 per cent – approximately 4 per cent from dividends (which can be taken as income or re-invested in more shares to compound your wealth) and 4 per cent from capital growth. The nature of stock markets is such that you will not see these returns every year. Some years will likely be amazing and others possibly quite dire, but over the course of a market cycle you should be able to compound returns by 8 per cent per annum, with potentially a pleasant surprise to the upside.

Investment returns can be volatile from year to year, but quality assets can compound over time.

Returns from property investment are a hotly debated subject. I am going to assume that you can learn the skills to generate around 6 to 8 per cent capital growth per annum from investment property on top of the rental income, depending on the state of the economy and the prevailing rate of inflation. Remember the rule of 72! This means that the value of the property you own would double approximately every 9 to 12 years.

Of course, common sense should tell you that it is not possible for the price of all property to outpace incomes forever. That would not make any sense, because if property prices continued to increase ahead of income growth eventually only those with existing equity could afford to buy. However, I certainly do not suggest buying any property. I only recommend buying the property types in locations which will easily outperform the averages over time, which takes a level of research. Over a long period as a property investor I have analysed what causes property prices to rise and fall, and therefore what types of property to invest in, as well as where and when, so I can help to guide you towards the right investments.

Times have changed since the subprime crisis.

When the global financial crisis hit, markets around the world, which had become overheated, including housing markets in Ireland, the Unites States and Spain, declined sharply and some speculative markets crashed dramatically. This led many pundits to declare the household debt super-cycle to be over and residential property a dud investment. This may appear to be a logical conclusion, and no doubt if you bought property at the peak of the market in a location where prices crashed you might justifiably take that viewpoint!

However, this is a matter of perception versus reality. The fact is that property markets will always cycle, for reasons explained later in the book. Your goal as a property investor should be to buy quality assets in the locations which perform well and outperform inflation through several cycles, while clearly you will also aim to buy counter-cyclically, meaning at the bottom of the housing market cycle and not the top! The most important thing is that you invest in assets which outperform the averages and outperform inflation.

While several housing markets from around the globe which had been in bubble territory did crash, after a blip quality, well-located investments in continually strong demand areas continued to deliver strong returns. Even within countries markets performed quite differently. In the United Kingdom, for example, certain regional and remote property markets corrected sharply and took eight or more years to recover even in nominal terms. In real terms, when adjusted for inflation, property prices in many areas have gone backwards.

Yet property prices in certain key suburbs of central London where we invest and we have always recommended investing simply kept on rising. In fact, price growth accelerated with the median London house price soaring to beyond half a million pounds. Similarly, median prices in certain key suburbs of Sydney doubled in the eight years after the financial crisis. Because my portfolio of investment properties is largely focused on Sydney and London, my returns accelerated through and after the crisis.

We have moved into a new economic era since the financial crisis.

Clearly property prices cannot continue to perform in that vein forever, but if you know what you are doing, if you can apply some market timing skills, and particularly if you can learn to carry out the research which I will show you in this book, it can be possible to attain capital growth of 6 to 8 per cent per annum on your portfolio over time, which can compound your wealth.

Notably, it has become clear that certain types of prime location real estate in global cities are being used as a store of wealth by international investors. If you can understand where these capital flows are increasingly being directed, particularly from China, as well as demonstrate the ability to time the market through buying investments counter-cyclically when sentiment is weak, you can comfortably outperform the median price growth of national property markets.

Just as in the share markets, you will not see such a level of capital growth every year, but averaged out over market cycles, it can be done. My wife and I have been doing exactly that for the past two decades with our property portfolios, and that includes straight through the middle of the greatest global financial crisis since the Great Depression of the 1930s. Because of the power of leverage – using borrowed funds sensibly – even if your returns are lower than this you can still multiply your wealth year after year to generate very substantial equity over time. However, since leveraged investing introduces risk, you must get the research right if this is to be your goal.

CHANGING TIMES

Times have changed since the financial crisis. The developed world has gone through a structural shift and, for now at least, has entered an era of lower interest rates, and lower inflation – perhaps softer global economic growth – and, for many developed countries, weaker national and household income growth. To achieve outperforming returns, you do need to be able to analyse property markets in some detail and I will explain some of the key demographic shifts and the dramatic changes in the use of household debt which you need to understand in more detail.

Belief systems determine everything.

Your belief systems are everything when it comes to investment and life. This is a great case in point. If you believe that it is not possible to create great wealth through shares and property, then this will be true ... for you. Yet others will continue to do so as they have done for decades. This may seem esoteric, but I have seen with my own eyes time and again how belief systems affect investment strategy. Someone who believes that property is a good investment can buy a quality asset and hold it through the inevitable bear markets and cyclical downturns in sentiment.

On the other hand, someone who does not believe it is possible to create wealth through real estate will panic and sell at the worst possible moment, that being the nadir of the cycle, thereby inevitably confirming their own belief that property is a dud investment. Owning property and the land which sits underneath can be an incredible investment for you over the next few decades, but only if you own land and the right types of properties in the right locations. You must learn how to recognise demographic trends to invest in the outperforming property types and locations or engage an expert to do so for you, but I assure you it most certainly can and will be done over time.

With the advent of the internet, there will of course be predictions of property crashes every year, without fail. And in some years, there will indeed be property market corrections. Of that there is no doubt. But if you can learn to understand economic data, demographic trends and household formation rates, you can still make outstanding returns from property markets through the cycles, while the corrections will present buying opportunities for the educated investor.

MAKING MONEY WHILE YOU SLEEP

When you invest in great assets, it is said that you make more money while you are asleep. Why? The answer to this is closely aligned to Warren Buffett's points on the snowballing of returns – the longer your own quality assets for, you the greater the opportunity for the snowballing or compounding effect to work its magic. The problem for so many people is that they invest in shares in companies and then watch them daily or even hourly as the share prices first tick up and then tick back down again. They fret over every news report and worry that they will be the next victim of a stock market crash. Therefore, they buy and sell too often, instead of holding quality assets for the long term.

It is important to build a strategy which brings you peace of mind.

This is the wrong approach to investing for most people. Instead, you need to have an approach to investment that gives you absolute peace of mind so that you do not need to watch the markets every day. I will discuss later in the book how to do this, firstly through investing amounts in the market regularly which averages out your entry cost, and secondly through owning great assets that you do not need to worry about over the long term. These include index funds, listed investment companies (LICs) and well-located residential property. It is true that you can make more money from quality investments while you sleep. Why? Because while you are asleep quality assets that you own continue to work for you and since you are not worrying about them you are far less likely to mistakenly sell in a panic!

HOW QUICKLY CAN I BE FINANCIALLY FREE?

Over the years while undertaking mentoring of clients there is one question a variation of which I have been asked more than any other:

'How quickly can I be financially free and retire?'

My advice is usually to try to think a little differently. Instead of having it in mind to create a certain amount of wealth, at which point you will quit your job and retire to the Caribbean or a caravan park (depending upon how and where you set your goals), try to consider how you can build a plan to snowball your wealth for the rest of your life … and even beyond your own lifetime.

This is a major mind-set shift for most people to make, but I believe that it may be an important one. One of the major challenges facing people today is to stop thinking of money as something to be earned and then spent. Instead, try to consider how the money you earn can be invested in assets which will grow and compound for you in perpetuity. If you can identify quality assets which will continue to generate return for decades and decades into the future, suddenly you can begin to maximise your wealth-creation plan. There will never be a need to sell and you can continue to multiply your wealth for as long as you live.

USING THIS INFORMATION PRACTICALLY

I have introduced some ideas in this chapter, but how can you use them practically? I am going to suggest that if your goal is to escape from the rat race of reliance on a pay cheque relatively quickly you probably need to use a buy-and-hold approach investment property as well as equities products or shares. In Chapter 5, I will consider how the number of dollars you would be likely to earn from a lifetime in employment could be far higher than you might intuitively expect, and consequently it is not so much a question of whether you can earn a couple of million dollars, rather whether you can keep that amount!

HOW CAN YOU ACCELERATE YOUR RETURNS?

What if you want to achieve financial freedom sooner than the traditional retirement age? The ideas introduced in this chapter should tell you that what you need is a portfolio of quality assets or investments which you can hold on to forever, which will continue to grow and compound for as long as you live. Then, if you so wish you can begin to focus on building a business to gradually replace your salary income rather than focusing on chasing an ever-higher salary which accrues ever-higher tax liabilities.

Buying and holding quality investments is the most efficient way to build wealth.

Let us look at some simple numbers. Suppose you can invest $5000 in the share market and attain average returns over 8 per cent per annum, re-investing your dividends, and each year you can invest an extra $5000 per annum. This is one of the most efficient forms of investing, because by not trading (continually buying and selling in a bid to try to time the market) you do not incur unnecessary transaction costs and you do not become liable for capital gains taxes each time you sell for a profit.

Figure 5.2 – Investing $5000 per annum

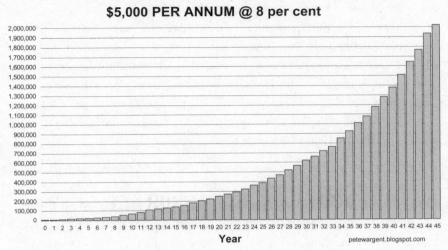

Even by only investing the same amount each year, the gains of 8 per cent per annum continue to grow and compound so that the size of the portfolio gradually begins to accelerate. Of course, the returns will not be as smooth as this because share markets are liquid – they are easy for investors and traders to buy into and sell out of as suits them – and therefore tend to be quite volatile. However, for those with a long-term outlook share market gyrations need not be a major concern. Indeed, the averaging effect of buying a set dollar value of shares at regular intervals means that you effectively buy more shares when the market is depressed and has careered lower, and acquire fewer shares when the market is exuberant and has bolted higher.

While the principle here is more important the absolute numbers, which will naturally vary depending upon your income and the amount of money you can make available to invest, you can see that over time it is easily possible to build a reasonable net worth. In fact, if you are planning to remain in the workforce for decades, you can easily adopt this approach of buying a diversified portfolio of quality shares hard and often and holding them for the long haul. It is a proven and time-tested long term route to wealth.

What if you could get money to work for you sooner and for longer? The results are quite eye-opening because of the sheer power of the compounding effect. In the above example $5000 has been contributed to the portfolio each year, and thus total contributions come to $225,000. What if you could simply invest $100,000 in the stock market today and leave it there for the long term? Surprisingly, over the course of a typical working career that amount invested could grow and compound to around $3 million, even with no extra funds invested. This is where the phrase 'money goes to money' comes from. The dice are very much loaded in favour of the wealthy who have more financial capacity to invest in quality assets for longer and they become richer and richer with each passing year.

The vital point to take away here is that if you want to achieve financial freedom sooner, then you will likely need to invest as hard as you can as young as you can! You need to have as many dollars as you can, working for you for as long as possible. When you consider the chart above, it makes one wonder how it can be that so few people truly retire wealthy. How is it that the average pension balance at retirement is so meagre and so many rely on government assistance after they retire?

One reason is that most people don't spend substantially less than they earn. Another of the reasons is that life gets in the way. A redundancy can happen, or some emergency expenditure comes along. Increasing numbers of folk these days become separated or divorced, which is one of the most effective ways of destroying your net worth there can be. The concept of compounding or snowballing your wealth is many times more powerful if you do not allow a major life event such as this to get in the way of your results!

Spend less than you earn, and invest the difference in compounding assets.

A key reason that retirement balances are often so paltry is that so few people truly understand the impact of compounding and therefore are quite content to spend every cent they earn and then some. Expensive holidays are particularly easy to justify after a hard year of work. New cars are deemed to be a necessity instead of what they are, which is a proven destroyer of wealth, a depreciating asset which declines in value from the moment you drive away from the garage forecourt.

The nature of pensions has also changed quite dramatically over the last few decades. We have lived through a structural shift from defined benefit pension schemes to defined contribution or accumulation schemes. What this means is that while pension amounts to be received at retirement were once guaranteed by the employer or by the government, today the pension fund is the responsibility of the employee.

Your pension is your own responsibility.

People are often confused on this point, thinking that because the management of their pension is delegated to a fund manager their pension is someone else's responsibility. This could not be further from the truth! Your pension balance is your own responsibility and you must decide how it is managed and by whom, or whether you decide to manage it yourself.

I posed the question as to why so few people retire wealthy. One of the reasons is that the pension system is not set up for you to win. Firstly, this is because the dollar amounts invested are not allowed to grow and compound in the most efficient manner, with pension funds churning over stocks repeatedly in a vain attempt to beat the market. Since institutional funds in aggregate largely are the market, this achieves very little except for generating transaction costs and triggering capital gains tax points.

Secondly, pension fund managers clip out a management fee in good years and in bad, with the management fee typically based upon a percentage of the amount you have invested, which means that the fees charged tend to increase over time as your pension balance increases. It is therefore little wonder so many pension balances at retirement are such a puny reward for decades spent in the workforce and the hundreds of months of contributions paid in.

If you want to become financially free sooner, the way in which this becomes possible is to invest as much as you can as young as you can in assets that you never need to sell. This very simple point is precisely why I believe that, if you want to escape the rat race of reliance or dependence on a pay cheque, you ideally need to own or invest in residential investment property. For the average investor, the leverage you can use is generally so much greater than that available in any other asset class that you can achieve results more quickly, provided you invest with an appropriate level of detailed research and skill.

To become financially free sooner, you need to invest more sooner.

Take the example where instead of investing $100,000 in the share market, the investor has used that amount as a deposit to invest in a $1 million property which appreciates at 8 per cent per annum. For the sake of simplicity, we will ignore transaction costs here, which can be a material dollar figure when in investing in residential property. Due to the snowballing or compounding effect the property doubles in value in only 9 years (remember the Rule of 72) and after a decade is worth $2.15 million, generating equity or net worth of over $1.25 million. The investor is comfortably a millionaire in only one decade through using leverage and allowing the value of the property to grow and compound totally unimpeded by transaction costs or capital gains taxes.

Of course, just as in the share market price gains do not occur in such a linear fashion, so it is with residential property. Instead in a typical market cycle capital city property prices tend to be flat or declining for a period of some years before entering a recovery and then ultimately booming, before again returning to a downturn phase. And indeed, the asset selected might take considerably longer than nine years to double in value! We'll return to how to pick the outperforming properties in due course. For now, it is the principle that is important, because the investor who builds equity is typically able to redraw a portion of it to invest in other assets.

Recurrent property market cycles tend to repeat due to the fundamental principles of housing market economics, whereby construction increases in response to rising prices until the market is fully supplied or over-supplied, putting downward pressure on the market. The cycles also recur partly due to the human emotions of fear and greed, which are always in evidence in financial markets.

I have already noted the tremendous impact of being able to invest more money sooner, which, all things being equal in terms of returns and holding period, achieves results far in excess even of the sensible approach of investing smaller amounts regularly over the years. So, what if you could learn how to invest millions of dollars safely? The short answer is that you can generate more wealth than you may ever have believed possible. This is true even if you cannot generate 8 per cent capital returns.

In fact, if you use the newly created equity to acquire more investments the equity you can build over a lifetime could potentially be boundless, providing you are sensible and always resolve to maintain a healthy buffer for the inevitable market downturns. Of course, people tend to scoff as such obviously over-simplified examples. However, note that if there is one single trait that all of those doing the scoffing invariably have in common it is that they have never successfully built a portfolio of investments themselves!

Observe where a consistent growth rate is achieved on an asset, the dollar value of returns is not constant – your wealth does not go up in a straight line. It accelerates because of the compounding effect. The implications of this are several. Firstly, if you want to achieve financial independence at a young age you probably either need to be investing in residential property or you need to be able build a big business.

Now don't get me wrong, shares can be a wonderful investment when you know what you are doing, and contrary to popular belief shares are also a safe investment for building wealth slowly but surely. If you are planning on earning a regular salary income for decades to come, there is no safer way to build wealth that I know of than to invest consistent dollar amounts into a diversified share market portfolio or product regularly.

Leveraged investing in an extremely powerful tool, but also a double-edged sword.

And the simple fact of the matter is that to invest millions of dollars into any market quickly introduces a level of risk which must be managed correctly. However, the way in which it becomes possible to use millions of dollars safely is by investing in the right type of property, which appreciates in value, to draw out some of the equity to use on further investments, but always maintaining a sizeable buffer.

At various times in the lending markets it has been possible to use 100 per cent mortgages. This can certainly work as a strategy over the long haul and I have even used 100 per cent mortgages myself previously. However, what the global financial crisis demonstrated neatly is that when banks are starting to throw around 100 per cent mortgages this is also likely to be the period in the cycle when there is an elevated level of risk in the market. It is far better to take your time and always maintain a reasonable buffer of cash to protect against market downturns or an unforeseen period of unemployment. You should also always maintain an equity buffer between the value of your property portfolio and investment mortgages to protect against adverse market movements.

More than anything else, it is important not to buy risky assets. There has been a proliferation of real estate books over the years which have taught 'investors' how to buy cheap properties in one-horse regional towns with lacklustre economic prospects due to the seemingly attractive rental yields. This is a risky approach to investing in property, in my opinion (and experience, in Europe). Instead you should invest in quality properties in landlocked and thriving city locations where the population of the city and demand for property is guaranteed to increase for as long as you live.

THE IMPORTANCE OF BUY AND HOLD

In every economic cycle and financial markets cycle it will be said that buy and hold is dead as a concept and you will need to be cleverer by trading in and out of markets faster than everyone else does. In aggregate, of course, this is not possible for all investors to do, and since this is a zero-sum game and most average traders achieve very little. Only the skilful and experienced traders with great money management skills will win at this game and everyone else gets 'ticket clipped' or sometimes wiped out entirely.

The problems with trading financial assets are threefold. Firstly, there are transaction costs involved in buying and selling most assets, such as brokerage fees, stamp duty or agent fees. Secondly, there are capital gains taxes to pay on the sale of an asset where you have made a profit. And thirdly, most people are generally far less skilful at timing the market than they think they are, this being a deceptively challenging skill to master.

Success happens neither overnight, nor in a straight line.

Building a retirement portfolio should be a relatively straightforward exercise. Buy quality assets and hold them for the long term! So how then do so many folks end up requiring a state pension? In most cases this is because for some reason compounding growth has not been allowed to work for them. Perhaps they traded their house half a dozen times and the transaction costs involved in doing so kept on piling up. If you came from a split family as I did, you will sadly know only too well the financial complications and setbacks that can eventuate from a divorce or other such significant life event, such as a period of unemployment. During recessions, jobs can be lost and financial buffers are eroded while a new job is sought. Other people simply spend every dollar they earn, which is the one sure-fire way to achieve very little financially!

For a wide range of reasons, wealth is not always built successfully throughout a working lifetime. I suggest that the best chance you have of continuing to compound your wealth is to invest in assets which you never need to sell because they will keep earning you more income and continuing to grow in value for as long as you live. You can make money while you sleep.

CAPITAL GAINS TAX

The buy and hold strategy is designed to lower risk by buying quality shares and holding them for the long term. One of the unavoidable consequences of a focussed approach to investing is that returns will be more volatile. A heavily diversified portfolio will tend to move in harmony with the market but an investor with all his net worth in a handful of stocks may see his paper net worth fluctuate significantly on a short-term basis.

One major advantage of a buy and hold strategy is the reduced impact of capital gains tax. Warren Buffett refers to unrealised profits – paper profits on shares that have not yet been sold – as an 'interest free loan from the Treasury'.[1] Although if you do sell in the future there will be tax to pay, the impact it has on your returns is likely to be proportionately less if you invest for the long term. Consider the following table, where a share trader has doubled $10,000 five times in five share trades, each time realising a gain within a year and incurring capital gains tax at an assumed rate of 30 per cent.

Figure 5.3 – Gains taxed at 30 per cent

Starting capital	Capital doubled to:	Tax at 30pc	Finishing capital
$10,000	$20,000	$(3,000)	$17,000
$17,000	$34,000	$(5,100)	$28,900
$28,900	$57,800	$(8,670)	$49,130
$49,130	$98,260	$(14,739)	$83,521
$83,521	$167,042	$(25,056)	$141,986

In the graphic above, after doubling his capital five times and paying his due capital gains tax at an assumed 30 per cent the investor has been left with a total capital of close to $142,000. Next consider the below table, where a share trader has again doubled his capital of $10,000 five times. This time, he has held each trade for more than a year and has thus only incurred capital gains tax at an assumed lower rate of 15 per cent (due to a capital gains tax discount for assets held for more than 12 months).

Figure 5.4 – Gains taxed at 15 per cent

Starting capital	Capital doubled to:	Tax at 15pc	Finishing capital
$10,000	$20,000	$(1,500)	$18,500
$18,500	$37,000	$(2,775)	$34,225
$34,225	$68,450	$(5,134)	$63,316
$63,316	$126,633	$(9,497)	$117,135
$117,135	$234,270	$(17,570)	$216,700

While he has incurred tax that has still eaten into his gains, his final capital of around $217,000 is more than the investor in the first example. Finally, consider the table below of an investor who has doubled his capital of $10,000 five times through one trade that he has held over a period of years. He will pay capital gains tax of 15 per cent on the whole amount of the gain in the final year:

Figure 5.5 – The power of compounding unrealised gains

Starting capital	Capital doubled to:	Tax at 15pc	Finishing capital
$10,000	$20,000	$-	$20,000
$20,000	$40,000	$-	$40,000
$40,000	$80,000	$-	$80,000
$80,000	$160,000	$-	$160,000
$160,000	$320,000	$(43,500)	$276,500

While the tax payment in the final year is undoubtedly painful, the final capital of $276,500 is an excellent result, and far outstrips the capital of the other two investors who have traded more regularly. This is the essence of successful value investing and it echoes the approach of the property investor who never sells in order not to trigger a capital gains tax liability. The tax bill in year five may be significant, but the final capital balance is a handsome compensation.

Buy and hold for efficient gains.

The numbers in the above table aren't all that realistic or important, but the principle certainly is. If you can adopt an investment strategy which involves buying quality assets and holding for as long as possible then the income and capital growth can continue to grow and compound for you in perpetuity. The more you trade, the more transaction costs and capital gains taxes will eat away at your ability to achieve the financial freedom you desire. Timing the market always seems easy in retrospect because you are reading the chart from right to left. In real time and when you are reading the chart from left to right, timing the market is much, much harder to do well.

Can you see why buy and hold is potentially so important? This is another of the key reasons why most people never achieve financial freedom. Too often people are looking for a fast buck or a quick windfall! They buy a stock or an investment property and hope it goes up in value. If it goes down in value they hold on to it in the hope that it goes up again, but eventually they sell for a loss and begrudge having made a poor investment. If, on the other hand, the investment goes up in value then they quickly sell to 'lock in' the gains. Unfortunately, there are transactions costs to pay when selling, and then there are capital gains taxes to pay on the profits. The common theme is that in both cases the investment gets sold. In today's more hectic world, all too rarely are investments stowed away safely in the bottom draw and held onto for the long term.

DESIGNING THE LIFE THAT YOU WANT

I have talked a little about my investing philosophies in this chapter, but this is not only a book about investing. It is also about how you can design the life that you want to lead and how you might consider turning your passion into your business, either through setting up a business of your own or getting a job in your field of passion.

However, it is true that life can be far more satisfying if you have your financial future secured before you replace your paid employment with your passion. Simply put, securing your financial future first takes the pressure off that area of your life. The numbers in this chapter merely form a broad overview of what might be possible, and later in the book I will show you in practical terms how you can achieve these outstanding returns. What this chapter demonstrates is the power of getting more money to work for you sooner – and therefore for longer.

Chapter 5 Summary

- Setting exciting and inspiring goals and linking pleasure to them is the key to making dramatic changes.
- If you don't know where you're heading, you won't know when you've got there.
- Commit to saving 20 per cent of your income for investment as soon as possible.
- Save pay increases and bonuses!
- Invest in quality assets for the long term to minimise capital gains tax liabilities.

CHAPTER 6
GET SET: ASSET ALLOCATION

ABOVE AVERAGE?

My oldest brother Nick passed his driving test at the first attempt at the age of 17. He was naturally a very competent driver, and had few problems with the test. My younger brother Chris has always been a highly observant character and took to driving very easily. Another of my brothers, Jack, has had a lifelong obsession with cars (despite inadvertently letting the handbrake of Mum's car when he was a toddler ... oops!), and today is an exceptional driver. And while I haven't seen my youngest brother Matt drive so much, I expect he is very competent too.

Alas, the only one of us who is probably not a driver of above average skill is me! I don't drive so much these days, but when I was young I drove too fast and then later I drove absent-mindedly (usually thinking about accountancy worries, or cricket, or share markets, or other nerdy things). Now I am older I have become risk averse and I drive quite slowly and carefully, but with only a pretty average skill level, it must be said.

Statistically, we cannot all be above average.

Studies have found that most drivers believe that they are above average, but logically they cannot all be correct. In fact, if you think about it only half of drivers can be better than average!

As humans, we often have a tendency towards overestimating our own abilities, and this is never more the case than when it comes to money and finance. It is quite clear that humans are hopeless at predicting the future, yet when it comes to financial markets for some reason we believe we can see patterns and make investment decisions accordingly. We also tend to think that we are better than average, but for at least half of us this cannot be true. If the market moves in our favour, we tend to pat ourselves on the back for a job well done. Yet if the market moves against us we look for someone or something to blame. The simple fact of the matter is most of the time our predictions will be wrong in one way or another.

INVESTMENT SKILLS (SHOULD YOU PUT YOUR EGGS IN ONE BASKET?)

There are some conflicting views on diversification. Some say that you should diversify broadly to reduce the risk of losing money. Others argue that you should become an expert in one field and invest heavily in the field of your expertise. So, who is right? As is so often the case, the answer is probably somewhere in the middle, or a combination of the two arguments. Let's look at this conundrum a little further.

10,000 HOURS TO BECOME A TRUE EXPERT!

In his 2008 work Malcolm Gladwell made the '10,000-Hour rule' famous.[1] Gladwell makes reference to the rule whereby he argues that the key to success in any field is a matter of practicing a specific task for a total of 10,000 hours.[2] Some key data behind the rule came from Swedish psychologist K. Anders Ericsson who discovered in a study that classical violinists all had one thing in common, that they all had undertaken at least 10,000 hours of practice before becoming a professional.[3]

Practice for 10,000 hours to become an expert.

Gladwell's book garnered a lot of criticism, but certainly makes some sense. As a young cricketer, I can remember that my peers who went on to become professionals dedicated thousands upon thousands of hours to becoming the best players that they possibly could be. Some went on to dazzling careers and are still playing professionally or internationally today. It was tough for those who didn't make the grade, however, or those who were released from their professional contracts after under-performance or injury. The huge focus that had been required to play professionally usually meant that studies, qualifications or developing networks of business contacts fell completely by the wayside. Today, the more progressive professional cricketing associations offer greater support to young players, to ensure that if their cricket career doesn't work out then they at least have alternative careers to consider.

WHAT DOES THIS MEAN FOR INVESTORS?

In short, it takes a great deal of time and effort to be a genuine expert in any field! This does not mean that it cannot be done, particularly if you are passionate about investing and finance (though many people are quite understandably more interested in other pursuits!). But if you want to become an expert investor this does require a great deal of dedication.

That's the bad news! The good news is that this doesn't necessarily matter provided you recognise your natural and inevitable limitations such as they are, and take mitigating action accordingly. It is a good idea to spread your risk so that you don't take too much exposure to losses from any individual investment. Remember as a rule humans are quite hopeless at making predictions, so what we need is a simple long term plan that we can follow in almost automated fashion, without worrying too much about the short-term gyrations of manic-depressive markets.

CONFLICTING ADVICE ON DIVERSIFICATION?

It's interesting how conflicting advice can be sometimes. Everyone knows the adage:

'Don't put all your eggs in one basket.'

Yet, how does this tally with what Andrew Carnegie said way back in 1885: 'Put all your eggs in one basket and then watch that basket. Do not scatter your shot. The great successes in life are made by concentration'? Famously, Mark Twain said pretty much the same thing, but then again, Mark Twain said most things. Even Benjamin Graham, the doyen of successful investing, said that: 'The really big fortunes in from common stocks have been made by people who packed all their money into one investment they knew supremely well.'

That was certainly an approach which did not faze Graham's protégé, Warren Buffett, who at one stage held 40 per cent of Berkshire Hathaway's common stock portfolio in just one venture, being the Coca Cola company.[4] Think of some of these household names on the rich-lists over the years: Sam Walton of Wal-Mart, Bill Gates of Microsoft, John D. Rockefeller of Standard Oil, Richard Branson of Virgin, Warren Buffett of Berkshire Hathaway. They built their wealth through tremendous focus on one company or brand. More recently, Steve Jobs became phenomenally wealthy as the founder and CEO of Apple, yet it is sometimes forgotten even as great a businessman as Jobs had his fair share of false starts and ventures which hit the skids in the past. It should be remembered that if you put all your eggs in one basket, dropping the proverbial basket can smash all your eggs.

It is hard to stay on the rich list.

Forbes columnist Kenneth Fisher highlighted just how difficult it is to remain on the Forbes 400 rich list. In 1982, the average net worth of members of the 'Forbes 400' rich list was $230 million.[5] For an average member of the 1982 rich list to have made it onto the 2002 version of the list, they would only have needed to have made on a 4.5 per cent return on their net worth to remain on the rich list.[6] And over that 20-year period stocks were running hot returning an annual average of 13.2 per cent. Yet only 64 out of the 400 members – a measly 16 per cent – of the rich list from 1982 remained on the list two decades later.[7] For the other 84 per cent, it seems that the industries and companies they used to make themselves so rich in the first place, failed to keep them at the top of the pile for a long period.

If your goal is to become one of the richest people in the world – if perhaps only temporarily – then you'll most likely need to concentrate on building a huge business, and you will probably fail at least several times. If, on the other hand, your goal is to become wealthy but safely, then it's wise to spread your risk.

SPECIALISE BUT DIVERSIFY

There is no question that becoming an expert in one area or field of investment is the route that many of the most successful investors take to becoming wealthy. But that said, it makes sense for most to spread their risk to some extent within their preferred asset class. Gambling 100 per cent of your money on one company, no matter how well you feel you know it, is likely to be a volatile and potentially risky approach to personal finance. This has been shown over and over in cases where employees invested their pension and retirement plans in shares of the company that employed them – corporate failures can and do happen.

In the property investment world, similar principles apply. Investing your financial future in one large property development might reap dividends, but it is probably healthier for the volatility of your portfolio (and for your disposition) to spread your risk across property types and cities.

ASSET ALLOCATION – YOUR REAL BUCKET LIST!

The very phrase 'asset allocation' may sound a bit too much like financial jargon, but if it helps to simplify the concept you can think of it in another way. Think instead of a series of buckets, with each bucket representing one of your investments. You can spread your risk by having a range of different investments in different wealth buckets - which is known as diversification. Here is an adage of investment:

'Asset allocation is the only free lunch you will find in the investment game'.

What does this mean? It means that all risk assets have different risk profiles and all asset classes go through highs and lows, good times and bad times. So, diversify! Don't have all your eggs in one basket! And here is another adage of investment:

'Asset allocation accounts for more than 100 per cent of investor returns'

How can it be so that asset allocation accounts for more than 100 per cent of investor returns? Because, as already noted, most fund managers are myopic, engaging in market timing, trading, and stock selection techniques, and they rack up untold transaction costs and tax liabilities. Furthermore, add in the management costs charged by the fund managers to individual investors and their returns are still lower again. The implication of this is that in aggregate fund managers achieve very little. This isn't too surprising when you think about it – institutional investors make up such a significant share of share markets these days that to all intents and purposes they are the market.

The truth is that there is no perfect portfolio or perfect balance of assets to invest in. The reason for this is that we all have different goals, time horizons for investment, and tolerance levels for risk. For example, someone who has just left university may adopt a very different strategy to a person who is approaching their retirement. Why? Because they have time on their side and can afford to take a longer-term view with respect to risk assets.

In my experience, most people have an affinity for certain types of investments. Some people love the share market because you can start small, it is easy to invest in, it is liquid (so that it is easy to sell assets quickly if required), and unlike investing in property you don't have to worry about heavy transaction costs, repairs, or dealing with tenants. Other folks prefer property because it is a tangible asset which they can understand, can see or feel, and because there is no daily quoted price for individual properties they feel more comfortable holding for the long term.

Figure 6.1 – Asset allocation

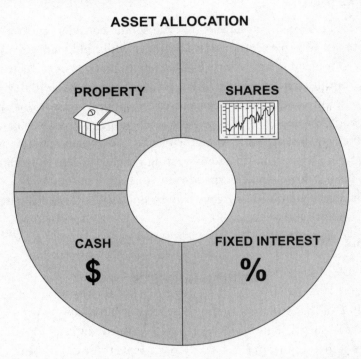

It is important to note that while the above graphic shows a possible diversification between asset classes, it is also both preferable and advisable to gain some diversification within asset classes too. For example, buying shares in two companies will lead to volatile results and is likely to entail quite a high degree of risk, because returns are entirely dependent on the fortunes of those two entities. However, if you own shares in a range of companies which operate in retail, the mining and resources sector, telecommunications, and financials, then you will have some diversification within the asset class. As we will see in Chapter 7, today it is easy to buy products such as low cost index funds, listed investment companies (LICs) or investment trusts which achieve diversification for you instantaneously. In the ideal but sadly non-existent world we would all have the perfect asset allocation mapped out for us, carefully tweaking and rebalancing our portfolio every year to minimise risk and maximise returns. The real world for most of us does not work like that. Another easier way to look at diversification is instead to again think of a series of buckets. Each time you have money to invest top up one of your buckets.

In this book, I am going to suggest that you should consider ignoring the great mass of hyperventilating stockbrokers and fund managers who continue to pretend to know what will happen to markets next. Instead, why not consider buying quality assets which you know you will never have to sell? Sure, there will be market corrections and 'drawdowns', but since nobody is consistently able to predict when they will be, you can instead focus on buying more when the market is cheap and holding for the long term. Better still, instead of wasting valuable energy following markets up and down, you can spend your time more productively elsewhere, perhaps by building your own business which will generate more income for you to invest!

Figure 6.2 – Wealth buckets

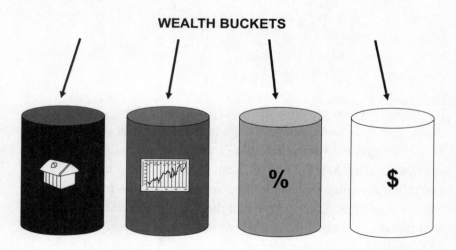

WEALTH BUCKETS

SPREADING YOUR RISK

Remember there are ways to diversify, including:

- across different asset classes
- over a portfolio of securities
- investing in different markets
- investing your capital across time

To keep your portfolio of assets balanced it makes sense to review how things are progressing for you, perhaps once each year. The idea of the passive investing strategy which I am introducing in this book is to keep things simple, and this particularly applies to asset allocation. Many fund management investment strategies call for endless rebalancing of risk, selling assets which are doing well to buy lagging assets. Although this sounds counter-intuitive, the theory behind this is that investments which have not done well may be due to perform better, while those which have increased in value may be due for a lean patch.

It does make sense to rebalance your investments regularly so that you don't have too much risk in any one part of your portfolio. However, since the passive investing strategy I'm suggesting is focused on not attracting transaction costs, instead of selling assets which are doing well (thereby attracting transaction costs and capital gains taxes), consider whether a better way to rebalance your portfolio is simply to buy new investments in asset classes to which you don't have such a heavy exposure.

Rebalancing: instead of selling, why not add more to the lagging asset classes?

Diversification is not just about improving returns - it is also about improving your emotional security. The ideas that I am discussing in this book aim to improve your life by giving you the sound knowledge that your plan will succeed over the long term. Through spending less than you earn and investing in quality assets that you need never sell, you can relax a little and allow time to be your friend.

By way of an example, I have quite a heavy exposure to property in London and Sydney. These are expensive property markets no doubt, and there is always a risk of correction. That said, I have never stressed about what happens in these markets because I have invested safely and within my tolerance for risk. I no longer waste time trying second guess when prices might rise or fall, I just aim to buy investments counter-cyclically and never sell them. I'm sure that there have been bubble and crash predictions every year since the mid-1990s – and sometimes prices do go down instead of up – but I still never sell quality well-located investments.

PREDICTABLY IRRATIONAL

Some years back now when I learned to drive I am sad to say that I didn't have one of those cards which designated that my organs would be donated to help others live. In the United Kingdom at the time there was a card which you could carry in your wallet which carried the simple explanatory tagline: 'Donor card – I want to help someone live after my death.'

Looking back this seems a shame, particularly as driving around the overcrowded London streets invariably seemed to involve a higher than satisfactory chance of one's organs becoming 'donatable'! By the time my daughter is old enough to pass her driving test, however, I expect that her organs will be made available for donation. Is this because she is a better or more thoughtful person that I was in my teenage years? To some extent, possibly, but it's not the real reason.

Allow me to explain. The consent rates data for the United Kingdom shows that less than one fifth of Brits are willing to donate their organs.[8] Yet in countries such as Austria, Belgium, France, Hungary, Poland and Portugal the figure is at least 98 per cent.[9] Why is this so given that those other European countries have similar culture and religious beliefs to Britain? The reason is simple. In those countries, would-be organ donors are required to opt out of participation. In Britain on the other hand one must opt in by checking a box on the form for your organs to be donated when you pass away.

Does this mean that Brits don't care? I don't think so. More likely they see organ donation as a complex or challenging emotional decision, and therefore they make no choice at all in choosing to leave the box blank. Whether we realise it or not, our environment tends to have a large effect on our behaviour. When faced with difficult or challenging decisions we tend to make no positive choices at all and instead adopt the default option. In the words of behavioural economist Dan Ariely, we are Predictably Irrational.[10]

FAILING CONVENTIONALLY

Due to peer pressure, it is easier for us to fail conventionally than it is to dare to take the different path. You may be familiar with what I mean. Try telling your circle of friends that you are planning to build an investment portfolio to target achieving financial freedom and note the responses. Often your peer group will be vaguely disapproving or even pour scorn on the idea. But why? I'll give you a clue: the answer is that it's more about them than it is about you! Taking responsibility for your financial future can shine on a light on the financial insecurities or even inadequacies of your friends. There is no value judgement to be made upon them, but you will need to be prepared for negative reactions and resolve not to let them stop you from taking command of your financial future. Resolve that you will have no reliance on the state pension in your retirement.

FEE FIGHTERS

The transaction costs generated by fund managers can be crippling to your overall returns from investment. Investing efficiently in low cost products is one of the ways in which you can forge ahead. Fund management products are cleverly designed to make the fees charged appear to be low. For example, there might be a fee charged of 1.5 per cent of your assets under management. It doesn't sound like much, of course, but the trick is that not only are the fees charged every year regardless of results, the fees you pay increase as the balance of your funds invested increase.

If the inefficiencies of investing in managed fees were limited to the management fees charged, this would be bad enough, but there is worse news still. Fund managers tend to churn over their holding remarkably regularly to beat the market (or at least try to). After all, if your fund manager is not generating better returns than the next guy, what are you getting for the fees he charges you? While this might seem to make sense, churning over stocks so rapidly often achieves very little except generating transaction costs and tax charges within the fund, reducing net returns. There are several ways in which this needless level of activity makes fund returns less efficient, including brokerage fees and slippage on entry and exit. If you are interested in the mechanics of why and how this happens, I explain this in a little more detail in my book *Get a Financial Grip*.[11] All you need to be aware of here is this:

On average, fund managers don't beat the market.

Indeed, the returns from funds may be even worse than advertised. Firstly, poor performing funds can be quietly merged or 'euthanized', meaning that the data may suffer from survivorship bias. That is, in the latest data reported we don't get to hear about the funds that have performed badly because they cease to exist!

Another word of warning: be wary when interpreting the returns that are quoted on your fund statements. Statements may quote 'average returns' but these can be an illusion. For example, the fund statements might record an average return for a financial year of 8 per cent. Be warned however, if you have been investing additional amounts into your pension through the year, then you time weighted returns could be lower because your dollars have not been invested for the full financial year. Average returns are an illusion, what you need are time weighted returns because you contribute through the year. If the calculations seem like hard work simply look at your opening balance, the amount you have contributed in the year, and the closing balance. How much value is your fund manager adding? Any at all? Ultimately the churning and trading of stocks is a zero-sum game. All this achieves is the generation of untold transaction costs in the form of brokerage fees and tax liabilities.

For all that, this book is not intended to be another one of those anti-fund manager contributions. Lord knows there are plenty of those out there already! Nor will I spend precious time and space citing the astronomical fees (as well as entry and exit charges) levied by some funds for very ordinary or underwhelming results. I'm not particularly keen on getting sued, after all! What I would be willing to do, however, is take a bet that if you take a glance at the returns from your pension or superannuation fund manager they haven't beaten the market by a substantial margin over the life of the investment. How do I know that? Because they almost never do! In fact, look at your annual financial statements when you get the chance. Are the results underwhelming?

Studies have shown that the cumulative impact of fund management fees and inefficiencies can act as a drag on annual returns to the tune of an astronomical 3 per cent or more per annum. The figure varies depending on the study and the data source, but the conclusions are usually similar. Now you may be thinking that a couple of per cent here or there is a small price to pay for somebody else managing your funds for you. You could be forgiven for thinking so, because that is exactly what fund management marketing departments are hoping you will think!

However, this is quite wrong. Look at the below chart where I have shown how the compounding growth rates of 5 per cent, 7 per cent and 9 per cent on a simple $100,000 invested over a working lifetime produce dramatically different results. As you can see $100,000 invested for 45 years at a 5 per cent compounding return fails to achieve a final balance of $1 million. Yet the same figure invested at a 9 per cent return continues to snowball to nearly $5 million over the same time horizon. This chart helps to explain why some people believe that fund management fees could rob you of up to 50 to 70 per cent of your returns!

Figure 6.3 – $100,000 investment over the long run

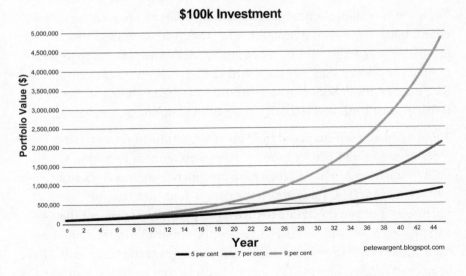

Remember, most fund managers don't beat the market. How then do they ever manage to command such huge assets under management?

The answer is simple enough – it's largely in the marketing. We are led to believe that managing your own money is too complex for an average person to do, and therefore we should pay somebody else to fail to beat the market instead! Which is pretty much exactly what fund managers want you to believe.

Funds are actively managed to attempt to beat the market, but they don't, largely because due to their massive size institutional investors to all intents and purposes are the market. Moreover, funds are too fearful of diverging far from the index return and therefore they hold dozens and dozens of stocks to reduce volatility (more transaction costs). The fund managers become 'index huggers'. Again, I don't intend to cite reams of statistics to prove the point. Simply check your pension or superannuation fund statements for as many financial years as you have the information available for. Have the returns diverged far from the average returns of the stock market over time? No, I didn't think so! You're paying for a fund manager to hug the index, which you could do far more efficiently yourself by buying a low-cost index fund!

MANAGING YOUR OWN PENSION

These are very important points in deciding how you are going to invest your money in the most efficient manner that you can going forward. It is possible to manage your own pension fund. I've been doing so for years myself. However, it does not necessarily follow that you must manage your own pension fund, because there are costs attached to doing so. Firstly, in terms of your time, and secondly in terms of administration charges.

That's because a self-managed fund takes some time to set up in terms of its structure, and you will need to pay an accountant to help you. Each financial year you will then have compliance costs such as audit and accounting fees. There is also the cost of your own time to consider, because even if you do choose to invest you pension passively in shares and property, you will still need to co-ordinate the administration of the fund. This is another way in which fund managers accumulate such a huge balance of funds under management – because they make it seems like the easy choice, the default option, or the path of least resistance.

If you have a small pension fund balance the compliance and

administrative costs make self-management an unattractive or unviable proposition. If you have a larger balance in your fund you are interested in managing your own pension fund, speak to an independent and licensed financial advisor who can advise you on whether this is a realistic proposition for you. Obviously, you don't want to find a financial advisor who will then recommend you invest in a fund with significant management fees! An independent financial advisor is what you want.

USING AN EXPERT

I've made the point strongly in this chapter of the book that fund management fees can have a devastating effect on your ability to grow and compound your wealth. Although the numbers sound small in percentage terms, the cumulative impact can be extraordinarily detrimental to your returns.

Don't get me wrong, however, I do believe that paying for expert advice can be a good thing in the right circumstances, and choosing an asset allocation can be one of those areas. Unfortunately, not all financial advisors are born equal, and the industry has had a long history of conflicted interest whereby some financial advisors only recommend products for which they can earn a trailing commission. This is not what I am suggesting. What may be worth considering is finding a financial advisor who charges a straight fee-for-service to get you on the right track.

What can a financial advisor help you with? Plenty! A financial advisor can help you to choose a sensible asset allocation which mitigates the risk of loss, and they can also help you with choosing low-cost products which will not clobber you with heavy fees year in and year out. If you decide to self-manage your pension or superannuation, then they may be able to advise you on the likely costs and appropriate structures too.

Remember there are different ways to diversify, such as into different securities, different countries and different asset classes – which can help to spread out your risk. You can also diversify over time by investing money regularly and not taking a higher risk by investing all your money at once. Remember look for an independent financial advisor who charges a fee-for-service, rather than someone who is only going to recommend products which they will earn a commission on, such as off-the-plan apartments or certain managed funds.

Chapter 6 Summary

- Don't put all your eggs in one basket.

- The more your plan is reliant upon successfully timing the markets successfully the less likely it is to be a success.

- Fund management costs erode your returns more dramatically than you think.

- Escape the fee factories by finding ways to invest efficiently in low cost products – this alone could be the different between achieving financial freedom and not.

- Using experts is fine – sometimes preferable even – just know what you are paying for, and don't get ripped off!

CHAPTER 7
GO!
TIME TO
INVEST

AND THEY'RE OFF …

Having done your groundwork, preparation and training, you are now at the starting line and ready to begin your race in earnest. Remember that your strategy is simple: to start slowly but surely, and to continue accelerating throughout your race, all the way to the finish line and beyond! You now know that you need to become a stakeholder or owner in the economy by becoming an investor. You also now know that due to fees and transaction costs managed funds on average will underperform the market. It's time to invest!

TIMING THE MARKET OR TIME IN THE MARKET?

When I wrote my first book *Get a Financial Grip* I devoted a full chapter to the concept of value investing, the strategy of buying shares in quality companies with an impenetrable economic 'moat' when they are undervalued and holding on to them until they are fully priced.[1] At that time share markets globally were priced very attractively as sentiment was only just in the process of recovering from the financial crisis shock. It was a great strategy for that time and it has literally paid very handsome dividends, as well as delivering outstanding price growth!

Value or focus investing certainly has its place in any investment strategy, but it does require a lot of work. In any case, over yearsmuch of the past decade-and-a-half, rock bottom interest rates have sent stock markets around the world soaring to all-time highs. By the time this book goes to print this may have changed, but presently as I write this, stock markets are generally not offering a great deal in terms of value, which is particularly the case given the mixed economic outlook.

Over recent decades an industry has grown up of 'buy side' and 'sell side' analysts hyperventilating over stock markets, with endless talking heads spouting forth opinions (which are frequently little more than educated guesses) as to what stock markets will do next. As often as not the guesses prove to be wrong, but by the next week a whole new round of commentary and predictions is underway. Time and time again we have seen that stock market predictions prove to be underwhelming, yet the media has column inches and screen time to fill, so it keeps coming back for more.

Other ideas spouted by marketing types include the idea that if you just managed to stay out of the market on the 10 worst days of the year then you could improve your result dramatically. It's an alluring idea, but nonsense of course. How can anyone know in advance when the worst trading days of the year will be? Obviously, they can't! The flip side to this is that if you are out of the market for the 10 best trading days of the year your returns will probably be wiped out. Incidentally, most amateur share market traders do precisely the opposite of what they should be doing, as I covered in more detail in my book *Get a Financial Grip*.

This is a book about investing in the market passively, which is a way to win the personal finance game with minimal fuss over the long term. Instead of worrying unduly about what is happening in markets you can thrive using an automated investment strategy which avoids the crippling effect of fund management fees that over time can swallow more than 50 per cent of your total returns.

INVESTING IN SHARE MARKETS

So, what are the benefits of a low-cost index fund and why are they so effective? Firstly, the management costs are very low – you do not have to pay a fund manager to try to outsmart the market for you, you simply hold a share in every stock in the index. This gives you instant diversification. While most people like to pick individual companies to invest in, it's close to impossible to know which companies will be around for the long term. Businesses, a bit like you and me, have a life cycle. They are born, some flourish, and eventually they die. It often seems that large companies must inevitably be around forever. Yet look at a list of the stock exchange companies from even just a few decades ago and see how many of them are no longer around. Where did they go? They may have merged, been taken over, dropped out of the index as they flail, or sunk into administration and been de-listed.

Many of us choose to self-manage our superannuation or pension because research has shown that over time, managed funds cannot or do not beat the market, so the management fees charged add no value. Managed funds cannot win over time because transaction costs, taxes and fund management fees drag down results. Of course, in individual years a managed fund may beat the market, but cumulatively the fund must beat the market by several percentage points each year to stay well ahead – to cover those transaction and brokerage costs, the fund management fees, the insurance charges, and the taxes. It can happen in some years, but over time, funds in aggregate fail to beat this hurdle consistently.

To some extent we can be a little harsh on the fund industry. Institutions hold such a large percentage of the market that aggregated fund returns must to some extent reflect the return of the market: for they essentially are the market. As a fund grows larger, asset elephantiasis limits the choices of stocks it can hold. Investors swarm towards funds which have experienced successful years thereby virtually ensuring that future returns cannot be as great. As fund transactions grow, funds suffer from market impact: large parcels of shares which are bought by the funds themselves impact the market (and they already are struggling to beat the bid-ask spread).

But these issues should not be your problem, so don't let them be your problem. Let them be someone else's problem! An index fund doesn't worry about trying to pick the next Microsoft, Facebook, Apple, or Nvidia. Once a company gets large enough you will own it anyway, and by owning a cross-section of industry you will own every stock worth owning. And when companies fall upon harder times and their value shrinks, they will drop off your portfolio during the periodic rebalancing of the index.

DUMB MONEY

Perhaps the biggest disadvantage of an index fund is simply that they are boring! You can never outperform the market and brag to people at parties, you can only match the index which you invest in. Yet perversely, the boring nature of index funds is also their greatest advantage. By using an averaging strategy, you can achieve tremendously effective returns over time by simply continuing to contribute each month or each quarter. For example, my wife and I have a UK index fund which has been contributed to for more than 25 years consecutively: very boring but over the long run it is effective. From time to time we might check in to see what the index is doing, but it generally doesn't matter whether prices move higher or lower. If the index goes down then we will simply be buying more units next month, and all the while the dividends increase over time as the economy and the profitability of the most successful companies grow. Warren Buffett once famously said that:

'Once dumb money recognises its limitations, paradoxically it ceases to be dumb'.

This is such a good quote that it should become your ninth new money mantra! What Buffett quite rightly implies is that in acknowledging that most average investors fail to beat the market, by reducing management costs and adhering to a sensible strategy of continuing to contribute each month, investors spread their risk both over time and over securities and achieve a fine result. Buffett also once said that time is the friend of quality investments and the enemy of mediocre, which equally applies to an investment in an index fund. The longer you hold the investment the more time you have for dividend flows to add to your returns and for the index to rise over time.

To some extent the same is true no matter whether you are investing in silver, modern art, diversified funds, property, or blue chip shares. The cleverer average investors try to be by outsmarting the market with timing, the more likely they are to come unstuck. While investors can always look to find value in their investments and buy high quality assets in a downturn, some level of diversification is important and acquiring assets over time has the effect of averaging the entry cost. This can reduce risk greatly.

OTHER LOW COST PRODUCTS

Realistically, most average investors are time-poor and do not take the time to learn the laborious process of how to analyse financial statements, nor do they have strong market-timing skills. Therefore, for most, the process of choosing shares to invest in is largely one of forlorn guesswork, which is reflected in sub-optimal results. What hope is there, then, for average investors who don't want to be slugged with expensive fund management fees, but also want to beat the index? There is another option, and that is to find a low-cost product such as an exchange-traded index fund or listed investment company (LIC) in Australia which has a long track record of strong performance. In other countries, similar low-cost products are available, such as investment trusts in the United Kingdom.

A quality LIC may have a focus on sustainable industrial companies rather than resources companies which have high capital costs and can only compete on price because they sell commodities. As such, these companies may perform well at certain points in the commodity cycle, but tend to have high capital costs and so pay weaker dividends on average through the cycles (although in truth this does depend a bit on the dates you choose to measure from and to!). Since the first edition of this book was released, the resources sector has performed very strongly, as government stimulus has created huge demand for commodities.

The advent of internet brokerage sites has seen a huge global increase in individual investors selecting their own stocks in which to invest. The answer is to promote an investment plan that is both repeatable and spreads your risk through averaging. That is, to contribute a regular dollar amount into a well-diversified product on a regular basis. When the market is low, you will effectively buy more stock, and vice-versa. But what product to buy? Here are a few of the reasons why you might elect for a LIC in Australia:

1. Diversification

By buying into a LIC which holds up to 100 or more stocks and trusts, you can be instantly diversified. The approach of not having all your eggs in one basket is a tried and tested approach to reducing risk over time.

2. Low costs

Returns can be improved substantially over time if you select an LIC with low administrative costs. What would represent a low administrative cost? This means that the LIC does not charge you a cripplingly expensive 'performance' or 'management' fee, and the costs charged for remuneration, office rent and other administrative costs, such as for the company's IT and stationery, represent lower than 0.2 per cent of the fund's average assets at market value.

Compare this with the fees charged on your superannuation fund and you will begin to see why LICs can be a superior choice. Remember that while fund management fees of 1 to 2 per cent may not sound dramatic, if you consider how much of your expected annual return this might represent the effect on your ability to create wealth over time can be overwhelming. A well-selected LIC does not trade hyperactively. Instead, it will aim to identify quality companies to invest in for the long term and will only rarely look to sell. This reduces unnecessary brokerage costs and taxes.

3. Outperformance over time

By choosing an LIC which is heavily weighted towards profitable industrial stocks and the banks you may be able to outperform the index over time. Why do industrial companies tend to outperform the resources index? Because the performance of resources stocks can be cyclical and dividends can be substantially weakened in the downturn phase! Resources companies also tend to retain large amounts of capital to source and re-invest in new projects which can hamper shareholder returns. At various points through the market cycles, industrial companies have tended to be more sustainable and more self-perpetuating, in contrast with resources companies with their diminishing reserves.

4. Dividend re-investment

You may have the choice in a LIC to receive dividends or to re-invest them to grow your portfolio in an efficient manner. Remember, your goal is to snowball or compound your wealth, and re-investing your dividends can be a great way to achieve this. A dividend re-investment plan (DRP) should not attract brokerage, stamp duty or other transaction costs and thus can be an effective method of allowing your portfolio to grow and compound.

5. Control over investment

As you can buy a LIC on the securities exchange it is remarkably easy to buy and sell, provided you select an appropriately liquid investment. This gives the investor great control, and while selling may be inefficient, the liquidity of such an investment can allow funds to be accessed easily in an emergency.

THREE ADDITIONAL CONSIDERATIONS ABOUT LICS

Above I have noted some great reasons for consider investing in an LIC. However, before doing so there are a handful of risks to consider:

1. Track record

When investing in an LIC you want to know that the company has a proven track record of success that has been delivered over a period of decades. I like LICs which have proven themselves over 50 or 60 years! At the very least, you probably want to look at investment companies which have a proven track record of increasing their dividend payments consistently over a period of three decades or so. Why so? Because this period should outlive the working lifespan of an individual CEO or portfolio manager, and thus you know you have found an LIC with the right philosophy. The company should not be reliant on the skills of any one individual because then there is a risk that the company could deteriorate when that individual departs!

Many people ask me about cryptocurrencies and other new asset classes. In truth, I'm not an expert in those markets, and I'm not that interested in investing in them because I have no idea where things will be headed decades from now. With stock market investments, I can look back at over a century of data to give me some comfort about the expected returns.

2. Liquidity

When you start out investing most of the LICs of a decent size will have sufficient liquidity for you. What do I mean by liquidity? The ability for the market to absorb your buy and sell orders easily. The way to check this out is to look at the volume of shares traded in a normal day on the stock exchange for the LIC you are looking at. When you are investing relatively small amounts this may not be an issue, but it can be a problem as the size of your investments gets bigger. If your shareholding is huge but only a relatively small number of shares are traded each day, then it may be difficult for you to exit the investment should you ever need to. Even those of us with a strong bias towards buy and hold never know when we might need to liquidate an investment for other purposes.

3. Leverage

As we have considered in other sections of the book, leverage in the form of debt can be a useful tool for maximising returns. If you look at the balance sheets of most successful companies you will find that they tend to employ a moderate amount of debt, and this can be true of LICs too. The key word here is 'moderate'. There is no problem with buying shares in a company which is using an easily serviceable amount of debt, but you should be very wary of investing in an entity which is heavily reliant on debt or might struggle with servicing interest charges. Moreover, a sensible investment in the share market should be able to return you a comfortable 8 per cent per annum over the long haul, and there is no need to invest in heavily leveraged companies to take on undue risk.

SUMMARY OF LICS

By choosing an LIC with a reasonably conservative and appropriately experienced management, you can take comfort in your investment approach. Through holding shares in all of Australia's major, profitable industrial companies, even in times of recession you know that the LIC will retain value and your averaging approach will ensure that you pick up more holdings when prices are lower.

Better still, if you can buy more heavily when the market has experienced a major correction, you can begin to move further ahead of the pack in an efficient manner which does not generate excessive brokerage and capital gains taxes through trading. The more repeatable an investor's strategy is, the greater the likelihood of its enduring success. If you are thinking of investing in a low cost LIC or an index fund, see an independent financial advisor who can recommend the best product for you.

In recent years, exchange-traded funds (ETFs) have made owning all of the top few hundred companies in an index very easy and very low-cost, and as such this has been an increasingly popular approach. The aim of this book is not to direct you to any specific product, but more to get you thinking about what the most appropriate product and strategy might be for your situation.

PROPERTY

The main advantage of property as an investment for the average investor is the opportunity to use more leverage, and this is particularly the case for residential property. Investing in property is a very different proposition from investing in the share markets! For this reason, in Chapter 8 I will discuss in more detail how you might best go about investing in property.

FIXED INTEREST

Traditionally it was said that fixed interest investments offered investors the benefits of a risk-free return. That is, investor could choose to allocate a portion of their portfolio in term deposits, bonds, notes or other fixed income investments to receive a steady return of interest payments. One of the challenges faced by investors since the financial crisis of 2007 is that globally interest rates have been cut to considerably lower levels, meaning that returns from most fixed interest investments are now often lower, unless you are investing in products of a perceived level of higher risk.

Indeed, in some cases during the pandemic period it was true that the return from fixed interest investments proves to be below the rate of inflation, leading some commentators to describe these asset classes today as providing 'return-free risk'. Remember, markets and economies are ultimately cyclical, and at some time in the future there will return a time when interest rates are higher once again. When that financial season comes around again there will be more of a place for fixed interest investments in the portfolio of most investors.

CASH

It makes sense to hold a reasonable amount of cash as a buffer. Because holding cash or cash equivalents is generally perceived a low risk choice, the returns on cash in a bank account tend to be low. Although holding too much cash in your portfolio acts as a drag on returns, it is sensible to hold a reasonable level of cash in case of emergency. Moreover, holding cash allows investors to take advantage of great opportunities when they do come around, such as in the aftermath of a stock market correction. Make sure you keep it in a bank account which is secure and pays a solid rate of interest.

TIME HORIZONS FOR INVESTMENT – SHORT TERM TO LONG TERM

What would you consider to be a long-term investment? If you ask people what they might consider to be a short, medium and long term investment, they will probably give you an answer like the following:

- **Short term** – one month to 12 months
- **Medium term** - more than 12 months
- **Long term** – five years or longer

In this book, I want to get you to rethink these preconceptions and instead consider a much bigger picture, where a long-term investment could mean the duration of your lifetime. Better than that, I want you to think of your investments are vehicles which can generate wealth through your lifetime and even way beyond your own lifetime. That is the type of bigger picture I am talking about!

Humans cannot predict the future accurately.

Am I being too outrageous if I say that humans cannot predict the future accurately? Of course, we can't! There are more than enough examples to prove my point. Yet what do you see when you turn on the news or the internet every day? Prediction after prediction! 'Stocks will fall tomorrow, interest rates will be hiked soon, the gold price will rise, and bond prices could get smashed.'

'Stock prices have reached what looks like a permanently high plateau.'
- Irving Fisher (1929)

Humans love to make predictions but it is clear that as a race we are generally quite hopeless at them. Could it therefore follow that any investment which relies upon an asset price moving in our favour over any period under, at the very least, a decade is to some extent something of a guess?

Longer term predictions can often be more reliable.

Over the longer term some things are reasonably predictable. Company earnings will generally move higher and the total dollar value of dividends from the share markets will rise. Property and land prices in the inner suburbs of large capital cities with strong population growth will increase over time. The currency in our pocket or stashed in our bank accounts will depreciate and be worth less. In developed countries with inflationary economies, it has ever been thus.

Although even these outcomes are sometimes not 100 per cent certain, they are nevertheless very likely in part because central banks plan for it to be so. Central banks and governments today are aware of the dangers of deflation such as was experienced in Japan and will therefore fight tooth and nail to maintain a steadily inflationary economy. If required the interest rates will be cut to near zero, as we have seen in recent years, central banks will effectively 'print' money through asset purchasing programmes and in truly desperate times they may even just give us money to spend.

Deflation can be staved off by 'dropping money from helicopters'.

The concept of dropping money from helicopters was conceived by Milton

Friedman and later quoted by the Chairman of the US Federal Reserve, Ben Bernanke, who became known colloquially as 'helicopter Ben'. While not to be taken literally, the notion is important. The key point is that central banks have powerful tools at their disposal to ensure that prolonged deflation does not take hold of the economy, and they will use them to ensure that it never happens.

Here are some more realistic time horizons for investment:

- **Short term** – one decade
- **Medium term** – 10 years to your lifetime
- **Long term** – your lifetime and even beyond your own lifetime

We have already established that we cannot reliably predict the future and therefore the length of our life is unknown. But we can certainly take a reasonable guess and work with that. True investing does not focus upon the immediate price action of a security or asset. Instead, investors focus on the fact that over the long term – yes that means a lifetime – quality assets that they hold will generate both strong recurring income and dependable capital growth.

Think beyond your own lifetime.

Although the concept of continuing to steadily build an asset base over time is simple to grasp, the mindset is not easy for many people to accept. In fact, for most it seems to be a totally alien, almost abstract concept. Think of how often you hear people with an opposite view:

- 'You can't take it with you.'
- 'You're only young once ...'
- 'Don't be so tight!'
- 'I plan to spend the last dollar on the day I die.'
- 'I'll take the lump sum on a long holiday and then live off the government pension!'

Unfortunately, the average pension balances at retirement ensure that for most, drawing the meagre government pension is the only option that remains. If you are not sure how much the state pension is (or, more accurately, is not) likely to pay for, take a quick look. The government pension doesn't go a long way in the modern world.

Perhaps we need to be able to move beyond the idea that money is simply something that you earn and then spend. Instead, a portion of what is earned should be donated to charity, some should be spent on moderate living costs, a reasonable buffer saved for emergencies and the remainder invested for the future. Better still make the charitable donations and investments first and then spend or save the remainder.

Through first grasping and then embracing these very simple concepts, over a lifetime of application perfectly ordinary individuals achieve results that can be staggering. Spend less than you earn and buy quality, appreciating assets with the difference. And as for what will happen to stock markets and property markets over the next few months or years? Rhett Butler said it best in *Gone with the Wind*:

'Frankly my dear, I don't give a damn.' – Rhett Butler

BUY LOW, SELL HIGH?

You will often hear in the financial press the phrase 'buy low, sell high'. It makes perfect sense, of course. Have you considered, though, that if it were that simple then everyone would do it? Remember that even many of the most experienced and professional of investors have not been able to consistently time the market well, so what chance is there for amateurs to time their entry and exit to the market accurately? Rather than building an investment plan around constantly trying to dip in and out of the market, you may wish to consider a buy and hold strategy, and choose to focus on the growing income or dividend stream? When the market crashes or corrects – as it will periodically – why not aim to buy more when the market is on sale?

By following this approach your investment place will be much more efficient. You will not attract regular capital gains tax liabilities in the manner of a trader. Meanwhile, dividend streams can be tax-advantaged in some circumstances when they are received with franking credits attached under prevailing dividend imputation rules. Alternatively, you can re-invest the dividends via what is known as a DRP (dividend re-investment plan) and not incur tax until you choose to sell.

In truth, almost everybody is a market-timer to some extent. Some of us choose to build up bigger cash buffers when we thinking markets are expensive. TAnd then when markets fall, we look to put more money to work in the stock markets. The debate about market timing versus time in the market is often a matter of degree rather than of principle. Often investors become more defensive or risk-averse as they reach their wealth goals, or as they approach retirement, and of course this may make sense.

AVERAGING IN PRACTICE

My wife has an index fund which she set up about 25 years ago with a direct debit which directed funds to buy new units every month. The idea is to fund higher education for the kids, if they decide to pursue University. This investment principle is founded in great common sense and the strategy is known variously as averaging or dollar cost averaging. It works because by spreading the entry times into the market the investor buys more units when the share market is low and fewer units when the market is high, thus spreading the risk and 'averaging' out the entry cost. Meanwhile the investor continues to enjoy income from the investment which typically grows each year, ideally ahead of the rate of inflation.

In his classic investment book *The Intelligent Investor,* Ben Graham talks of such a strategy as being one of the most sensible and straightforward approaches for the averaging income-earning investor to employ.[2] And it's not hard to wholeheartedly agree with that. While in hindsight timing the market always seems to be very easy and obvious, in real time when you are reading the share price chart from left to right it is not. Even professional fund managers have shown themselves to be poor on average at exploiting a market-timing strategy, so what hope is there for the everyday investor?

Spreading your entry into the market can reduce risk.

The concept of dollar cost averaging earned something of a bad name through the financial crisis as markets crashed, leading many commentators to suggest that market timing is the only way to go. In theory, this is fine, but what typically happens is that investors sell in anticipation of a forthcoming market fall and then the market roars upwards – and the same happens at the bottom of the stock market cycle too, but in reverse.

The simplest way to create wealth through shares is to choose an appropriate investment product or products – suggestions I make include index funds or listed investment companies (LICs), as I will explain later – and to write yourself a contract such as the one opposite, agreeing with yourself to continue to buy at regular intervals. This key concept is elaborated upon further in *The Intelligent Investor* by Warren Buffett's mentor Ben Graham[3], which is one of my favourite books:

DOLLAR COST AVERAGING – CONTRACT

I (name)..

Hereby commit to investing the following amount: $...................

Every month/quarter (delete as applicable)

I will invest the amount noted at the interval stated above in the following equities products:

....

....

....

....

Signed..

Date ....

WHY DOES THIS WORK?

Why does this simple approach work so effectively for average investors? Firstly, it is due to the averaging effect and a natural smoothing out of your entry prices which helps to make up for a lack of market timing. When the market is depressed and prices are cheap your dollars automatically buy more shares, helping you to buy more when the market is on sale. On the other hand, when the market is expensive, exuberant or over-priced, your dollars do not go as far and purchase fewer shares.

The simple genius of averaging is that the automatic stabilising effect of smoothing your entry price helps to eliminate or reduce risk. The share market can be risky if you engage an approach of pushing large sums of money at the market too quickly since you are then reliant upon the market moving in your favour at any given point in time.

Buy quality assets for the long term.

By instead committing to investing an affordable amount of money regularly into the market, in doing so you can give yourself peace of mind that over the long term you will prosper regardless of short term gyrations in the market, provided you buy quality, well-diversified investment products. In an inflationary economy, a basket of quality, profitable companies will continue to generate larger profits and pay greater dividends to you over time, which you may elect to receive as income or simply re-invest into the market to continue snowballing your portfolio.

In the next chapter of the book, we will consider whether you might re-invest dividends or take them as income, but for now, it is only important here to recognise what a powerful tool dollar cost averaging can be if it is used smartly.

MOST PEOPLE ONLY HAVE TWO SUCCESSFUL INVESTMENTS

It seems to be the case that in many developed countries the majority of everyday folk only have two genuinely successful investments which account for more than 80 per cent of their wealth – their house and their pension. Why is that? Generally, it is because they see them both as long term investments which they can 'set and forget' for many years or even decades. Like shares, real estate can be an excellent investment if you buy well and hold for the long term – long enough for household incomes to increase, dwelling construction costs and labour costs to increase and resultantly for dwelling prices to do the same.

Residential property tends to be an effective long term inflation hedge if you buy in a capital city with a growing population. This is because new dwellings must be built to house the growing population and the new dwellings will always be built at today's prices and with today's labour, construction and materials costs.

However, capital growth in real estate never occurs exactly in a straight line. In the simplest terms as the population grows this puts upwards pressure on the housing market – vacancy rates fall and property prices start to rise as more people compete for the existing stock of dwellings. As prices rise, developers see the potential for profit and begin to develop some of their land-banked holdings with new dwellings which they can sell for a reasonable profit margin at the prevailing higher prices.

Nobody rings a bell at the top (or bottom) of the market.

Unfortunately, nobody rings a bell at the top of the market and the rate of construction tends to overshoot. Construction continues beyond the point which it is desperately needed and an oversupply of properties ultimately eventuates. As the population is now competing for more properties on the market vacancy rates rise, rents tend to ease and prices begin to soften or decline. This in turn leads to a slowing of construction until vacancy rates tighten once more and upwards pressure on the market eventually returns.

Of course, the property market cycle is far more complex than this and engaging an expert can help you to recognise how different sectors of the market behave in markedly different manners regardless of the stage of the cycle, but the basic principles described above are correct. If you can begin to recognise how safe and profitable an investment property can be if you understand the market, you can begin to turn this to your advantage to generate very substantial wealth.

Property does not tend to be a great short term investment, however, unless you happen to be a highly skilled renovator or developer, because of the material transaction costs involved when buying and selling property such as taxes and legal fees. However, over the long term, by which I mean 15 to 20 years or more, very substantial gains can be made if you can learn the appropriate skills to significantly outperform the averages.

SET AND FORGET

Experience shows that most average investors experience the greatest success when they can adopt an automated approach to their investing and adopt a set-and-forget attitude. One of the key themes of this book is to consider how you can buy assets which you can hold onto forever – it is the most efficient way to build wealth there is.

ARE STOCK MARKETS RISKY?

Have you ever heard it said that successful people have views which are opposite to those of the crowd? It is often true. Popular consensus would have you believe that share markets are risky, and this may be true if you do not know what you are doing. If your approach is to pile large sums of money into shares in a handful of companies in the hope that you have guessed the direction of the market correctly, then indeed engaging in the share market is likely to be a risky venture for you.

What people seem to have forgotten is that the point of buying shares is to buy a share in great businesses and a claim on the future earnings and distributed profits. These days, largely thanks to media commentary, too many investors (or, should one say, speculators) are instead buying a number on a chart without carrying out any due diligence worthy of the name into the company that they are buying shares in.

As previously noted, when I began writing my first book some years ago I devoted a full chapter to the concept of value investing, partly for the simple reason that there was a good deal of deep value to be in the market back at that time. And what a successful strategy that has proved to be for anyone who followed those simple principles of buying quality companies at a value price! Since that time, we have lived through a roaring bull market across global share market indices with more than a dozen years of rollicking gains being recorded in the US, the United Kingdom, Australia and elsewhere. Even the pandemic crash of 2020 lasted only a matter of weeks before markets roared back, since recapturing record highs.

Consequently, as I write this there is far less value to be found in stock markets with lower interest rates and fiscal stimulus having pushed market valuations higher, with US indices having hit new heights. In short, depending upon when you are reading this book, it is probably not such a good time to be pouring a huge amount of your net worth into the stock market while valuations are so stretched. If you are interested in the Warren Buffett approach to investing of buying value stocks, then you need to be able to carry out detailed analysis of financial statements, including ratio analysis and profitability forecasts, as well as understanding the industry outlook for the companies you are investing in and how each company will fare within its own field. The statistics don't lie on this – even some of the great investors have struggled to beat the market averages over the past couple of decades, so you can save yourself a lot of time and energy by accepting the market return, and focusing your energy on saving more, and on your career or business, and self-improvement, for example.

'Price is what you pay. Value is what you get.' – Warren Buffett

I have come to appreciate the conclusion that the great majority of investors who claim to be value investors are in truth no such thing because they do not carry out any genuinely detailed research at all into the companies that they are buying. Researching a company's financials can be painstaking work and at times quite dull, which is why, one supposes, most people do not bother to do it. Others do not have the financial education or the expertise.

It is no secret that one of my favourite books is The *Intelligent Investor* by Ben Graham. If you want to understand the principles of value investing this might be a great place to start. The trouble is today that too many people want to ask 'what do you think of XYZ stock?' instead of taking the time to analyse and understand the criteria for what makes for a sound investment and what denotes a good value proposition.

The beautiful thing about the share market is that this does not necessarily matter provided you can adopt a sensible alternative approach for the long term of diversifying and dollar cost averaging. If you genuinely want to learn the skills of value investing read my book *Get a Financial Grip*, but if you do not have the time or inclination, please do not kid yourself about what you are doing, adopt a sensible averaging approach using diversified products which give you peace of mind, and instead apply your efforts to other more productive pursuits … like setting big and exciting goals for the future!

THE INDEX

When my wife Heather went to work at Deloitte after graduating from University, in one of her early training courses the facilitator asked the new graduates a simple question: 'At what level is the stock market index approximately today?' only to be met with blank stares all round. Not only did no one in the room know the answer, none of the new trainees knew the answer to within hundreds of points. So much for accountants having their finger on the pulse!

The interesting thing about averaging is that you don't really need to know what the index is doing on a day-to-day basis, or even a week-to-week basis. It's not all that important because of the natural smoothing effect of buying a set dollar value of shares regularly. When shares are cheap you naturally purchase more, and when shares are expensive you acquire less.

However, that said, it might be worth me explaining again here what an index is! A market index is a measurement of the market value of a cross-section of the stock market which is calculated using the weighted average of last traded prices. It is essentially a way to ascertain the sentiment across a section of the wider stock market but it can easily disguise the price of individual components or stocks acting a markedly different manner from others within the index.

'The best way is just buy a low-cost index fund and keep buying it regularly over time, because you'll be buying into a wonderful industry, which in effect is all of American industry. People ought to sit back and relax and keep accumulating over time.'
– Warren Buffett

Investing in an index fund can be an efficient way to invest because instead of paying a percentage of your money to a fund manager to churn over stocks for you (which creates further transaction costs and taxes) you simply hold the top companies by market capitalisation and liquidity – it is the ultimate form of simple buy and hold investing for share market participants.

Most people overestimate what they can achieve in a year, but hugely underestimate what they can potentially achieve in a decade or a lifetime. If you truly understand how compounding works then your potential can be almost limitless over the long haul, but you do need some time to allow compounding to work its magic.

The long-term trend in most stock markets tends to be upwards for a few reasons. Generally, over time, successful companies tend to increase their profits, which is reflected in higher share prices, while unsuccessful companies eventually disappear off the bottom of the index or become completely insolvent and are wound up – thus there can be an element of survivorship bias in some indices. Inflation plays a role too, as profits in dollar terms are pushed up by the depreciating currency. The thing to remember for long term investors is that market crashes, far from being something to be feared or panicked about, can represent great opportunities to load up on more quality stocks at an attractive price.

WHAT ABOUT WHEN THE MARKET CRASHES?

But what about stock market crashes? Stocks markets are liquid and thus they can and will crash from time to time. It is a natural part of the cycle. During the pandemic lockdowns, for example, the Aussie stock market fell by more than 35% from peak to trough, before recovering all of the declines comparatively quickly.

Of course such violent swings in your portfolio can be scary, which is why most of us tend to keep some cash on hand, to be able to buy more when the market is down significantly. Remember that crashes are not permanent and the long-term trend in stock market indices is up. Even if it sometimes takes years for markets to recover to previous years, you're still getting the dividend income, and you do get the chance to buy more stocks when the market is lower. I once asked stock market guru and author Peter Thornhill about the impact of share market crashes. He discussed with me the emotional impact of investing through the financial crisis and said:

'When the market crashes, you would have to be dead not to feel it.'

Presumably this is particularly so for someone like Thornhill who has invested in the market for decades and thus commands a large portfolio of assets. It is interesting to note that during the most recent crash even the most experienced investors felt the psychological impact of share market movements. Incidentally, Thornhill is a strong advocate of the principles of investment described above, a fair chunk of which I learned from reading his book. Why? Because he worked for years in the fund management industry and he fully understands the folly of fund managers attempting to churn stocks over all the time to chase instant returns.

What is most important about market corrections is not only how you feel but how you react. I have noted elsewhere that success in life is frequently far more attributable to how you interpret and respond to events than what happens to you. Perhaps most inexperienced market participants panic when the stock market falls and sell their assets at the most inopportune moment to the professional investors.

Experienced investors know that sizeable stock market corrections which bring price-earnings ratios down to single digit territory are great buying opportunities rather than a reason to panic. They will continue to acquire shares in the normal fashion, but the true and experienced experts will have set some money aside to buy even more when the market falls to irrationally low levels, because they understand that markets are cyclical.

Stock markets are liquid and therefore can be volatile.

Remember my key principle of investment is to buy a quality investment that will pay you income forever and offer you growth potential. Recall the Pleasure-Pain Principle – investment is something which you should associate with the pleasure of knowing that you are building a nest egg for your future. If you associate investing with pleasure you will do more of it and do it better. Too many people associate investing with pain, stress and loss, and they do less of it, and do it badly. If you have adhered to this rule then stock market corrections are something to be embraced rather than to be feared – they offer you the chance to buy more of a wonderful thing at a mouth-watering price!

THE YIELD TRAP

People often tell me they have found a good investment because of its high yield or income. However, yield can be a very misleading indicator of the quality of an investment. We need to understand the dimensions of yield and growth and how they interact with each other. This is neatly illustrated by Thornhill himself in his share investment book *Motivated Money*.[4]

Back in 1980, he notes, term deposits were paying around 10 per cent interest, so on the face of it were far more attractive investments than, for example, a portfolio of industrial shares, which were yielding only around half of this percentage. High yield (and supposedly low risk) investments tend to attract retirees who seek certainty of income. There is a hidden trap, however, and it is this: a high yield is not the same thing as a high income.

HIGH YIELD DOES NOT MEAN HIGH INCOME

A yield is simply a spot figure calculated at a point in time. Income of $100 on an investment of $1000 gives a yield of 10 per cent, which is superficially attractive. Income is the dollar figure that the investment pays you over time. Suppose a retiree invested $100,000 in term deposits in 1980. Income of $10,000 in the first year may have seemed more attractive than the lower percentage dividend yields of shares.

Yield and income are not the same thing.

By 1993, however, an initial $100,000 portfolio of industrial shares, whilst still paying a 'weaker' dividend yield of around 5 per cent, was paying income of closer to $20,000, and by 2006 a huge dividend income of around $75,000 on a portfolio value of a massive $1.75 million.[5] Even after the stock market downturns of 2007 to 2009 and again in 2020, the market has continued to deliver the goods over the long term. Now what happens to the capital value and income of a term deposit over that timeframe? Oh dear, not much. So much for the initial high yield!

Investing in investments upon retirement such as term deposits might only be a good investment if you plan on dying quickly. What we want, rather than high yield, is high income over time. The percentage yields on shares over the long term tends to fluctuate with prevailing sentiment and prices, so yields do become comparatively higher when share prices crash and lower when prices boom. Thus, a stock market meltdown is a great time to buy both for yield and future capital growth.

CONCENTRATE ON POTENTIAL FUTURE CASH FLOWS FOR FINANCIAL FREEDOM

In the simplest terms when you have income which flows to you and is greater than the sum of your financial commitments then you are financially free. Therefore, if you can learn to focus on continuing to invest in shares and equities products which pay you a strong and increasing dividend stream, then eventually you will become financially free. This can take a long time which is why young investors often look to property and leverage to accelerate the process, but it's important to note the key lesson here. Just as the true value of a company is ultimately the discounted present value of its future cash flows so it is with the value of an investment.

Share prices gyrate from day to day and from month to month, but an investment which increases its income streams in perpetuity will also see its price increase over the long term. When investing in the share markets learn to take a longer-term view and watch the ever-growing income streams rather than fussing over haphazard movements in the share price. What is remarkable about this approach is that when done successfully share investors can see more income from their dividend streams in retirement than they ever earned from their salary incomes during their entire working career.

> **Chapter 7 Summary**
>
> - Fill up your buckets with quality investments which you can hold for the long term.
> - A lengthy time horizon for investment means your lifetime and beyond!
> - Returns from investment come in two forms – cash flow and capital growth.
> - Concentrate on growing future cash flows for wealth and financial freedom.
> - The capital growth should follow in time.

CHAPTER 8
PROFITABLE PROPERTY INVESTMENT

LOCATION, LOCATION ...

At the time of writing, we've been through a highly tumultuous four years for property markets Down Under. During the pandemic in 2020 and 2021 Australia experienced lockdowns and border closures, and the international borders were closed, effectively halting population growth for a time. Interest rates were cut to zero, and regional markets boomed as the property market experienced a wild 'race for space'. Then interest rates were rapidly hiked to decade highs to curb inflation, and employers began trying to entice employees back to the office.

Despite everything, property prices have held up well, and in many cases experienced solid increases. There are always market cycles and periods of rising and falling prices, but over the long run property tends to be remarkably resilient.

Consider these eight famous (or in some cases infamous) quotes about real estate, and what they might mean for property as an investment:

- 'Buying real estate is not only the best way, the quickest way, and the safest way, but the only way to become wealthy.'
  – Marshall Field

- 'The best investment on Earth is Earth.' – Louis Glickman

- 'Don't wait to buy land, buy land and wait.' – Will Rogers

- 'The major fortunes in America have been made in land.'
  – John D. Rockefeller

- 'Buy land, they're not making it anymore.' – Mark Twain

- 'Land monopoly is not only monopoly, but it is by far the greatest of monopolies; it is a perpetual monopoly, and it is the mother of all other forms of monopoly.' – Winston Churchill

- 'Ninety per cent of all millionaires become so through owning real estate. More money has been made in real estate than in all industrial investments combined. The wise young man or wage earner of today invests his money in real estate.'
  – Andrew Carnegie

THE 6 BASIC CHARACTERISTICS OF PROPERTY AS AN INVESTMENT

Before drilling into some analysis of how and where you need to acquire property in the future to secure strong capital growth which can multiply your earnings and wealth, let us first take the concept of property ownership right back to basics and consider the simplest aspects of what investing in property means.

1. Property is immobile

Most, though not all, properties are immobile. If you like your house but not your suburb, the chances are that you will need to move suburb and leave your house behind. Lenders like this! You cannot easily default on your mortgage and disappear while taking your house with you, and even if you could somehow manage this, the land will still be there. This tends to make lenders more comfortable and therefore they can offer very long mortgage terms, often at relatively low interest rates, and frequently only relatively small percentage deposits are required.

This is a unique triumvirate of lending conditions and as such it makes residential real estate unique as an investment prospect. Everyday Mum and Dad investors can use significantly more leverage to invest – they can borrow more capital – than is the case in any other asset class. Leverage is a double-edged sword, however, for it magnifies both capital gains and losses, so it must only ever be used wisely!

2. Property is durable

It is often said that real estate is durable because buildings can stand for centuries. While this may be true to a point, one disadvantage of property (as compared to, say, parcels of shares in self-sustaining, dividend-paying industrial companies) is that if you do not re-invest money in repairs and maintenance, your property will tend to deteriorate, and eventually it could even fall over!

This may not always be a problem. Some investors buy property for its land value and as noted above, for the land itself is virtually indestructible – it will always be there, and if it is in a prime location then land tends to appreciate over time. Nevertheless, property which is rented out to tenants usually requires some maintenance expenditure. Because real estate can be durable, in most market sales tend to consist primarily of existing stock rather than new builds.

3. Property markets can be illiquid

It can take a long time to buy or sell a property. This makes it extremely important where real estate is bought as an investment that there is a continual high demand for the type of property that you buy. The worst-case scenario in an illiquid market is owning an asset which is sliding in value with no buyers available. I've seen it happen to people who bought property in mining towns during the mining boom, at the recommendation of advisors. When the bust came, there were no buyers at any price.

Illiquidity in a market may be both a good and bad thing depending on how you look at it. In most years, only a very small percentage of capital city housing stock is transacted, which tends to keep property markets relatively stable. However, where a market is illiquid it can be very difficult to sell a property quickly if you need to, and in a declining market there may be no buyers of your depreciating asset. This can be nerve-wracking to say the least! Therefore, I recommend only owning quality properties in capital cities for which there is a strong and growing demand, and strongly suggest that you do not buy junk properties that nobody wants or needs out in the sticks.

4. Property incurs high transaction costs

Buying a parcel of shares is simple. You might pay a few dollars as a brokerage fee but there is presently no stamp duty to pay in Australia, although this is not true in all countries. It is not so in property! Transaction costs when buying property can be hefty: stamp duty, legal fees, lenders mortgage insurance, mortgage transfer fees, and more. There can be other costs when selling too, such as agents' fees and capital gains taxes, for example. The inescapable implication of this is that property as an asset class is nearly always better suited to long term ownership than short term flipping or trading.

5. Residential housing: both a consumption and an investment good

Residential property is a truly unique investment proposition, for it serves both as an investment and as a consumption good. Sometimes people buy property as an investment, others buy it purely to have a roof over their head, another factor which can promote market stability. Others buy property for both purposes, or they might buy property as a holiday home. People will always need somewhere to live, so a well-located property investment which is in strong demand should generate a growing income stream in the form of rental income.

6. Property is heterogeneous

Each individual property is different, so ascertaining the exact fair market value of an asset can be difficult and thus some level of experience and access to the full suite of sales data is very important. Use an expert's advice if in doubt! Market values can be somewhat easier to determine where there is a block of similar apartments with recent sales which can be used as a guideline. At the top end of the market in the premium sector a fair market value can be very subjective and much more difficult to be sure of. Consequently, the property market is imperfect and smart investors with access to all the available data can profit from this.

WHAT MAKES DWELLING PRICES MOVE?

Of course, there are many factors which can shift the market value of real estate, such as the growth in population, the availability of mortgage financing, the prevailing level of interest rates, and so on. In the very simplest terms, prices are dictated by supply (the properties available on the market, or in the construction pipeline) and demand (how many people are willing and able to buy those available properties).

So, who buys residential property? There is a range of categories of buyer, including owner-occupiers, domestic investors, overseas investors, developers, and renovators. Demand is driven by demographics, the size and location of the population, and its ability and willingness to pay for real estate. Consequently, investors in property should invest where the population is growing in wealth – generally, quality suburbs of the capital cities are the best bet – and in larger capital cities where the population is growing.

Where demand exceeds supply, prices rise ... and vice-versa.

Investors typically only have very limited control over the new supply that comes to market. The cost of new property coming to market is determined by land prices as well as the costs of building materials and construction, and the ability of buyers to pay. If prices and rents are to move higher as investors hope, then it makes sense to invest only in areas with a growing population or demand, but a limited supply of new land available for development. In the case of medium density dwellings such as apartments, oversupply can be a risk as developers build upwards as well as outwards, so look towards areas where huge new tower blocks cannot be built due to planning restrictions. City centres, central business districts, and sometimes transport hubs can have relatively few restrictions on the height of residential buildings, and therefore cyclical oversupply in these areas can be a risk.

LEVERAGE – MOVE THE EARTH!

To recap, what does leverage mean? Leverage essentially means being able to do more with less. What do you do when you have a tin of paint with the lid stuck on it? Answer: employ leverage. If you are anything like me you find a spoon or a fork (though not from the kitchen draw, of course!) to use as a lever to generate the extra power to force the lid open. In the financial world, leverage often refers to borrowing. A company which is highly leveraged is one with a lot of debt on its balance sheet. When it is used sensibly, leverage can be beneficial to the borrower who uses the extra capital to fund profitable projects. Sometimes, however, companies may overuse leverage and get themselves into financial dire straits. We saw this during the global financial crisis where companies that were over-stretched could not afford to service their debt and became insolvent. We can see that leverage is a double-edged sword, and so it is for property investors.

Leverage is a powerful tool, but only when used wisely.

Leverage has the potential to be the greatest advantage that a property investor has over investors in other asset classes. The basic principal is simple enough. Let us say you have a pool of capital of $100,000 and decide to invest in shares which then appreciate over the forthcoming years by 25 per cent. You have done very nicely and made an unrealised gain of $25,000. If you have chosen a profitable company, you will receive dividend income of perhaps $5000 or so each year too.

Alternatively, you might choose to use your $100,000 as a deposit to invest in a $500,000 investment property. If you can achieve 25 per cent capital growth on the property it would result in an unrealised gain of $125,000. It is possible that you may take some time to see the 25 per cent capital gain and there may in some cases be holding costs, of course, but look at the difference in the absolute size of the gain!

Leverage magnifies both gains and losses.

In an ideal world, we would never have to borrow money for anything, including investing in property, and borrowing money does introduce some risk into our investing. In our hypothetical but sadly non-existent ideal world, we would simply take funds out of our hugely healthy bank balances and invest in a diversified portfolio of shares, commercial properties, farmland, commodities, bonds, and other fixed-interest investments, which would pay us a healthy and increasing income from now until the end of time.

Naturally if we all started out our financial life with a vast pool of capital available to invest, you would not be reading this book and I would not be writing it! Leverage is potentially so important for the average investor. It presents the opportunity to invest with some of our money and much more of the bank's money to super-charge returns. In plain English, you have a better chance of generating significant wealth with millions of the bank's dollars than a few of your own. The leverage offered by residential investment property is the number one reason that property offers the average investor the best chance of not being average.

THE RULE OF 72 REVISITED

Remember that the rule of 72 can help you to calculate how long an asset such as a property will take to double in value. Just to remind you, here is how it works: take the number 72 and divide it by the growth rate per annum of the property, and the answer you get is the number of years the property will take to double in value. In the table below an asset appreciating at 10 per cent per annum doubles in 7.2 years (72/10 = 7.2).

COMPOUND GROWTH IN REAL ESTATE

You have already heard the Albert Einstein quote on compound interest.

It is a neat quote but what does it mean for property investors? Another way of describing what compounding is might be growth upon growth. In nature, water lilies only cover a small part of a pond for some years but in subsequent years they begin to run rampant and suddenly cover the entire surface of the water. Think of the incredible spread of the rabbit population in Australia – from just a handful of bunnies shipped over from England to there being millions of them in a relatively short space of time. And so on!

Figure 8.1 – Compounding growth

Year	Value at 7.2 per cent capital growth per annum ($)	Growth in year ($)
0	500,000	-
1	536,000	36,000
2	574,592	38,592
3	615,963	41,371
4	660,312	44,349
5	707,854	47,542
6	758,820	50,966
7	813,455	54,635
8	872,024	58,569
9	934,809	62,786
10	1,000,000	65,191
11	1,072,000	72,000
12	1,149,184	77,184
13	1,231,925	82,741
14	1,320,624	88,699
15	1,415,709	95,085
16	1,517,640	101,931
17	1,626,910	109,270
18	1,744,047	117,138
19	1,869,916	125,571
20	2,000,000	130,381

Intuitively, you might expect an asset that is growing at 7.2 per cent each year to take about 14 years or so to double in value. It would seem to make sense, wouldn't it? Yet in fact, as you can see above, in only ten years the asset has doubled in value, and in 20 years it has doubled in value twice! The reason for this is the compounding growth. As you can see, in the first year the property has grown in value by $36,000, but in the twentieth year the property has grown in value by more than $130,000. Each increase is greater than its preceding equivalent. That is, there is growth upon growth – which is what investors use to multiply their earnings.

Believe it or not, at such a rate of growth by year 30 the property would be worth $4 million! The gains accelerate over time. These returns may or may not be realistic depending on the prevailing market dynamics, inflation rate, and the health of the economy. What is important is the principle, and particularly that you invest in assets which outperform the rate of inflation over time.

Figure 8.2 – Compound growth in property

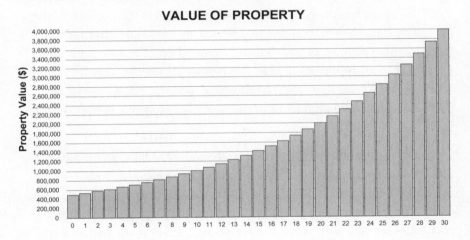

Simply investing $100,000 in the share market at a compounding rate of return of 8 per cent could turn the initial investment into $1 million over 30 years. Impressive! It's worth noting again that the absolute return is not actually the most important thing. What is crucial is that the returns beat inflation – whether inflation is high or low – so that your money invested is worth more to you in real terms over time. The reason that property investors who get it right can achieve financial freedom is that instead of investing with only $100,000, they can potentially use those funds as a deposit to invest in property worth $500,000.

If they then achieve 6 or 7 per cent capital growth per annum they can generate enormous equity over a few decades. And if they do not achieve 6 or 7 per cent capital growth? Well, they can still outperform the returns from other asset classes provided they can achieve reasonable capital growth ahead of the rate of inflation, due to the leverage involved.

Of course, property prices will never appreciate in such a linear fashion, and you might not achieve 6 or 7 per cent per annum growth if you invest in the wrong asset. What tends to happen in reality is that values remain flat or slightly falling, perhaps for some years, before surging upwards in value. There's a market cycle at play. However, the principle remains the same: over time, compounding growth can work in your favour to help you build very significant wealth if you choose the right assets to invest in.

Meanwhile, inflation makes the real value of any mortgage debt effectively worth less with each passing year. The implications of the previous chart are quite clear, and this is something which my wife and I have found having owned properties and shares for more than 25 years – with each passing year, an appreciating asset can begin to make the associated mortgage debt look very small, while rental incomes can easily rise to double or even more than triple of the mortgage repayments over the long haul.

Of course, as the old saying goes there are no free lunches in investing, and the cost here is that the use of leverage introduces risk and therefore you cannot afford to get it wrong. For this reason, I strongly advise using an expert such as a property buyer's agent to buy your investment properties for you, with specific expertise in managing the purchasing process and knowledge of the key areas they buy in. There may be a cost attached to this too, it is a relatively inexpensive price to pay to avoid making potentially very costly errors. Importantly, you pay the fees once rather than annually, whereas the benefits of choosing a high quality and high growth asset should continue to multiply returns in perpetuity. If you're going to invest in property, you only need to make a few great decisions, but you must not buy a dud asset!

THE ECONOMIC BACKDROP

Through the 1970s and 1980s much of the developed world was living through a period of relatively high inflation. In terms of what this meant for property, nominal prices almost everywhere seemed to rise quite consistently, largely because the price of everything rose. That is not to say that it was an easy era for property owners, however. At times interest rates ran very high, while recessions and unemployment also made life very difficult for some homeowners.

The compensating good news for those who hung onto their properties throughout this period was that the high rates of inflation saw much of the value of household debt inflated away. However, not all property types outperformed inflation significantly – many poorly located properties did not.

We have undergone a structural shift into an era of lower interest rates and low inflation … at least until the 2020 pandemic!

The 1990s were a different matter entirely where we moved through a structural shift towards lower rates of inflation and lower interest rates as central banks began to target inflation rates or bands. The result of this was an unprecedented rise in the levels of household debt as banking systems were deregulated thus allowing lenders to create debt more freely at competitive rates. There were also more dual income households over time as more women entered the workforce.

The net result was that for different reasons dwelling prices continued to rise relentlessly through each of those three decades with some corrections, and until around 2007 this trend looked set to continue through another decade unchecked. Times had been so good for so long that folk began to believe in dwelling prices as a one-way bet, while in the US lenders found ways to write loans to people who previously had not a prayer of seeing a mortgage. Some real estate pundits were duped into believing that even properties in regions with weak economies could keep rising in price, seemingly defying gravity. Unfortunately, in many cases lenders issued loans to people with little chance of ever repaying the loans, known in the United States as 'subprime' lending.

The property investment landscape has changed radically since 2007.

The global financial crisis, which played out from that time, saw another dramatic change in the landscape and we have moved into a new era once again. Before the financial crisis some market commentators had been head faked into believing that because property prices had risen so consistently over such a long period, the location and the property type that they chose to invest in was unimportant.

In certain cases, advisors recommended buying the worst types of property, those which were in very low demand and in secondary locations. These properties can be superficially appealing because they are cheap to buy and their historical lack of strong capital growth can mean that the rental yield might at face value be higher. Since 2007, a great many of these regional and secondary markets have performed poorly.

The property markets have once again moved into a new era.

Today there is no longer such high inflation to inflate away the value of mortgage debt, at least for now, and the structural shift towards lower interest rates and the associated boom in household debt is essentially behind us. Other trends such as the growth in dual income households have also now taken their full effect and will not be repeated. In short, the easy gains in property which we as investors have benefited from over recent decades are no more, and you need to genuinely understand how times have changed if you wish to continue multiplying your earnings in the future.

The best long-term outcome for most remotely located properties or those in secondary suburban locations is that they increase in price in lockstep with the growth in household incomes, perhaps at a few per cent per annum on average at best. In many cases, even this may be wishful thinking. The problem with small regional towns and cities is that weaker population growth can easily be absorbed by land release, jobs and income growth tend to be weak, and consequently there will tend to be very little sustained upwards pressure on property prices. To outperform in the future, you will need to implement a different strategy.

POST FINANCIAL CRISIS AND PANDEMIC PROPERTY INVESTING

Large and growing capital cities and regional cities within two hours commuting time have a built-in and significant advantage over smaller towns and cities and this advantage is becoming greater with each passing year. If you understand a little about economics and demographics you will quickly understand why this is the case and can use this information to your advantage. Large cities such as Sydney, London, and some others around the world have long had an inherent advantage of attracting migrants and new inhabitants, which is indeed why I have invested so heavily in these markets myself over the years. In many cases these are the only cities which migrants are familiar with within their respective countries, and the larger cities offer greater potential for employment which also encourages internal migration.

This is a global trend. By 2030 some two thirds of the world's population will live in cities. In Western economies, cities across Europe are attracting population growth in their millions as employment shifts from manufacturing to services. In China, meanwhile, the urban population is rising inexorably towards 1 billion from less than 200 million in 1980.

Figure 8.3 – Urbanisation

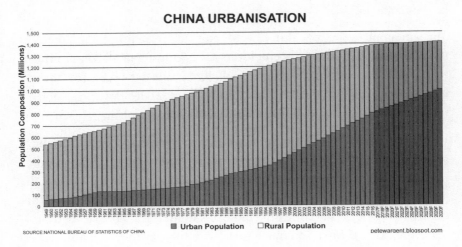

SOURCE:NATIONAL BUREAU OF STATISTICS OF CHINA

petewargent.blogspot.com

Over time, the populations of the cities we tend to recommend investing in grow at a fast pace, presently tracking at around 100,000 persons per annum in Sydney's case, which will see close to another 1 million people living in the harbour city in another decade's time. Demand is likely to grow in cities such as Newcastle, as buyers are priced out of Sydney. Melbourne is growing at a similar pace, though Melbourne has also found it easier to build and sprawl than Sydney has, due to Sydney's geographical constraints and surrounding national parks. The Greater Brisbane and south-east Queensland (Gold Coast and Sunshine Coast) region is growing even faster on a percentage basis.

London is also expected to see its population swell to some 9 million persons by 2021 which equates to a truly massive new demand for housing. By the way, I practice exactly what I preach and own a large portfolio of properties mostly comprised of investments in Sydney and around London. Of course, not everyone can afford these markets, at least to begin with, but the principles are important to take note of.

These are huge population growth numbers which create great strain on infrastructure and consistent upwards pressure on the existing stock of dwellings. The problem for small regional towns and cities is that rather than larger employers and inhabitants seeking out cheaper alternatives in regional locations, they are continuing to focus on being located in the larger capital cities.

The pandemic saw a huge shift towards working from home, but now as the unemployment rate rises employers are encouraging worker to return to the office, at least for 3 days per week. It remains to be seen how these trends play out in full, but it seems that a hybrid model of working both form home and in the workplace will be where things ultimately land.

While big cities tend to be expensive for leasing office space and this may seem ill-advised, studies have found that there are some sound economic reasons behind the decision-making process, largely related to the fact that productivity tends to be higher in densely concentrated capital cities. This is partly to do with the ability of employers to fill roles more easily from a diversified labour force and much to do with the way in which businesses in proximity interact with each other. The larger capital cities are self-sustaining jobs magnets, with immigrants mostly heading to Sydney and Melbourne, while internally Aussies move to Brisbane, south-east Queensland and some other favoured coastal and regional locations.

When investing in property look towards capital cities with sustained and assured huge future population growth.

Just as we have seen elsewhere, compound interest is an extremely powerful force, and the virtuous cycle is becoming self-fulfilling in favour of the largest cities. For every 100,000 new persons that choose to call a city their home, we need to build approximately 45,000 more homes, more hospitals, more parks, shopping centres, more junior schools, senior schools and further education units, more roads, more infrastructure, more service stations and more restaurants, more entertainment outlets, and more supermarkets.

Dwelling construction itself tends be very effective at creating employment, not only for construction workers, but also for retailing and shopping centre staff, healthcare staff including doctors and nurses, schooling and teachers and other sectors besides. As previously noted therefore, construction can itself have a strong multiplier effect across the local economy. For every $1 million spent on dwelling construction, this tends to create around $3 million of additional output in the local economy, representing an economic multiplier of three.

In decades gone by, and until recently again through the resources investment boom, many Australian state economies were largely reliant upon natural resources for to generate income and therefore prosperity. However, developed countries have gradually shifted towards more knowledge and services based economies over time, with mining in Australia now accounting for fewer than 2 per cent of jobs. Large cities have another great advantage in this regard too, as they serve as the financial and service sector hubs for their respective countries.

Developed economies are transitioning towards knowledge and services based industries.

London, for example, has been Britain's greatest success story, becoming a major financial centre for the European region, partly thanks to its location in the world and its time zone, being unique in its ability to service transactions between America and Asia. Over the decades

Britain has generated some wealth from its coal and North Sea Oil, but increasingly financial services have been the driver of Britain's economic growth and prosperity.

In Australia's case, if you look back only three decades, around three quarters of the stock market by value was accounted for by resources companies, yet today mining and resources companies account for only a quarter of the value of the index. It is true that commodities are still of great importance to Australia's economic standing and do account for a significant proportion of the national income. However, overall the largest sector of the economy is now services, and with the construction of the new suburb at Barangaroo, Sydney is setting itself become a major new financial hub for Asia.

Sustainable property price growth must be founded upon real wages growth.

Ultimately, sustainable growth can only be sourced from productive enterprise and value being created. Three decades ago in Australia this simply meant ripping an ever-greater volume of minerals out of our weeping planet. However, today much of our wealth is created through technological ingenuity and intellectual expertise, while jobs growth has been particularly strong in healthcare and social assistance, and in financial services. About 80 per cent of employment is now accounted for by the services sector, up from around 40 per cent in 1900, with the percentage share continuing to rise. Sustainable property price growth needs real wages growth and growing demand. Speculating in remote areas, outlying cities or tourism-dependent regions where real wages growth is negligible carries a material risk premium.

As the readership of my daily blog and other books would testify, I have spent a great deal of time over the last decade studying demographic and economic trends in detail and I have only just begun to scratch the surface here. The key takeaway for the point of this book is that larger and growing cities are self-sustaining jobs magnets which generate far more wealth than small regional centres or smaller cities will ever be able to.

TRENDS WITHIN THE CAPITALS

As noted in the preceding section, I have spent a huge amount of time studying economic and demographic trends, and what I have found is that even with the large capital cities, specific and measurable new trends are increasingly evident. The internet has made the world less reliant upon being in a certain location. Before 2020, there were more Australians looking to base themselves at the regional cities withing a couple of hours from the capitals. These areas included Newcastle, Central Coast, Wollongong in New South Wales, as well as some of the popular coastal cities such as Byron Bay, Geelong, Morning, Bendigo, and Ballarat in Victoria, and Gold Coast and Sunshine Coast in Queensland.

The COVID-19 pandemic and associated restrictions suddenly and massively accelerated the regional shift. Although some of this has reversed by the time of writing, living withing a couple of hours from the major conurbations has retained more popularity than pre-pandemic. Most new arrivals into Australia continue to head to the capital cities, and this have created a painful shortage of rental properties at the time of writing.

REAL ESTATE AS AN ASSET CLASS

Just as is the case with equities over short periods of time residential real estate can be an unpredictable beast – there are simply so many factors and sub-factors which can impact markets. Over longer periods of time, however, property markets in larger cities with well diversified economies can be much more predictable as generational demographic waves flow through.

The greatest advantage that residential property has for average investors over other asset classes is that it allows the use of more leverage. That is, investors can borrow significant sums of money to invest because of the perceived safety of housing as investment. Share markets tend to be liquid, meaning that you can buy and sell shares very quickly. This has the advantage that you can get hold of your money quickly by converting it into cash. A disadvantage of the share market is that so can everyone else, and therefore markets can be quite volatile, sometimes swinging wildly from day to day, and sometimes even from hour to hour.

Property markets are generally far less liquid. It can take a long period to sell a property, particularly when sentiment is weak, and therefore it is important to invest in quality properties which are in continual high demand. Markets tend to be less volatile than share markets, and because prices are not quoted daily this makes it easier for many average investors to mentally 'switch off' the market, helping them to take a long-term view without undue concern.

Property investment tends to incur material transaction costs, which is another factor that discourages rapid buying and selling. There are taxes to pay when buying such as stamp duty, and there are agency fees and potentially capital gains taxes to pay when selling too. Transaction costs do help to discourage speculative trading or flipping of property which tends to make larger city markets more stable. As discussed in earlier sections of the book, if you want to become wealthy you need to find ways to invest efficiently, and therefore property lends itself ideally towards buying quality assets and holding on to them for so long as possible.

PROPERTY MARKETS ARE INEVITABLY CYCLICAL

Property prices are always cyclical for the reasons explained in more detail in the next section of the book. That said, over time prices will always be driven by the underlying fundamentals of the market which determine the respective levels of supply and demand:

- Population growth
- Wages and income growth
- Tax and monetary policy settings
- Construction and the supply of new dwellings

While land and dwelling prices are cyclical, the long-term trend in a thriving city economy where the population is growing strongly will typically be higher over time, while the level of mortgage debt is gradually inflated away. This is not accidental – central banks deliberately target inflation bands today to ensure that we have a steady inflationary economy. The alternative scenario where prices are falling, known as deflation, causes consumers to delay purchases in the expectation of cheaper prices in the future, and this can lead to a deeply undesirable deflationary spiral. Therefore, property cycles tend to look something like this over time.

Figure 8.4 - The property price cycle

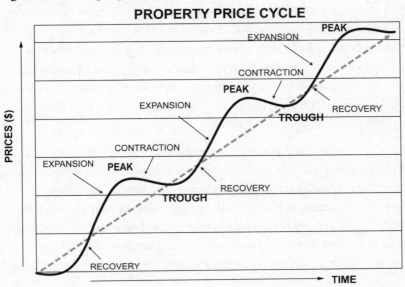

Due to the heavy transaction costs involved in buying and selling property, the asset class is often most effective as a long-term hold, since this allows the value of the asset and rents to grow and compound for the longest period. By inference therefore, property investors with a long-term outlook will inevitably experience cyclical market downturns. Of course, you can try to time markets too, but it's rarely quite as easy as it sounds! I only ever recommend investing in quality, well located property for which there will always be a high level of demand.

PROPERTY INVESTMENT AND LEVERAGE

Property investment is another way in which you can accelerate your returns because it allows you to use leverage, or borrowing to super-charge returns. However, leverage is a double-edged sword. It can get you to your goals faster, but if you make mistakes then it can also set you back. I sometimes use the analogy of a powerful race car. Used correctly and skilfully, with appropriate care and attention to safety, a powerful car can get you to your destination more quickly than usual. On the other hand, if the extra power is misused or not used carefully it can cause you to spin off the track and you can get hurt.

When done sensibly and when following some basic rules, investing in property can be a powerful tool for creating wealth over time. Remember, due to the heavy transaction costs involved in buying and selling property, it is best treated as a long-term investment. Indeed, just as in the share market, the longer you can hold an investment property the greater the returns can be, because the capital gains of the growth in prices can be allowed to snowball or compound. The ideal time horizon for holding a quality investment property is forever.

There are many different types of property which you might choose to invest in, including various types of commercial property, industrial units, retail property, agricultural property or office buildings. Each type of property has its merits, and some niche properties can command higher rates of rental return for those with the time to commit and the expertise to make them work. For most average investors, residential property is easier to understand, has a lower risk of vacancy, and represents the lowest risk.

WHERE? LARGER AND GROWING CITIES

Wherever funds allow, it's usually best to invest in a larger and growing city, don't invest in a small town. While investing in smaller towns and cities can seem attractive because it is cheaper and the rental returns can be superficially attractive, as a rule this can come with additional levels of risk. Since property investment is best treated as a long-term investment – and it is very difficult to predict what will happen to economies and industries over time – the more reliant a town or city is on one or two industries, the riskier the proposition for property investment. In Australia, for example, mining towns can be highly cyclical, and therefore risky.

An extreme example can be seen in Detroit, a city which was once known for its automobile manufacturing prowess. The population of the city boomed to nearly 1.9 million by the time of the 1950 Census, yet today the population has shrunk to just 680,000. Between the Censuses of 2000 and 2010 the population of the city collapsed by an incredible 25 per cent. It must have seemed in 1950 that Detroit's population could never fall, with the city in boomtime. Yet the city was heavily reliant on a narrow range of employment and as car manufacturing failed an exodus followed. When the population of a city falls into decline property prices will eventually follow, and once populated neighbourhoods saw vacant houses becoming worthless.

Detroit is an extreme example, but it does show why investing in a large and growing city with a diverse range of industry is always a far preferable proposition if you can afford the entry price. Over the years my focus has been investing in and around London in the United Kingdom, and in cities like Sydney and Brisbane in Australia. While some people like to make the case for investing in much cheaper areas, over longer periods of time landlocked areas in larger and growing cities with strong population growth and a well-diversified economy prices may outperform. This is due to the lack of available land for release in the land-locked inner and middle ring suburbs, while the growing population increases demand and pushes up prices.

The chart opposite, for example, shows the enormous differential in performance between house prices in London and the rest of the United Kingdom. The chart also shows that house prices in the less desirable outer metropolitan suburbs significantly underperformed the city, although they still tracked better than prices in the British regions. While I've used the example of London and the United Kingdom here, you will find that the same often holds true elsewhere. For example, house price growth in Auckland has outperformed in New Zealand, and so on.

Figure 8.5 – Capital cities outperform[1]

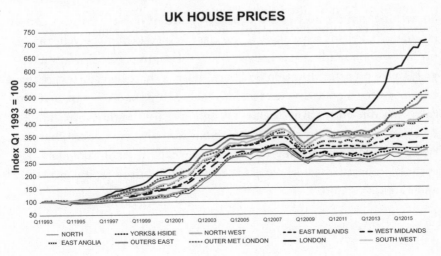

UK HOUSE PRICES

The key point to take away here are that the drivers of price growth are a strongly growing demand and increasing household wealth, typically found in a growing city, and constrained supply of land which drives up prices. Land-locked inner and middle ring suburbs which are easily commutable to the central employment hubs tend to fit the criteria best. There are some exceptions to this rule. In Australia, coastal locations can be highly sought after (I live in one of them – postcode 4567 in the Noosa Shire), but you need to choose carefully.

THE YIELD TRAP IN PROPERTY

There is much talk of the benefits of investing in properties which generate a high gross percentage yield. We do need to note, however, that high yields tend to exist in residential property where capital growth has been restricted due to uninspiring levels of demand or in more niche property types (short-term rentals, rooming accommodation, or retail commercial premises, for example). Very similar investment principles may apply to property as they do to shares.

When property market prices are high, percentage rental yields tend to be lower (and vice versa), but over a longer time horizon we might expect rental yields to revert to something close to a mean or average, and therefore what we want is properties which experience great capital growth. The rental income will generally take care of itself over time if you buy well, so look for the property types in the highest demand not poor quality properties located in regional areas.

Something to remember is that counter-cyclical property investors can attain decent yields regardless. If you elect to invest counter-cyclically in property when sentiment is low, you can still attain reasonably attractive yields even on prime location property – just as share investors who invest after a crash get great dividend yields on blue chip shares. Smart investors can find sufficiently strong yields through investing counter-cyclically. By electing to invest in property which has recently experienced sharply rising rents but not capital growth, just like share investors, counter-cyclical property investors expect to receive both future capital growth and a solid yield too.

Counter-cyclical investors can achieve strong enough yields.

Smart investors tend to secure rental yields above the quoted average and manufacture higher yields too by adding value to properties through cosmetic renovation. Quality, well-located boutique blocks of apartments in the inner suburbs of Sydney, for example, will over the coming decades experience a sizeable increase in demand due to population growth, while construction will continue to remain inadequate and tremendously costly.

OK, so I may have bored you with the theory. What does it mean in practice? What can growth do for us as investors? Being an Anglo-Aussie myself I frequently refer to what is happening in England for clues, as some of the property markets there are more developed. While many property investors in the UK regions who bought in the period after 2005 are the unfortunate owners of property with negative equity, prices in London continued to surge to the highest they have ever been.

Prime location suburbs of capital cities and favoured regional cities outperform over the long term.

Ask people who bought a house back in the 1980s and 1990s in Britain or Australia how they've fared and they say: 'I have done well'. Why? Because the property is worth more in dollar terms than they paid for it. Buy have they done well? Most likely they have no idea because mostly they have few other investments and no worthwhile benchmark against which to measure performance.

Typically, house prices moved upwards through the inflationary 1980s, and appreciated further again as credit growth expanded in the 1990s, but have tailed off in most areas outside London over recent years. Expect to see similar trends unfolding in Australia, with properties in prestige suburbs of the major capital cities over time being significant outperformers both in terms of rental income and capital growth. Lower yields, maybe, but far, far higher income and more robust capital growth. Understand this fundamental difference and you can be a winner too. Most important of all, remember that it's the compounding capital growth of residential property which creates wealth, not the moderate rental income.

WHERE SPECIFICALLY, AND WHAT?

We have already established that property is typically best treated as a long-term investment. Therefore, it should logically follow that you should buy the types of median-priced property that are guaranteed to be in extremely high demand over the very long term. In doing so, you are buying yourself time, and if you choose to do so you can hold onto the asset in perpetuity, safe in the knowledge that it will continue to be a strong performer for you over time. The safest property locations are generally in the areas where people will always want to live. In suburbs within easy commuting distance of capital city employment hubs, ideally close to good schools and direct train links as populations grow and traffic worsens.

WHEN? THE PROPERTY MARKET CYCLE

Over time and with experience you will come to recognise that there are always market cycles when it comes to residential real estate. Always. And indeed, you will also come to understand that in growing towns and cities there can be no other way. As new jobs are created and household incomes rise, the population of a city tends to rise, which puts upward price pressure on housing and rents. The growing population of the city drives a requirement for new infrastructure, and the building of more roads, schools, shopping centres, service stations and hospitals.

Eventually as house prices rise it becomes more attractive for developers to build new housing, since it becomes more likely that new dwellings can be sold on with a profitable margin. The new housing helps to cool rents, and as the construction cycle peaks this tends to bring the market back into equilibrium, and then as developers flood the market with supply prices flatten out or begin to fall.

Figure 8.6 – The real estate construction cycle

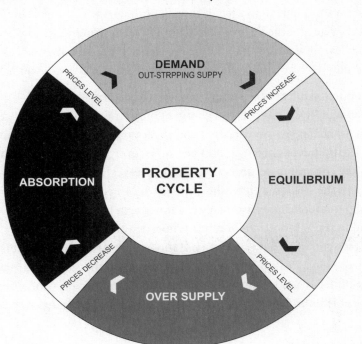

This cycle has always repeated in populous and expanding cities, and will always continue to do so. Although invariably folks complain about it, there can be no other way. Indeed, as an investor market cycles can be your friend as you have the luxury of being able to choose to buy when sentiment is depressed and prices are cheaper in anticipation of the next upturn. Of course, just as is the case in the share markets, it can be almost impossible to time the market perfectly, but this need not matter. Instead, investors should aim to buy as the market is bottoming out when fear abounds and it is possible to make low offers to vendors. Alternatively, more risk-averse investors may wait until the market has begun its recovery phase and look to buy in the early stages of the market's upswing.

USE OF AN EXPERT

Investing in property is one course of action for which I recommend that you use an experienced and independent buyer's agent as your property market insider. If you're switched on you will be thinking: hang on, can't

I grow my wealth more quickly by doing it all myself and not paying any fees? It's a valid question! One of the big problems with fund management fees is they get charged every year without fail, in good years and in bad – regardless of whether the fund has returned a profit. Moreover, as you contribute more to your fund and it grows, the fund charges you more.

When purchasing an investment property, I recommend using independent buyer's agent who charges you a straight fee-for-service. The reason for this is that they charge you the fee once and it is not recurring, and a skilful buyer's agent should be able to mitigate the risks of property while helping you to secure an outstanding investment at a good price. Unlike in the stock markets where mistakes can easily be reversed by selling parcels of shares, property is a long-term investment in a relatively illiquid market. Moreover, because properties are often the biggest purchases you ever make and are usually bought using leverage, it is simply too big a deal to get wrong. That's why you should consider paying a once-off fee to get a property market insider working on your side. They may be able to find you 'off-market' deals through their industry contacts too.

What you certainly should not do is go to someone who tries to sell you something for a commission. Unfortunately, this type of activity is rife in the real estate industry. Property 'advisors', and sometimes even accountants and financial advisors, often recommend buying brand new or off-the-plan properties for which they are paid a commission by developers to sell. Buying new properties tends to involve paying a hefty developer's premium which means that it could be years before you recover the capital growth needed to get the investment back to a break-even point. Developers often factor in a percentage of the price for marketing and sales, and advisors can often receive up to 6 per cent or more of the purchase price as a commission. All the advisor then needs to do is to find a willing investor and explain to them why a new investment is 'just perfect' for them so that they can paid their commission.

The process is often highly disingenuous, and all kinds of glossily produced statistics and reasons are given for why buying new property is the best approach, ranging from 'it's for the tax benefits', to 'lower repairs costs', to 'it's easier to find tenants who will pay strong rent' or any number of other lines. Of course, all the advisor cares about is that they get paid their hefty commission. If these matters are a concern, buy established property that is nearly new, and bypass the price premium. Just as buying a new car comes with a hefty cost, so it is with new properties.

Demographic studies have found similar themes to be playing out. The higher-paying services sector jobs growth are largely to be found in the larger cities, and this is particularly so in Australian capital cities, while public transport from outer suburbs is unable to service long-distance commuters effectively. Furthermore, employment and population growth remains heavily focused on inner- and middle-ring suburbs. The combination of these two factors is putting huge pressure on inner- and middle-ring dwelling prices, to the extent that land and dwelling prices are continuing to rise in inner city and middle-ring locations as compared to outer-suburban locations.

This trend is likely to continue. Demographic studies have concluded that since outer suburb locations in capital cities have poor access to jobs, even where an hour is allowed for public transport or driving time, urban sprawl should be curtailed and more land should be made available for development where possible in inner- and middle-ring suburbs.

There has been a generational shift towards placing a premium on living in suburbs with great schools and access to the city.

One key generational change has been that younger employees do not want to commute too far for work and are prepared to pay a premium to rent property located close to the centre of capital cities. In many cases, they could afford to buy a starter home in a distant outer location and then look to trade up later, but often they simply do not want to.

Often they would rather forego the starter home for a more exciting life closer to the city, and in many cases their first step on to the property ladder is via buying an apartment closer to the city either to live in or as an investment property. There is nothing inherently wrong with living close to the city of course, provided young people do remember to set some money aside for the future by investing it wisely, although I fear that often this last point is forgotten (looking at the inexorable rise in retail spend on cafés, restaurants and takeaways, the evidence appears to be quite damning).

Rightly or wrongly, this is the way the world is heading. The population is prepared to pay a premium for the privilege of living in our most popular cities. I suggest that if you want to escape from the rat race, rather than mortgaging yourself to the hilt to do the same you should consider owning a portfolio of investments and rent them to this growing demographic which wants it all and will pay a premium to live in the most popular areas.

This is only a starting point for consideration, of course. You still need to time the market and there remain a wide range of factors which you need to consider to make sure that you buy the right property, and look for locations and property types where the supply is effectively capped but demand is growing rapidly. But focusing on properties from which the inhabitants can commute to the employment hubs within 15 minutes or less by train is likely to be a very good starting point.

SMALLER HOUSEHOLD SIZES

We have just begun to consider above of the types of locations which you might consider for buying investment property. Let us now drill in a little further. There has been a trend over the last century of falling household sizes, from well above four persons per dwelling to under 2.5 persons.[2] This trend of falling household sizes may or may not have run its course, but what has gone before will have some key impacts.

Figure 8.7 - Smaller household sizes[3]

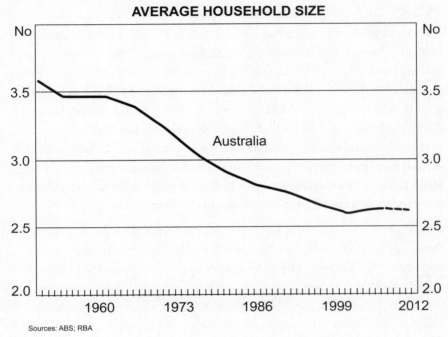

AVERAGE HOUSEHOLD SIZE

Sources: ABS; RBA

Firstly, and most obviously, with smaller average household sizes, we need far more dwellings to house the same number of people. This is creating tremendous pressure on the existing stock of dwellings. Secondly, there is a greater demand for medium density dwelling types such as townhouses, flats, units and apartments than there has ever been before. In some areas, though, high-rise apartments are being over-built, so it's imperative to buy the right property in the right location.

This has partly been due to affordability as the population places a premium on the most favoured suburbs close to the city centres and popular regional lifestyle locations, and it is partly to do with a generational shift towards this style of living. Living in a flat or unit was once seen as a secondary choice only for those who could not afford a house. Cleverly rebranded as apartments in a stroke of marketing genius, these attached dwelling types are often now seen as a favourable choice whereby they can allow tenants to live close to the city with a great deal of low-maintenance and secure convenience.

Houses and apartments can both be great investments depending upon your goals.

This is not to say that houses are by any means an inferior investment. Due to their inherent scarcity value and high land value content a capital city house close to the city centre will likely generate the highest level of capital growth over the course of a cycle, and always remember that it is capital growth which creates the most wealth in property, not cash flow. However, if owning houses is to be your strategy then you need to find houses that will be in increased demand, which means relatively close to the employment hubs and likely this will mean a high entry price and a low yield. Houses on a quarter acre plot in distant outer suburbia are unlikely to be the most popular property choice of the future.

One of the key reasons that you might look towards medium density dwellings is affordability. A house might be the best investment you can ever make, as I know from my own experience, but if you cannot easily afford to service the mortgage then you will be limited in how many of these investments you can hold. Rental yields for well-located houses can be significantly lower, and finding tenants for prime location houses who are prepared to sign up for high-cost leases can be more difficult too. Periods of vacancy for these higher-end property types can be very painful.

TYPES OF APARTMENTS TO BUY

There is another adage in property investment:

'Land appreciates, and buildings depreciate.'

I am often fascinated by traditional sayings and adages and wonder where they first came from. In most cases, you find that they exist for a good reason. What this adage is hinting at is that there is only ever a finite supply of land in locations where people want and need to live close to employment centres. While some cities, including Sydney, have used small amounts of reclaimed land to reasonable effect this is sometimes offset by rising sea levels reclaiming land in other parts of cities. In cities with growing populations the supply of desirable land is effectively fixed yet the demand for that land grows, and in an inflationary economy this inevitably pushes land prices higher over time. So far, so straightforward.

As for the buildings depreciating part of the adage, there is more than a grain of truth in this too. If you leave a building alone for long enough without paying good money for it to be maintained and repaired, eventually it will fall into complete disrepair and fall over. Property ownership can be a liability to the extent that there are ongoing costs of this nature associated with it. For this reason, to get compound growth working in your favour you simply must buy property which is in increased demand resulting in capital growth. For this property type rents tend to increase and compound over time too, leading to a happy outcome for the landlord.

Looked at another way, however, the building does not necessarily fall in value. The replacement cost of a dwelling increases with inflation as labour costs and materials costs rise, and therefore a house which was built 50 years ago for a few thousand dollars has not depreciated in terms of its absolute dollar value. So, how to use this information to your advantage? The answer is often to buy apartments that are in prime locations in capital cities, but those with a high land value content which means buying a property with a level of scarcity value in a relatively small or boutique block.

Capital growth is sourced from high demand and scarcity value.

Take the inferior investment proposition of a high-rise tower block which has 500 apartments in it. The block of land is generally relatively small and the land value content of each individual unit is likely to be very low, perhaps representing only a few per cent of the market value of the property. This is not the type of property to buy. Almost by definition, there is very little scarcity value in this type of property, because there are hundreds of other properties exactly like yours! When you come to sell, there may be half a dozen or more units on the market exactly like yours.

Some people insist that a house is always a better investment than an apartment because a house sits on more land. While this may be correct in theory, in practice if the land location is a secondary outer suburban or regional area where demand is lower, prices will still probably only increase in line with household incomes in the best-case scenario. If you do not believe me or are unsure about this, take a drive out to some remote areas and see how cheap a vacant lot of land is compared to the capital city! Do you see what I mean? Real capital growth after inflation is non-existent where there is a relatively low demand for the land. The property value in secondary locations is all in the building, which does not appreciate in real terms, especially after costs. I would take a prime location apartment over a distantly located house every time provided it fits my other criteria for purchase. The capital growth over time will be much stronger because there is a much higher and growing demand for living close to the city and employment hubs. Note, however, this will not hold true if you buy in locations where the market can be flooded with supply, such as former industrial suburbs where great swathes of land are rezoned for residential use, or locations without a heights restriction on the construction of new apartment blocks.

Finally, look for something unique or a point of scarcity. Harbourside or beachside apartments can be great, or properties with a protected view. The immutable laws of supply and demand are always the key to outperformance.

REGIONAL PROPERTIES: YES, WITH A CAVEAT...

Here is yet another adage of real estate:

'Cheap today is cheap tomorrow.'

The problem with buying cheap property is that it is usually cheap for a reason. Just like gold investors who buy gold and still only have a bar of gold at the end of the process, folks who invest in very cheap regional properties because of a seemingly tempting initial rental yield still only have a cheap property at the end of the process. While inflation can see the value of associated mortgage debt decline steadily over time, only rarely will outer regional properties significantly outperform the growth in inflation and household incomes over the long haul, and therefore it is very hard to build wealth in such a manner. And that is before you even consider that holding properties for a long period tends to incur repairs and maintenance costs.

On the other hand, if you can buy property in a more sought-after location for which demand is growing, then the rental income can continue to grow in perpetuity and dwelling prices can continue to grow ahead of inflation too. If you cannot afford to buy property in a capital city then you might choose to look at regionally located property, and this may be preferable to taking no action at all, but history shows that capital growth over time will be longer in capital cities with strong population growth.

Given the trend towards falling household sizes – and an increase in the number of divorces and thus middle-aged singles – I typically favour buying an apartment in a boutique block in a quality capital city location in a city such as Sydney over a house in a poor or remote regional location, the capital growth results will be better over time. A spacious apartment can be suitable for a young or downsizing couple too.

Successful property investment requires an understanding demographic of shifts, and the available research shows that as thriving capital cities develop they become self-sustaining jobs magnets which attract further population growth. Companies become compelled to locate their headquarters and offices close to each other in the centre of cities. As we have seen this can become a virtuous circle. Remember that as the population of a large capital city expands and more jobs are created, we also need to build more schools, dwellings, hospitals, parks, shopping centres, transport links, train stations, and other infrastructure, which in turn creates further jobs in the construction industry.

The impact of the new construction has a beneficial multiplier effect across the city economy, creating demand for building materials and transportation. For every dollar spent on construction, three additional dollars of demand can be created across the economy. Remote regional locations historically have not benefited from such strong jobs growth, wages growth or population growth and as such property price growth has always lagged way behind over any meaningful period of time.

CAPPED SUPPLY

On the supply side, prime location land in the inner suburbs of capital cities tends to be fully built out. New development can only take place through demolishing existing dwellings or rezoning industrial sites. While this can be achieved, land remediation tends to be an extremely costly exercise in the modern era with such high compliance, health and safety, labour and materials costs, and this underpins the value of established dwellings at a relatively high level. With no new vacant land to be released close to the centre of capital cities demand outstrips supply placing further upwards pressure on property prices in those locations.

Look for properties which are restricted in supply but where demand is growing.

Many regional locations can suffer here as there almost invariably exists significantly more land to be released for development. While statistically median prices can appear at times to rise as new homes are built, the actual capital growth rate in established regional properties is generally poorer as compared to those in the cities.

Indeed, in outer suburbs and regional locations construction of generic project style homes may become cheaper over time as new construction techniques are used such as 3D printing, increased use of mass production for certain building materials or, for example, concrete being poured on site in the style of old prefabricated buildings first seen after the war. While in theory this could happen in inner suburban locations too, rising land prices and particularly land remediation costs ensure that the price of new dwellings remains elevated. Over time, the difference between the haves and the have-nots of the property world is becoming more pronounced, and the trend is for this gulf to keep becoming wider and wider.

INNER, MIDDLE OR OUTER SUBURBS?

We have briefly considered above whether you should you invest in inner suburbs or outer suburbs of capital cities. There are multiple considerations here, but basic geometry tells you that inner suburb property should outperform. One of the key characteristics of real estate is its fixed location, hence the popular quotation:

'Location, location, location.'

While property rights can be exchanged over time, the location of a property remains constant and the ongoing demand for the land constitutes a prime determinant of prevailing market price. There is a geographical economic theory in real estate circles known as the bid-rent theory, which dates back some decades, it being derived from a Ricardian theory on the most productive agricultural land.

In the simplest terms, the original theory and bid-rent curves implied that the price and demand for property was highest within the concentric rings located closest to the central business district (CBD) and decreased the further away from that central point you travelled. Location theories hold that centrally located land is commonly worth more as retailers aim to maximise profitability and therefore will bid more for the land close to the city. Land on the outer is often deemed to be more viable for industrial use and demand is lower. Meanwhile, as different land uses compete, residents are also prepared to pay the highest rent for land close to the city where work and entertainment is traditionally located.

Land values often appreciate faster over time in inner suburbs.

All else being equal, prices could be highest in the inner city and gradually recede the further from that point you move out to the inner/middle rings suburbs and the outer locations. High prices in central locations also encourage a higher density of building as compared to the lower density and more sparsely populated locations further from the city's centre. Over time, however, it should be expected that improved transport links can increase demand from higher income earners further from the centre of the city, increasing demand in the well-located middle ring suburbs too.

Despite some obvious limitations, there is some reasonably sound logic behind the bid-rent theory. For one thing, simple geometry shows that when looking at concentric rings or something approximating thereto, there must be far less land in the inner zone of a city. Correspondingly, there is a significantly greater supply of land available to be developed in the outer, which you can clearly see with your own eyes as you drive through any capital city.

Look for a scarcity of available land.

The original grid system in Australia created an artificial land scarcity and the standardised city blocks encouraged rapid resale and speculative activity. As you can see on any map of the country the artificial land scarcity in Australia was also exacerbated by the earliest cities being located beside water. If you travel away from the city in the wrong direction, you'll quickly end up in the blue stuff.

Over time it has become clear that in countries like the US and Australia, all is not quite equal when it comes to residential property. Even from the 1880s you can find clear references in original sources to residents in Australia having a strong preference for suburban living slightly away from the centre of the city. Social housing is often located in the inner-city zones, for example, while wealthier households have often sought space in the middle-ring suburbs. Further, the traditional bid-rent curve is distorted by other factors such as households preferring to be located near favoured schools or other recreation. One of the true experts in housing market economics Michael Oxley observed that[4]:

'A major objective of rational land-use planning is to take account of the external cost and benefits. If land-use planning achieves its objectives the actual pattern of land use will differ from that predicted by simple market-orientated location theories.'

Another artificial barrier is in place with our city land supply, which is related to zoning and land release. And herein lies Australia's greatest challenge. Look, for example, at the population growth in some of Sydney's leafy inner- and middle-ring suburbs and you will find that the population levels are remarkably static for a capital city with such a burgeoning population growth. Manly and Woolllahra are two areas where the housing supply has remained essentially fixed. On the other hand, Parramatta has seen a huge boom in high-rise apartment construction.

While new construction and renovation does occur to some extent and significantly so around certain transport hubs and urban activation precincts, the total supply in certain popular suburbs is often all but fixed due to effective height restrictions on new builds. Even on land which is zoned as 'high density', it is often difficult to build upwards due to blocking the views of other existing residential buildings. Sydney homebuyers and investors are piling into this type of stock because they understand that the supply will be fixed with the demand increasing by the year. London has never really embraced high rise living, and as such the supply of new homes consistently fails to keep up with demand.

The challenge for countries like Australia and the United Kingdom is to convince people that living close the central business areas is not essential, which means providing quality transport links to places of employment (the cities are not monocentric as is often argued, so this includes transport links to and from secondary business areas and other employment hubs), improved infrastructure and other entertainment.

There have been a great many suggestions as to how this might be achieved and affordable housing can be provided for our growing populations. Ultimately, in aggregate, demand is growing, so if you can own well-located property you can do well over the long term through real estate. , and the route we are presently embracing is simply people paying ever.

THINKING BIG

Why not think big? When you start out investing the concept of building a multi-million-dollar property portfolio may seem like an impossibly distant goal. However, consider what you now know about compounding. If you can choose assets which increase in value year after year, your gains gradually become larger and larger. The journey gets easier every year. One of the magic things about real estate as an investment is that if you choose the assets which you invest in very specifically and very carefully, you can secure enough capital growth to withdraw some equity to use for further investments.

'You only have to do a very few things right in your life so long as you don't do too many things wrong.' - Warren Buffett

A word of warning here, however. I have read plenty of books which talk about the so-termed 'fear of debt' holding back investors and that they should in fact use as much debt as they possibly can to invest in more and more properties. Perhaps it is right not to fear debt, but debt is a powerful double-edged sword should always be respected and only used with great care. Just like our belief systems, debt has the power to create wealth, but it also has the power to destroy it.

5 KEY ELEMENTS TO BUILDING A MULTI-MILLION-DOLLAR PORTFOLIO ... SAFELY

1. Discipline

The first key element in being able to build a very sizeable property portfolio is discipline. Without the discipline required to save your first deposit or two, you will not be able to start investing in the first place.

2. Always buying well – not having a single dud in your portfolio

The next step is buying the right property. I noted earlier in the previous chapter that I believe investors should use an experienced buyer's agent to secure the best possible investment for capital growth. While a beginner may save some money by not using a buyer's agent, the likelihood of making a key mistake is multiplied tenfold. Probably more so.

Property can be a forgiving asset class at times, in that most properties will show some capital growth over the long term. However, I know from years of my own experience the pitfalls that can be experienced by investors. When I look back at the early investments I bought, I cringe at some of the many mistakes I made. As I said, provided you buy in strong capital growth areas, over time, most mistakes will be forgiven over time by a rising market, but if you want to achieve financial freedom quickly you should make as few mistakes as possible, and this is particularly so in the modern era where capital growth rates will on average be lower than those seen in the past. Remember the way in which it is possible to build a sizeable property portfolio quickly is to find areas which deliver capital growth quickly so that you can draw out a moderate amount of equity to divert towards new investments.

Make a few big financial decisions and make sure you get them right.

There was an unusual theory doing the rounds some years ago that it did not matter where you bought property because capital growth cannot be predicted. The theory was that you should buy for a strong cash flow and spread your investments all over the place so that some of them should get good growth.

This is wrong, and back-to-front, and today the amount of credit extended by financiers may be constrained, so you simply must buy well. The greatest advantage you have as a property investor rather than a homebuyer is that you are not compelled to invest anywhere unless you believe that you found a superior location where capital growth is assured. You can choose your suburb from thousands of possible choices and you can elect to invest counter-cyclically in cities which have not recently experienced a boom. To say that you should invest anywhere and just hope for capital growth is not the right approach today.

3. Time

Note that we should only be interested here in how to build a multi-million-dollar property portfolio safely. In theory, you could 'build' a multi-million-dollar portfolio immediately, simply by borrowing the full purchase price – if, of course, you could ever find an institution who would lend you such an amount! However, you could not do so safely and the transaction costs would put you immediately behind the eight ball. Property investment is a long-term game and the only way in which is possible to build a large portfolio safely is through the use as time as your friend rather than your enemy and to maintain a reasonable buffer.

Time is the friend of the outstanding investments and the enemy of the mediocre.

In all my years of investing in real estate, I have never sold one property. I have just continued to hold them for so long as I possibly can to continue to benefit from the compounding effect of capital growth, for year after year. Unsophisticated? Whatever, very efficient and devastatingly effective! When I look back at the purchase price of some of the earliest investments my wife and I own, I can scarcely believe how cheap the prices were! Yet, I can also absolutely assure you that the prices always felt very expensive at the time.

In fact, that is forever the case when buying property and prices never feel cheap at the time of purchase. Yet through allowing time to compound your wealth, you can undoubtedly succeed. There is no risk at all in the earliest investments I bought today, because the mortgages held against them as so small in relation to the value of the asset, even when I have refinanced them to buy new investments.

4. Patience

To build a very large portfolio of assets, you need to demonstrate patience. This means that you need to be able to hold on to assets and wait for them to deliver you capital growth rather than buying and selling frequently. Buying and selling property attracts significant transaction costs in the form of stamp duty, legal fees, estate agent fees, capital gains taxes and other costs. You should avoid the temptation to try to do too much too soon. If you leverage yourself up too strongly, you may speed up the results from your investing and reach your goals sooner, but you also introduce more risk. Property markets can and do fall in value. In fact, they do so regularly through each property cycle, and therefore it is important to always keep a reasonable buffer.

5. Review your strategy and portfolio's performance regularly

I know that I have said that in general you should never sell an appreciating asset, but what if you have a genuine dud in your portfolio? This can happen if you bought poorly, especially if it is outside a capital city in a remote region. For example, sometimes industries suffer which impacts a certain region adversely. In this instance, it may make sense to sell your asset and redeploy your capital into a more productive property investment. Finally, you will need to stay motivated, and resolve to keep on going no matter what happens!

GETTING IT RIGHT EVERY TIME – ANALYSE THE KEY DATA

Building a huge property portfolio is fundamentally very simple in nature, but not necessarily easy to get right. Firstly, save hard and buy a quality investment property in a suburb which you expect to boom in value. Secondly, when that property has increased in value, contract the bank to refinance the property and draw out some equity. And thirdly, use the equity created as a new deposit to invest in further properties which you expect to experience capital growth.

Building great wealth through property is straightforward, yet it is clearly not easy. The statistics on the number of successful investors prove it. If it was easy, why do the overwhelming majority of investors only own one or two investment properties and fail to achieve financial freedom? The short answer is that they do not carry out the right research, they buy the wrong properties and thus they never achieve the accelerated capital growth they need to create the equity they need to buy further investments. That's pretty much it!

Chapter 8 Summary

- The use of leverage in property can accelerate returns ... or losses.
- Property markets move in cycles, which can be anticipated.
- For big profits, aim to play in a big pond (meaning larger capital cities)!
- Invest in quality, well located assets for the long term for growing rent and capital growth.
- Use an experienced and independent buyer's agent as a property market insider to help mitigate the risk of investment.

CHAPTER 9
CONTROL THE CONTROLLABLES

FINDING YOUR HIGHER PURPOSE

If there is one thing that I have learned about personal finance and building wealth it is that you need to find a higher purpose for your money. What do I mean by that? A cause to contribute to! And why so? Because if you don't find a cause with meaning to you making money itself will never be truly satisfying to you, and you will never have enough because someone will always be wealthier than you, or have a better car, house, or toys than you do. Find your meaning, or a cause.

THE UNIVERSE IS UNBALANCED

The Universe is not balanced – it's out of whack! Although it is fashionable to speak of the importance of balance or the twin concepts of yin and yang from Chinese philosophy, successful people intuitively understand that in truth the dice in business, investment and in life are loaded.

A key golden rule to understand and then use to your advantage is the 80/20 Principle, a concept which was first written about more than a century ago. Way back in 1906 the Italian economist Vilfredo Pareto noted that 80 per cent of the land in Italy was owned by only 20 per cent of the population.[1] It often also proves to be the case that more than 80 per cent of the wealth of a nation is held by fewer than 20 per cent of its inhabitants.[2] The world we all inhabit is curiously, yet surprisingly consistently, unbalanced.

A small number of inputs cause most of life's outputs.

Pareto went on to develop his principle by observing that 20 per cent of the pea pods in his garden contained 80 per cent of the peas, and the famous Pareto Principle was born. Today, people often instead refer to the 80/20 Rule or the 80/20 Principle (or sometimes even the Law of the Vital Few), but the name you prefer to attach to this concept is of far less importance than how you choose to apply it to your own life.

Consider the potentially huge implications of this simple rule! Most of your personal wealth will likely be derived from only a handful of your business and investment decisions. In business, it is often the case that only 20 per cent of customers account for 80 per cent of revenues and profits. Meanwhile 80 per cent of customer complaints are frequently derived from only 20 per cent of the customers (and it is unlikely to be the same 20 per cent of customers that are generating most of your turnover!). The examples go on and on.

What does the 80/20 Principle mean for us as individuals? It means that nearly all the genuinely significant results in your life will be derived only from a vital few of your actions! On the other hand, most of what you do achieves very little. The significance of this is that if you can harness the power of this simple concept and apply it across the way you live, work and invest, you can radically improve the quality of your life including your wealth, health, relationships, happiness and more.

Better still, if you can make a few good decisions, observe very carefully what is working most effectively for you and then resolve to double down by doing even more of it, your results can get better and better. The 80/20 Principle can be a phenomenally powerful tool when it is thoroughly understood and applied effectively.

GETTING THINGS 80 PER CENT RIGHT

One of the reassuring things about the 80/20 Principle is that there can be plenty of headroom for mistakes. You do not have to get everything right all the time. This is fortunate, because we are all human and we all make mistakes every day. I know for sure that I do! You by no means must be perfect, and nor should you necessarily even try to be. After all, to err is human. However, you do need to resolve to learn from genuine mistakes, ensure that you get the big decisions right and, above all, aim to be the best you that you can be. Most of your best results will come from getting the basics right. The rest is just fine tuning!

'Tell me and I forget, teach me and I may remember, involve me and I learn.' – Benjamin Franklin

Remember, living the 80/20 way does not mean only taking the key actions which are getting you results and ignoring other parts of your life. The 80/20 Principle is a more empowering concept than that which requires that you study which of your strategies are achieving results and doubling down on them. The 80/20 Principle also implies to me that you should focus on your passion. This is in part because what you are passionate about you are likely to become a great expert in, and just as crucially, this is because doing what you are passionate about should also make you happy and fulfilled.

MODELLING, THE 80/20 WAY

One of the most useful and effective tools in your entire armoury – if your goal is improving your life – is modelling. That is, to find someone who has achieved the goals that you want to achieve and to model what has worked for them – to learn from what has worked so effectively for them and what has not and apply the learnings from their experiences yourself.

If your goal is to become the CEO of a large company or a Partner in a professional services firm, find CEOs or Partners who have achieved the success you want, and study how they became successful. If instead your goal is to found and then run a riding school, find someone who has achieved just that. Through modelling their most effective actions, strategies, performance and demeanour you can begin to achieve the same results, perhaps even more quickly and effectively than they did themselves. You can learn from them the potential traps and pitfalls too!

Having established myself as a property investor in London and in Sydney, one of the key mentors I chose to take my property investing skills up to the elite level was the best-selling author and leading property expert and advisor Michael Yardney.[3] Why did I choose him above all the other possible real estate gurus? Mainly because he had a proven record of achieving results over a period of forty years and was most certainly not a flash in the pan.

Find mentors who have already achieved your goals.

There were plenty of other real estate experts selling their wares, but many of them seemed to be relatively new to the property game or were claiming to have discovered some new angle or fad. That is not typically what you want from a financial or investment mentor. Instead you want someone who has been there and done it over a prolonged period, through the highs and the lows of more than one market cycle, because all asset classes have summer and winter seasons. The full gamut of their experiences, which have been gleaned through good times and bad, can be priceless. I still learn something new from Michael every week, directly or indirectly.

In the world of share markets and investing, I have read and learned from hundreds of books over the years and probably tried every approach to investing and trading at some point in time. And my word, there are lots of them! Eventually I came across one short book by top-selling author and investor Peter Thornhill which brought it all together and made share investing make perfect sense.

I quickly realised that Thornhill must be a man worth seeking out, and getting to know him I learned more from his words of wisdom than from reading thousands of pages of moderately useful information elsewhere or watching the endless dozens of talking heads on the television. This is another great example of the 80/20 Principle in action! What this book helped to clarify for me is that the share markets have become plagued by speculators, always wondering, hoping, or praying that they know which way the market will dive next. His book puts into black and white what I had intuitively felt. It need not and should not be that hard.

Invest in shares to compound your income as well as growth.

Invest in properties to snowball your asset base and equity.

Shares are an income asset. Great companies will pay you dividend income every year. If you can find low-cost investment products that invest in a well-diversified range of great companies, with a proven record over multiple decades of paying investors increasing dividends every year, then you can focus on the ever-increasing income stream and not on the day to day gyrations of the share price. Instead of spending each day or week worrying about what the stock market is up to, you can continue to receive your dividend cheques safe in the knowledge than when a company increases its dividends every year, over time, the share price will also take care of itself.

The best time horizon for holding a quality investment is forever.

What I learned from these true experts in their respective fields was that true power and peace of mind can be found in quality investments which can be held forever. Continuing to accumulate income-producing, appreciating investments is the simplest, most efficient, and most effective method of becoming wealthy. As we have already considered, gains can grow and compound unimpeded by transaction costs or capital gains and your wealth can snowball while you sleep.

USING EXPERTS

One of the great things about you having picked up this book is that you have made a choice to educate yourself in how to become financially free, how to design the life you want to live and to escape from the daily grind of the rat race. Don't underestimate the power of taking this step!

One of the key reasons I achieved my own financial freedom at the age of 33 is because I realised that this was a goal I wanted to achieve and I read prodigiously, some hundreds and hundreds of books in total. Granted, some books were considerably less useful than others, but over time having educated myself through huge amounts of reading I chose key mentors I could learn from to help me achieve my goals.

'Not all readers are leaders, but all leaders are readers.'
– Harry S. Truman

While it may not be feasible or even desirable to read hundreds of books, I do recommend that you attempt to read regularly and commit to learning new things. The world is ever-changing and evolving, and while the principles of success remain the same the specifics do shift subtly over time. It also sometimes makes sense to employ the use of an expert in investment.

In fact, most employees already do so by paying for a fund manager to manage their pension fund. They may not physically pay the cash, but the fees are simply deducted from the fund each year, regardless of whether the fund managers have made money or lost money for the fund. Others, including myself, deem the value to be added by fund managers as unacceptably low and thus elect to self-manage our pension and invest in different share market products which do not attract hefty or punitive fees. When it comes to investing in the share markets, as you know I believe there is a solid case for considering investment companies which incur only very low management and administrative costs, or simply investing in index funds.

Experts can help in investment.

Does that mean I would never pay for expert assistance? No! In some instances, such as when in investing in property, it absolutely makes sense to have a team of experts on your side: a property buying agent or expert investment advisor, a solicitor, an accountant, and a property manager, for example. While it is always admirable to determine to learn from your mistakes as you go, using leverage to buy real estate is too big a deal to get wrong.

Statistics show that the overwhelming majority of property investors never progress beyond owning only one or two properties, which is certainly not enough to achieve financial success for most people. One of the salient reasons for this is that they simply do not get it right in the early days – through inexperience they do not carry out the right research to buy the right property. They become disillusioned and never create the equity they need to generate new deposits for investment in further properties and therefore snowball their wealth.

If you make a successful property investment, however, the power of leverage can see you attain returns that can be leveraged relatively quickly into further investments through redrawing the equity created. That is why you simply must get it right and why I recommend that you should probably enlist the help of an expert to ensure that you do so.

The principle reason that property investment is such a powerful tool when it is done well is that the leverage involved can be such that a relatively small number of investment properties can make a huge difference to your personal finances. What this does mean, however, is that if you are potentially only going to own half a dozen investment properties, you simply cannot afford to get any of those investment decisions wrong if you want to accelerate your results.

NEVER-ENDING IMPROVEMENT

Back in the 1980s, it was common for business leaders in the west to look to Japan for clues as to how success could be achieved. Largely thanks to catastrophic policy errors Japan has been through some tough times in recent decades and has become something of a template for what not to do with respect to central bank monetary policy and intervention against deflation. Despite these major macroeconomic challenges, Japan has nevertheless been an industrial powerhouse and a country which has long prided itself on excellence in business. In Japan, there is a fascinating word that is often used in industry which has no direct equivalent in English

– kaizen. In English, the word is probably best described as a process of consistent and never-ending improvement. What a powerful concept that is for the way we live our lives!

How often do we feel or say that we are 'stuck in a rut', as though we are 'taking two steps forward and three steps back' or we are 'going around in circles'? These are powerful metaphors, and we should be careful with the language which we use because on an unconscious level we may begin to act in a congruent manner with the metaphor. Be mindful of the vocabulary and the metaphors which you use in your life and to describe it. Successful people tend to use positive vocabulary and empowering metaphors.

'Every day, in every way, I am getting better and better.'
- Émile Coué, French psychologist

A far more powerful way to think of our lives is to think of the concept of kaizen. Every day make a commitment to learn and improve in any way you can. One of the reasons this is such an effective manner to approach life with is that people tend to believe that they can successfully make small improvements and therefore they are achievable. In Chapter 5 we looked at choosing your own adventure through the setting of big and inspiring goals. Although setting big goals may appear a daunting task, it is vitally important, for if you set yourself goals which truly inspire you, then you will have the motivation to take the consistent action necessary to move towards them.

Another worthy analogy is to think of a large sailing ship progressing towards its destination. The sailor does not simply point the ship in the general direction of the target and then hope for the best as the ship progresses along its voyage. There will be unpredictable winds and weather and there may be setbacks along the way, but the experienced sailor will not fret. Instead, the sailor will continually make small adjustments to the ship's course as the voyage continues, constantly updating and reacting to movements in currents and the prevailing wind. The most important thing is to make sure you leave the port in the first place!

Do the one percenters.

When Steve Waugh was the captain of the Australian cricket team, he often spoke about the team 'doing the one percenters', by which I believe he meant every member of the squad being committed to doing everything possible to improve performance.[4] Again, small improvements are believable and therefore they become achievable. I sometimes look back at where I was ten or even five years ago, and am amazed at how far I have come. How about you? Are you progressing at the speed you want to? Are some areas of your life going better than others? Are there things you would like to achieve in the next five years?

It is difficult to know all the answers to these questions without sitting down for a moment and reviewing your actual progress. A useful exercise for you to carry out may be to consider how each part of your life was a decade ago to assess in which areas you have made progress (often we don't give ourselves enough credit!) and in which areas of your life you appear to have stalled, as this may be a signal that you need to take corrective action. I do this exercise every year, and it's always enlightening.

INVEST IN YOUR HUMAN CAPITAL

In investing we talk a lot about expanding financial capital which is a simple idea, really. You save some of your income each year and invest it for your retirement. Although one must make an allowance for a future increase in the cost of living, provided you invest enough and invest wisely, thanks to the compounding growth effect your retirement should be a comfortable and well-funded one. In the ideal but sadly non-existent financial world where nobody becomes ill, dies, gets divorced, goes on a spending spree, loses money on bad investments ... then building a retirement portfolio is very simple.

Let us now think instead about human capital. Invented by economist Theodore Schultz in the 1960s, in purely economic terms human capital is said to be 'the sum value of our human capacities'. This is a very useful concept. Just like other forms of capital, you can invest in your own human capital, through education, practising skills and professional training.

Figure 9.1 – Human capital

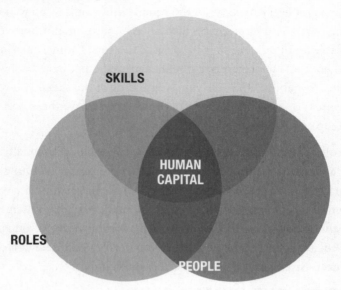

A purely academic economist would tell you that human capital is a way of measuring an employee's skill set, for the more skills and experience you can get under your belt, the greater your earnings potential. If, therefore, the value of your human capital is said to be the present value of your future earnings capability, you might expect that at the age of 18-21, while your financial capital might be low or even negative, your human capital might be at its highest point since you have decades of earning power ahead.

In practice, what often happens is that as we move through education, higher education, and professional training, our skills and therefore the salary we can expect to command in the future increases. When you are younger and you have time on your side, when allied with professional skills, this can make the level of your human capital high.

Human capital increases and then can decrease again later in life.

The basic point is that while human capital tends to be high when you are younger, it then tends to decrease as you approach retirement, since you have fewer earning years remaining. Consequently, from an investment point of view you should aim to be an accumulator with your long-term investment capital (including your pension) in your younger years while tending to take a more conservative approach as you move into the income phase as you approach retirement.

The old rule of thumb used to say 'subtract your age from 100 and put this percentage of your portfolio in shares, and put the balance in bonds'. But you will know that in the real world individual circumstances differ and no such hard and fast rule can be applied! Just like financial capital, human capital has different rates of risk and therefore potential returns. Some occupations, such as Chartered Accountancy, are expected to be relatively low risk and steady in terms of income flows, which makes formulating a regular investment plan straightforward. Meanwhile other occupations (such as acting or training as a musician, for example) may be perceived as riskier but potentially with greater rewards, both financially and personally. Other occupations are commission based and can see more earnings volatility. One thing which I have made a part of my reality over the last decade is to continually expand my skills and qualifications, and to aim to learn something new every day. There is an old saying that 'leaders are readers', and I believe that there is a good deal of truth in that.

RISK ASSETS

Typically, a younger person might be more inclined to invest heavily in the so-termed risk assets since they have the benefit of a longer investment time horizon. Apparently 'safe' term deposits may produce a reliable though small income, but over the long term tend to be much riskier since they provide no growth potential. Upon approaching retirement, your financial capital should have increased as your human capital gradually decreases, and the focus often tends to shift towards income investments.

TIME HORIZON

This is an important point, particularly in the light of day-to-day commentary which focuses almost unstintingly on recession risk, economic headwinds, investment market corrections, and so on. Remember that what is risky for one investor is not necessarily risky for another. Risk is often largely related to financial goals and time horizon. Stock markets will periodically boom and crash, but for those who invest wisely in dividend-paying investments the long-term risk is greatly diminished. By way of another example I read the story of a property investor aged 100 in 2015 who retired 55 years back having invested heavily in properties around North Sydney and the northern beaches of the harbour city. Since the median house price in Sydney in 1960 was around $4,000, these were clearly not risky investments for him, although they may of course have appeared to be so at that time!

Diversify your risk.

Diversification is one of the key rules of investment and since human capital is a form of investment, then you should avoid having all your eggs in one basket here too. To go back to the example of my own career, I recall that when I worked in mining, many of us were offered shares and options as long term incentives in their remuneration package from the company. When commodity prices tanked some years ago, the company was forced to make some executives redundant, while the value of their shares also dropped at the same time, and their options flipped out of the money too.

This represented for those executives a leveraged bet of both human and financial capital on one outcome – that is, one company successfully mining, selling and shipping commodities off to China at high commodity prices. While this focused approach can certainly pay off handsomely for some, for most of us it is often better not to have too much correlation between your human capital and financial capital. If you are specialised in one career, it may be wiser to invest your financial capital in non-correlated investments.

Take out appropriate forms of insurance.

When investing in the share market you might opt to you have a form of insurance (e.g. put options) and so it is with relation to your human capital. Life throws up unforeseen events such as illness or disability which can severely impact earnings potential and therefore there are forms of insurance that can be taken out to protect against such an adverse event. Investing in your human capital has many similar principles to investing financial capital. Invest in your skills and compound your education and the value of your human capital and your future earnings potential goes up. Aim to have some level of diversification, limit your downside risk, and invest in yourself for the long term.

GETTING BACK ON THE HORSE

It is perfectly normal to become interested in something for a period and then lose interest in it. When I was in junior school I became strangely compelled by the idea of playing chess for a couple of years, but then when I reached an intermediate standard, I lost interest again and went back to football. As an early teenager, I was totally obsessed with golf and got my handicap down to quite a low level, but then gave the game away when the sheer intensity of my University studies took on an increased importance (or something like that, anyway!).

There is nothing particularly unusual in that. As humans, we are designed to have a range of different interests and learn new things, and that is healthy. However, investment does not lend itself well to people who take a passing interest in a certain asset class before moving on to other investments, because it will often be the newcomers to the market who get wiped out when the market inevitably reverses, as it always does. To some extent I believe that investors can be successful in almost any asset classes provided they resolve to master the basics.

Aim to learn from people who have achieved the goals you want to achieve.

More than that, taking care of your financial future is something which you must remain committed to because its effect can be pervasive on the quality of all parts of your life. If you see an author write a book on finance or a new investment fad and then move on to write about other unrelated subjects this is probably a warning signal, if not a red flag. I understand why it can happen – I would like to write books on other subjects myself in the future – but be very wary of passing fads or crazes in investment. Be even more wary of apparent experts who have never built an investment portfolio of their own. They rarely fully understand what is best for the average investor because they have not been through the process themselves, with all the emotions this entails.

What I can tell you for certain is whatever your investment strategy is there will be days when you experience downturns, adverse results, mistakes and failures, because that is simply a part of the process. Success does not occur in a straight line and even the greatest investors of all time look back at some of the decisions that they have made (or often decisions they have not made – errors of omission rather than commission) and cringe. There is nothing unusual about this. It is normal! But it is important to re-emphasise that what determines success or failure is having a solid long term plan for success and resolving to get back on the horse and never, ever giving up. There may be no more important lesson than this in life. Never, ever give up!

LEARN FROM YOUR MISTAKES

We all inevitably make mistakes. The great challenge is to learn to treat these upsets as an opportunity for education rather than make them a reason to fear making wrong choices in the future. This is what former table tennis player, journalist and author Matthew Syed refers to as 'black box thinking'.[5] In aviation, accidents and mistakes are analysed in obsessive detail so that lessons can be learned. It can be human nature to make excuses for mistakes, but we would be far better served to resolve to learn the lessons from our mistakes, for we all surely make them. It's what makes us human.

Never say 'oh dear'. Instead say 'ah, interesting!'

Some days the world seems to be against you and everything can seem overwhelming. If that is the case – and on some days, it will be – resolve to get some small successes under your belt. Taking a first step inevitably leads to bigger things, bringing you both satisfaction and increasing your confidence. Success in life and investment is achieved by setting yourself big and inspiring targets but breaking those targets down into smaller and more achievable tranches. More achievable means more believable. One practical tip is at the start of each day to draw up a to-do list just for that day. It is amazing the difference that this simple action can make to the way in which you view your progress and the satisfaction which can be drawn from the knowledge that you are simply getting things done.

Culturally, we tend to be embarrassed by our 'failures' and mistakes. But we should take heed of the aviation industry which sees accidents and even tiny mistakes as precious learning opportunities. In personal finance, investing, business, and life, there are really two ways to achieve success. One is the top down approach of designing a detailed plan to succeed. This can be a great start, and it's partly what this book is here to help you with. But you can also achieve great things through trial and error, by drawing the lessons from your successes and failures along the way. I recommend that you use a combination of both approaches, by finding mentors and modelling their key strategies, while also resolving to learn from what is working for you and what is not. And most importantly of all, never, ever giving up!

DEALING WITH ADVERSITY

Perhaps the biggest determinant of how successful you will be in life is how you deal with failures, and how you treat adversity may be the single biggest influence on the results you can achieve. If you respond to failures or adverse results with a sense of resignation and begin to believe that it is not even worth trying, then you will have almost lost before you have even begun.

Success rarely occurs in a straight line and failures are not personal to us.

The past does not necessarily equal the future, yet too many folks become resigned to failure after comparatively few attempts, and worse, they take their failures personally. They begin to use phrases like 'this always happens to me' or 'I never seem to make the progress I want'. The problem is that such learned helplessness becomes self-fulfilling, because they stop trying and therefore stop achieving, thus confirming their previously acknowledged belief that they cannot succeed. It becomes a vicious and insidious circle.

Everyone experiences failure so it is how we respond to adversity that counts.

If you experience a failure or adversity, consider instead what you can learn from the situation. Actively picture yourself doing better next time. If you can change your beliefs to believe that success is reachable you can certainly achieve things that others believe are impossible – but you will inevitably experience hurdles and setbacks on the way, and it is how you respond to these setbacks which determines your eventual outcomes. Achievers in life do not see problems as permanent, they do not see failure as personal, and they do not believe that their problems are pervasive.

THE 5 KEY STEPS TO MAKING DRAMATIC CHANGES IN YOUR LIFE

With the above points in mind, I assume that there are areas in your life within which you would like to see greater results. If not, there should be! Remember we should think of our lives as the Japanese treat their business efficiency – a masterpiece which is a work in progress for constant and never-ending improvement. To achieve greater results, you will need to make changes to your beliefs and strategies accordingly. There are five key steps which you need to take to make dramatic changes to your life, and, in order, these are:

1. Decide what it is that you want

Consider setting some huge and inspiring goals. This is the first key step to making a dramatic change to any area of your life – that being, to decide exactly what it is that you want to achieve. After all, to misquote and paraphrase *Alice in Wonderland*, if you do not know where it is that you want to go, how will you know when you have arrived? You must also then consider what exactly it is that is currently preventing you from achieving your goals and consciously remove your limiting beliefs.

A client of mine told me that it often feels impossible to save any money to invest. I am, of course, always a big advocate of thrift and finding ways to save money through looking for trade discounts, using cinema vouchers, or using public transport instead of paying for taxis. In fact, I always try to link pleasure to seeking value for money in whatever it is that I do. A self-conducted review of his bank statements showed that the big-ticket items outside of his rent and taxes were:

- Cars
- Luxury holidays
- Nights out

There is nothing particularly unusual about this in the modern consumer economy. Contrary to how it might sometimes feel, people on average today have more disposable income than did any generation in the history of the world. Unfortunately, advertisers are very clever types and have tricked us into associating pleasure with using their products and pain with living a life that is apparently inferior in quality to that of our peers. Advertisers send us subliminal messages that the answers to our insecurities, frustrations and inadequacies lie in buying ever more of their products.

If you have ever spent time living in a developing country, you would quickly come to realise what utter nonsense this is. Consumerism is cleverly designed to bring you short term pleasure, but these results and feelings are transient and contribute very little to lasting happiness.

2. Link pleasure and pain to the right behaviours

The next step in making dramatic changes to your life is to change exactly what it is that you link pleasure and pain to. You need to link massive and immediate pain to whatever it is that is stopping you from achieving your longer-term goals. You need to link pain to sabotaging actions which you may be using as a crutch or for short term comfort. Conversely you also need to link great pleasure to making the changes you need to make to create a better outcome over time.

'There are plenty of ways to get ahead. The first is so basic I am almost embarrassed to say it: spend less than you earn.' – Paul Clitheroe

3. Break the existing pattern!

At some point if you are going to make a dramatic and sustained change to your life you need to break the pattern, to smash the existing routine to pieces! The problem with the way in which we link pleasure and pain to our actions is that often we have been doing things the same way for so long that the linkages we have created are virtually hard-wired into our brains. It can be very difficult to unscramble the existing subconscious process of linking pleasure to short term comforts.

If you keep doing more of what you have always done, you will get more of what you have already got.

The adage states that if you keep doing what you have always done, you will get more of what you have already got. While this seems an obvious truism, it is vital to understand that if you want to get different results, eventually you need to decide to change your behaviours, and you will need to find a way in which to break or interrupt the existing behaviour pattern.

4. Create an empowering new choice

It is usually possible to break a habit for a while. Smokers quite often manage to stop smoking for a few days, for example. But what can be challenging is putting an absolute stop to behaviour patterns which you formerly turned to for pleasure, comfort, or as a crutch, as this can seem to leave a gaping hole in your life. For any dramatic changes that you make to your life to be effective and lasting you need to create a new and empowering alternative.

Create alternative choices – empowering choices!

What I am suggesting here is that if you want to break a limiting or destructive behaviour pattern you need to find for yourself a stimulating, exciting and empowering alternative. Be guided by your passion!

5. Repeat the new pattern until it becomes hard-wired

The final step to making dramatic and lasting changes to your life is to fine-tune and condition the new behaviour patterns as regularly as possible until they become your new reality. It appears to be very difficult to change facets of your life dramatically but eventually if you condition the new behaviour in your life regularly your brain will recognise the consistency and the new behaviour pattern will become hard-wired.

'You can, you should, and if you're brave enough to start, you will.'
– Stephen King

An interesting aspect to this is that these small changes can have knock-on effects that you had not expected or intended. I find it interesting how these small flow-through effects can have unforeseen consequences, sending ripples out into your world. Remember, condition your new empowering behaviour patterns until they are consistent and become a part of your reality.

Chapter 9 Summary

- Find a higher purpose for your wealth creation plan – it will make it both more satisfying and sustainable.

- Success leaves clues: aim to model what has worked well for others.

- Invest in yourself and read widely.

- You will make mistakes, so resolve to learn from them.

- To create lasting and powerful change, link pleasure and pain to the right behaviours.

- Once you have constructed a solid portfolio of assets, you can find ways to follow your passion.

CHAPTER 10
ACCELERATE: PEDAL TO THE METAL!

PEDAL TO THE METAL!

We have looked at the fundamental principles of building wealth in a sustainable, tax efficient, and highly effective manner. You have the tools at your disposal to start the snowball rolling in your favour, safe in the knowledge that you will be making progress towards your financial freedom. That's great! But what if you want to get to your goals sooner? Can you accelerate towards the finish line? You can, in different ways.

Firstly, you can do more of the same, but do it even more vehemently. And secondly, you can employ some leverage which can help to magnify your returns. In this context leverage often tends to mean borrowing in one capacity or another, which is only something which should be done with great care. There are many ways to accelerate your wealth creation plan. Let's look at six of them.

ACCELERATOR #1 – EARN MORE!

Well, it sounds obvious enough, hey! If you want to become wealthier more quickly, earning more is one good way to go about accelerating your investing plan. Remember it is not your salary or business income which itself will make you wealthy, rather it is what you can do with those extra dollars of income in the investment sphere that will create your cash machine.

How can you go about earning more income than you already do? I can guess what you may be thinking – I already earn as much as I can, I work hard, and I have a plan to get promoted. This may be a great start, depending on which industry you work in and the opportunities it presents. How can you get paid more for what you do? Napoleon Hill said that the way to make more money is to make yourself more valuable to more people.[1] Try to make yourself invaluable to your employer. Can you become more efficient so that you are as productive as two people? Or even three people? Or five? Another way in which you can add more value is to become a true expert in your field. Can you become a specialist, or an authority in your field of employment? This may require that you undertake training or go the extra mile to learn new skills and knowledge.

The financial crisis resulted in many redundancies and layoffs. Many of those jobs in the manufacturing and other sectors are not coming back.

In developed countries, most of the new jobs are now being created in the services sector. The world will continue to change, as it always does. Therefore, to thrive it is important to embrace change and look for the opportunities that are presented by change, rather than to fear it. If you work in an industry which is in decline or your skills are becoming obsolete, then you may need to educate yourself in new skills, or even retrain. Of course, this can be a scary prospect , but change brings opportunities.

THREE TECHNOLOGICAL REVOLUTIONS

When I left school my first job was in a timber factory, and it pretty much involved putting timber through circular saws and moulding machines for 40 hours per week. It was often said that in the future such tasks will be performed by robots. It hasn't necessarily happened for all such roles, but the business did close some years later – small production and manufacturing business in developed countries often struggle to compete with their comparatively high labour costs. The book *Who Moved My Cheese?* is a simple parable which explains that the world will change whether we like it or not.[2] To earn more need to adapt to the new world order and make yourself more valuable.

Although for economic historians it was once commonplace to speak of The Industrial Revolution (as though there has only been one such revolution) more recently it has become fashionable to speak of three technological revolutions in modern economic history. Each of these revolutions represented genuine structural shifts. Put another way, although economies continue as ever to move in cycles, the revolutions fundamentally changed the environment so that things would never be the same again thereafter.

The Industrial Revolution was the first of the three technological revolutions and it took place in Britain in the middle of the 1700s. Prior to the Industrial Revolution, the British population predominantly lived in rural areas and endured a lifestyle that barely extended beyond subsistence living. People tended to work in agriculture and lived very much a hand-to-mouth existence. The invention of new machinery such as the steam engine and the Newcomen Engine (if I remember my Year 9 history lessons correctly!) saw humans for the first time being able to use automated processes and Adam Smith's famous division of labour in factories to create greater output.

Suddenly, Britain's Gross Domestic Product began to increase, which it had not been doing through the Middle Ages and through the period before the revolution. As the newly mechanised processes spread throughout Western Europe and to America, developed nations escaped from the assumed Malthusian Trap (Malthus had suggested that the growth of the population would be restricted by our ability to produce adequate food supplies to sustain growth). The Industrial Revolution led to continued inequality, although the wealth moved into new hands – those of the capitalist factory owners. As vast swathes of the countryside migrated to the rapidly growing and industrialising cities, the factory workers endured a tough existence and often dreadful working conditions in the new factories.

The second revolution was the technical revolution, and it came about as humans learned to master the power of electricity and metallurgy, including the widespread use of steel. Other resources such as oil were better understood and exploited to create petroleum and gasoline and the world harnessed its resources with more effect than had ever been the case before. Increased sophistication with regards to mechanisation saw the rise of the motor car and the world began to mobilise itself. Sadly, for the Brits, it was the Americans who embraced this revolution with more gusto and America became the world's leading economic superpower in the first half of the 20th century – a status which the US continues to cling to today.

The third technological revolution has been the internet revolution. Back in the 1980s we started to hear about a new 'information super-highway' that was apparently going to change our lives forever. Nobody seemed to be quite sure how or what it would do, but sure enough the internet and the age of electronic communication has totally revolutionised the world we live in. Even though from 2007 the world slipped into a major recession triggered by the subprime crisis, and yet it seems that this communications revolution, just as those before it, will again represent a structural shift in how we live our lives and will see the world more prosperous. This will be particularly so in those developing countries which are beginning to grow at great speed such as Brazil, China and

India.

The working from home revolution has changed the way some of us view work, though it has not eventuated in full. It is the capital cities in which the hundreds of thousands of new migrants are choosing to live in, and for those of us that already live in Australia … well, we are choosing to live in the capital cities too, or move up to some of the coastal locations along the eastern seaboard. Human beings are odd creatures. Individually, we like to believe we are different to most other people, and yet the truth is that we are far more similar than we care to admit. The internet and communications revolution is seeing us live closer together rather than further apart.

As for future revolutions? Well, they are almost always unpredictable. There is an argument to say that the next revolution will come through greater understanding of genetic modifications and cloning. So perhaps in the future we will be even more like each other than we are today! The key point here is that the world is changing and it will continue to change. If you want to earn more in the future, accept change. In fact, learn to embrace change! As well as threats, change brings opportunities!

ACCELERATOR #2 – RE-INVEST ALL YOUR PROFITS

The second accelerator you can use is very simple, and self-explanatory. The fastest results in wealth creation will always come from a combination of leverage and compounding growth. Thus, to accelerate your financial plan, don't reward yourself for successes by spending your profits on luxuries and treats such as a new car or a holiday. Instead, to accelerate your results, aim to re-invest all your profits!

ACCELERATOR #3 – SPEND EVEN LESS!

Just going 'cold turkey' and not spending any money is not a strategy which will work for most people. If you begin to feel as though you are giving something up, then you will unconsciously be relating saving money to pain instead of pleasure. And although you may be able to adhere to such a plan for a while, it is unlikely that you will be able to do so sustainably. Nevertheless, curbing your spending for a period is another way in which you can accelerate your results. Just as the 'secret' to losing weight is essentially to eat less and move more, the secret to building wealth more quickly is to spend less and invest more!

ACCELERATOR #4 – SAVE ALL PAY INCREASES

Have you ever been on a treadmill which is going just a bit too fast for you? I have! It's not a very pleasant experience at all, is it? You must clumsily reach forward to press the button to slow everything down, but because your legs are pedalling away flat out to keep up with the speed of the belt, it's hard to get everything under control.

Interestingly in today's consumerist society this is how perhaps most people spend their money. Each time they earn a bit more money, their expectations are raised a little higher and their spending increases accordingly. The treadmill starts off at an easy walking pace, but you get that first pay rise and it begins to spin a little faster. Then you get a bonus and you need to upgrade your car, and the treadmill gets a little faster again.

The scariest thing about this is that there is almost no limit to how fast the treadmill can go – no matter how much you earn the treadmill can get faster. Trust me I have seen people who earn extraordinarily high incomes for much of their careers yet they still don't manage to save or invest because their spending treadmill just kept on speeding up. Another simple way in which you can accelerate towards your goals is to save and invest all your future pay increases and bonuses. One of the key dynamics which keeps people trapped in the rat race of paid employment is that with each pay rise they receive their lifestyle expectations and therefore their outgoings increase accordingly.

Figure 10.1 – Save your pay increases and bonuses!

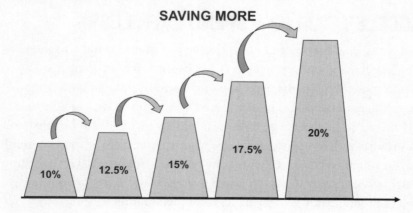

SAVING MORE

10%   12.5%   15%   17.5%   20%

ACCELERATOR #5 – USING LEVERAGE

You can use leverage to invest in either property or shares. In fact, most property investors choose to use leverage in the form of a mortgage. It is possible to use leverage in the share markets too in different ways. What often happens in the share market is that investors use some leverage which improves their returns when the market is rising, and then as soon as the market reverses they receive margin calls from the lender and get wiped out. If you want to see what I mean, look on the internet at the number of people who became full time traders of Contracts for Difference (CFDs) or used margin loans in the lead up to 2007.

Are they still full time in the share markets today? Almost invariably the answer is no, because they were wiped out. This is all too common in the share markets for average investors. When the market goes up they make money, but when the market turns they get caught out. This needn't matter provided you have a sensible long term investment plan in well diversified products which pay you a good income, but it's probably not a strategy which lends itself too well to the use of leverage. Borrowing to investment in quality property can be an effective strategy. Borrowing to invest in shares can be too, provided you know what you are doing.

ACCELERATOR #6 – INVEST COUNTER-CYCLICALLY

When something is not popular, it is cheap. You can accelerate your results from investment by aiming to buy quality assets when they are cheap. It's not as easy to do as it sounds, because when assets are cheap this means that sentiment is low, and all anyone can seem to talk about in the media is doom and gloom. Of course, when everything in the media is roses, this is likely to mean that the economy and asset prices are overheating, and so may be due for a correction. For this reason, timing the market can be counter-intuitive and almost impossible to do with any real precision, but it can accelerate your results if you can invest more when markets and assets are favourably priced.

DOW THEORY

In this book, I have promoted the idea that the best and most efficient investments can often be those which you can hold onto indefinitely. If you want to understand in more detail how share market cycles develop and play out, and how you recognise what stage of the market cycle we are in, I recommend reading my book *Get a Financial Grip*. Summarily, there are three phases of a typical share market cycle:

- accumulation phase
- public participation phase
- distribution phase

The accumulation phase is when professional investors are actively buying stocks against the general sentiment of the market. During this phase, stock valuations do not change much as these investors are in the minority, absorbing stocks that the market at large is supplying. Eventually, the market catches on to the moves of these astute investors and a rapid price change occurs, which indicates the second phase. This happens when the crowd begins to participate in the market, and this phase continues until eventually rampant speculation occurs. At this point, astute investors begin to distribute their shareholdings to the market and prices begin to fall.

Sophisticated investors aim to be fully invested through the bull market before lightening their holdings before the market reverses. In practice this is far more difficult to do than it sounds, because within each secular market cycle there are smaller movements and cycles within cycles which consistently head fake market traders and investors. A great example was the share market crash caused by the financial crisis, which threw up a couple of epic bull trap scenarios. A bull trap occurs when a market which has been falling levels out and then begins to rise again, tricking investors into believing that a new market cycle has begun.

The grim truth is that even professional investors have a great deal of difficulty in analysing market cycles, so unless you have a written plan and a great deal of discipline, an averaging approach suits most average investors best. That said, there is absolutely no reason that even an investor adopting an averaging approach shouldn't look to add more to their share investments when the market is demonstrably cheap on a historical basis. How do you know when a share market is cheap? There are different measures, but two of the simplest are to look at market-wide price/ earnings or PE ratios and to consider dividend yields.

If PE ratios are historically very cheap, then it is likely to be a good time to load up on quality equity investments. At the time of writing share markets appear to be only offering moderate value so you need to have a plan which allows you to survive a potential downturn. In other words, it may not be a great time to pour all your money into the market quickly!

In a similar vein, if dividend yields are historically high, then it is also likely to be a more attractive time to buy. You will never be able to time the market perfectly since that is not possible to do, even for the greatest of experts. However, what is possible is to adopt a sensible long term approach to investing in quality assets and buying more when the market is clearly on sale. To learn more about the different approaches to investing in the share market, I recommend reading my book *Get a Financial Grip*.

WHY PROPERTY MARKETS CYCLE

There are common explanations of why property markets move in cycles:

- It has been seen that monetary policy, particularly the tightening of interest rates, has been effective in the past at stifling undesirably strong levels of property price growth
- Governing bodies have been blamed at times for becoming addicted to the 'feel-good factor' or wealth effect associated with rising dwelling prices
- Construction activity can increase rapidly during a house price boom as developers chase profits, leading to a temporary oversupply thus exaggerating market downturns
- Construction activity can decline rapidly and be quelled during periods of falling prices leading to a tightening market and eventually an undersupply – and the next upturn begins

One of the most compelling factors, however, is simply the human psychology element. Not only does each new generation see an influx of new market participants who have never experienced a housing bust, humans are emotional creatures: we tend to extrapolate the present into the future in an irrational manner. When times are good, we think they will be good forever which sends the market up to an irrational and overvalued peak, which then inevitably must correct. Each boom sets us up for the next bust, just as each bust sets up for the next boom. The long-term trend of quality well located property investments, however, remains an upward one.

Investment markets are forever impacted by fear and greed.

All investment and financial markets are to some extent impacted by fear and greed. When markets are falling, fear abounds and those presently invested frequently look to sell in a panic, concerned that prices will be cheaper again next month or next year. When prices are rising, greed begins to take over and market participants push prices higher and higher. The market often the moves into the rampant speculation phase as a fear of missing out ('FOMO') kicks in.

Eventually the irrational exuberance comes to end and the market begins to fall again. It is these very human characteristics which cause markets to overshoot both on the upside and on the downside and why markets will always continue to cycle despite the best efforts of central banks and governing bodies to keep markets stable or in equilibrium.

THE PROPERTY MARKET CYCLE IN MORE DETAIL

I am now briefly going to delve a little deeper into the concept of property market cycles and housing market economics to help you understand why the market behaves as it does and how you can use this information to your benefit. Although there is often a disapproving tone from market pundits about dwelling prices rising and falling in cycles, there are good reasons why market cycles occur, and indeed to some extent cycles are beneficial to the functioning of a healthy market.

A market which is perfectly in equilibrium should see prices remaining steady in real terms, yet what happens in practice is nearly always somewhat different. Take the example of Sydney. The population of Greater Sydney could rise by anything up to around 85,000 or more persons in any given calendar year. The growth in the population naturally puts pressure on the established housing stock and an increasing shortage of existing dwellings puts pressure on market rents, forcing monthly rentals and market yields higher.

Dwelling prices tend to rise following increases in rental yields.

As rental yields rise, being a homeowner or a landlord becomes comparatively more attractive than being a renter, altering the investment decision in favour of purchasing a dwelling as a homebuyer or an investor. As more participants enter the market by buying a dwelling, prices begin to rise. Due to the human emotions involved in all markets, prices can begin to rise relatively quickly eventually becoming detached from the underlying fundamentals.

Property developers study market cycles very closely and land-bank holdings in anticipation of the market cycle moving upwards. Developers aim to release new housing developments to the market when prices are at attractive levels allowing them to generate an acceptable return on their invested capital and reasonable profit margins. For these reasons, the construction sector of the economy cycles too.

If, for example, a central bank wants to stimulate dwelling construction to offset weaknesses in other sectors of the economy, it will need to cut interest rates to push dwelling prices higher, financing costs lower and bring developers back into the market. Markets do tend to overshoot on the upside and on the downside, and if development continues too far then an over-supply of dwellings eventuates.

Markets overshoot irrationally on the upside and on the downside.

All of this sits against the backdrop of the wider economy which has implications for movement in interest rates, the strength of the labour force and myriad other factors which impact household confidence. The way in which the economy interacts with the housing market at both a macro and micro level can appear to be quite complex, and it is these very factors which I attempt to elucidate for readers in my free blog page each day.[3]

There are a few key points of note here. Firstly, housing markets in large capital cities are a very different beast to those in smaller cities or regional towns. Housing market economist Michael Oxley explains how in a large capital city a boost in dwelling construction will rarely have the same impact on supply that could eventuate in a small or regional city since the ratio of new stock to established stock in a large city tends to be relatively insignificant.[4]

'With only 6 per cent of all houses in London being newly built, the idea that there being an increase in the building of new houses, even a massive increase, will influence prices, is highly implausible.'

For example, if Sydney is in the middle of a construction boom it might still only be adding 50,000 new dwellings in a year, which is a small proportion of the established dwelling stock for an existing city population which is now passing 5 million. Further the new supply can easily be absorbed by the growing population over time. On the other hand, observe what happened across parts of Ireland through the financial crisis property bubble. With near full levels of employment, house prices had nearly tripled in a short period and unprecedented levels of over-building took place. Ireland also suffered because it didn't have its own currency, as Australia does, meaning that the economy took years to rebalance.

When the inevitable Ireland crash eventually did finally take place, some housing estates had to be demolished. I have met Irish property investors in Sydney who have told me that they have owned a property in Ireland for nearly a decade that has never once been let to a tenant! This is an extreme example and accentuates why I believe that real estate can be too risky a proposition not to engage an expert. You need to be able to identify inner capital city locations – not city centres or old industrial areas where there is no height restriction of tower blocks – where dwelling supply is effectively fixed, but demand is growing due to a rapidly expanding city-wide population growth.

Strong population growth can underpin capital city property markets.

If there is one situation you never want to be in as a property investor it is owning property in a town or city where the population is declining. If you want to see examples of what can happen to dwelling prices in cities where the population is declining, check out how dramatically prices have fallen in parts of Detroit, which is to say effectively down to zero in many cases. I have seen similar outcomes in parts of regional towns in the United Kingdom (while London prices simply kept on rising soon after the financial crisis), which should have been a salutary lesson to promoters of regional property.

If you want to succeed in real estate investment over the long haul, I suggest that you ultimately need to be playing in a large pond. It can be a reasonable strategy to start out investing in a small city if that is all you can afford, but capital growth over the long term will always be more robust in landlocked inner suburbs of large and thriving capital cities.

SHORTER CYCLES?

Typically, a property market cycle might take around six to eight years or so to play out in full, with prices flat or in a downturn for a period of two or three years, before rising again. Historically it was reasonable to expect that each trough in prices would be comfortably higher than its preceding equivalent, but in this era of lower inflation this may not always be so in the future. Indeed, we should expect average dwelling price growth to be lower in the future too as we are in an era of higher household debt and lower inflation.

In today's faster moving world with more instant feedback, combined with the fact that high inflation will no longer carry housing markets forward in long and sweeping cycles, it seems reasonable to expect that housing market cycles might be shorter and more staccato in nature than was the case in times past. Boom cycles will still occur periodically but may be of a lesser magnitude than was the case historically. To create financial freedom through real estate investment, you will not only need to own a portfolio of properties, you will need to own those well-located capital city property types which will comfortably outperform the averages.

Chapter 10 Summary

- Times will always change, you need to accept and embrace this fact, and learn to adapt.
- To earn more, find ways to make yourself more valuable to more people.
- Markets always move in cycles: try to invest counter-cyclically to improve your returns.
- Make as many positive changes as you can to your plan to accelerate your results.

CHAPTER 11
THE
BUSINESS
END
OF THE RACE

'MAKE YOUR VACATION YOUR VOCATION'

The title above refers to some very wise words from Mark Twain. If you can make your vacation your vocation, then you will never feel as though you have done a gruelling day of work in your life! If you think back to your school days and the so-termed extra-curricular activities that you undertook such as playing sport or a musical instrument, you may recall that people tend to be far more successful when they are passionate about what they do.

It tends to be little use if a parent instructs a child to undertake violin practice at home five nights every week if what they want to be doing is playing sport outside with their mates. Why? Because the child will see the violin practice as a chore rather than something to be enjoyed and approached with fervour, and as soon as they are old enough to do so, they are likely to give up the violin playing altogether. If on the other hand the child wants to play music instead of sport, then the reverse of course applies!

How often do people fall into careers which they never felt any passion for even before they started out? All the time! I know more than a little about this myself. I trained as a Chartered Accountant, which at times was great fun, but I am still doubtful as to whether many people grow up with a burning desire to be an accountant. Over the years in my career I enjoyed various parts of my job, but I found it lacked the opportunity to be creative, the hours could be horribly long and inflexible, and the further up the corporate ladder I climbed, the more of my week I spent dealing with appraisal meetings, profitability conferences, efficiency drives and other corporate stresses!

The remuneration was admittedly very good as I moved up the pay scales from Manager to Director, but all research into the subject shows that remuneration tends to only motivate people so far in a career. Job satisfaction surveys repeatedly show that levels of pay only have a relatively small input into happiness in the workplace. In short, you need to be passionate about what you do! While it does not necessarily float everyone's boat, what I was passionate about was finance, economics, writing, share investment, and real estate. I practised these things in my spare time regardless of whether I was paid for them because I am genuinely passionate about them, and so I resolved to plan to make my vacation my vocation. What would you be doing on a normal day if money were no object? This may be a clue as to what you might target as your future career!

THE ZULU PRINCIPLE

An English accountant and author (there are a few of us around!) by the name of Jim Slater argues that it is possible to become an expert in a defined field relatively quickly. After Slater's wife read a book about Zulus, she was quickly able to demonstrate a superior knowledge to him on the subject, and an idea was born![1] Slater rationalised that if his wife could then read every book she could find concerning the subject of Zulus then she could become an expert in that field, and perhaps even a leading authority! The principle holds that if you can identify a narrow and clearly defined area of knowledge then you can profit from your expertise. While there are of course some limitations to this idea, I nevertheless believe that it has a good deal of merit.

The Zulu Principle holds that you can become a true expert in one field.

In my line of business, for example, I know more than anyone else in the world about how to profit from investing in Sydney apartments in certain price brackets in a certain range of very carefully identified inner ring suburbs. On the other hand, I do not know very much about strata-titling blocks of apartments in the Whitsundays, but then nor do I particularly care to. If you can become a true expert in one field, then you can add value to others in this area of expertise. Following Slater's premise, it is possible for you to become an expert in your field of passion. If you can do so, then you can resolve to turn your passion into your business.

'BUT I CAN'T GO INTO BUSINESS ...'

I have talked in some depth in my previous books about the power of belief systems both to create and destroy achievements. I have done so because it is clear to me that whether an individual can transition from full time employment into business successfully is ultimately decided by their beliefs. So many of us have been trained through our upbringing and formal education to believe that a professional career is the only valid path to success (and perhaps that entrepreneurship is somehow a slightly less acceptable path) that we do not fully question the underlying assumptions.

A key theme of this book is that while setting up a business may be challenging for those who have been conditioned by years in the workforce, by first building a portfolio of assets which can go out to work for you in perpetuity, you can gradually begin to focus upon expanding your skill-set so that you can generate substantial income in your own business or area of passion too.

THE ADVANTAGES OF BEING IN BUSINESS

One of the inescapable problems with being an employee is that your salary remains linear. Each day you must wake up and return to work anew to earn your pay cheque. You only get paid once for each day of work, and if you stop turning up for work, it will not be very long before you stop getting paid! The same is true if you lose your job in a recession or due to corporate lay-offs. Regardless of whether you are an employee or a business owner, if you want a pay rise or more revenue then you must find ways to make yourself more valuable to more people, and do so more efficiently. If you want to become very wealthy, you must learn to make yourself invaluable, by honing your skills to dramatically improve the lives of others.

Going into business is another way in which it is possible to use leverage to your benefit. If you can develop a product or service that adds huge value to the quality of the lives of others, you can then create more value for yourself. A business has the potential to generate recurring income as well as potentially leveraging other people's time and money to increase profitability. If you can find ways to reach more people, more quickly and more effectively then money can begin to flow to you.

To create more value for yourself, find ways to create more value for others.

Another problem with salary income is that it tends to be more heavily taxed as you move up the pay scales, with around half of an employee's gross earnings in the top slice of income ultimately forming part of the government's sizeable tax take. Tax levied on salary income is deducted at source and there are relatively few defences for the employee. Broadly speaking as an employee, you go to work to be paid, the government takes its share of your income leaving you to spend the balance.

A business owner may instead deduct legitimate expenses from their revenue and only pays tax on the net profits after deductible expenses. Another of the key messages of this book is to find ways to minimise your expenditure to free up capital for investment. If you are a business owner, you should do the same, and try to ensure that most of your expenditure is directly attributable to your business so that it becomes a legitimate deduction for your business.

THE WELL-TRODDEN CAREER PATH

You may know some people who are natural born entrepreneurs. At school, they often stood out as kids who were always interested in making a bob or two from some profitable scheme or other – at my high school, selling chocolate bars for a small profit was all the rage! Natural entrepreneur types can perform reasonably well in high school exams, but often lack enthusiasm for traditional higher education, instead wanting to get 'out there' into the real world of business. In some senses, young entrepreneurs are the lucky ones, for they know that they do not want to be stuck in an office for their whole lives and can afford to take chances when they are young with nascent business ideas and ventures. One of my housemates in my Uni days set up a business even before he finished his University course – he had no time for a degree, he wanted to get out there and set the world alight (and, to be fair, he did exactly that!).

'Fortune sides with him who dares.' – Virgil

Most people, however, believe that realistically they can only operate as employees. As they move further up the pay scale, the more entrenched this belief inevitably becomes, for the pay cheques generally become larger and thus harder to walk away from, and the financial commitments also increase. Once there is a mortgage and children to think about, even the very notion of giving up full time work becomes a distant dream for many. This need not be so, but it is probably true that you would want to have a solid portfolio of investment assets behind you before you consider taking a leap into business.

MOVING AWAY FROM FULL TIME WORK?

Can the dream of moving away from full time employment to part-time employment or business owner still be achieved in these circumstances? The answer is yes, absolutely, but for many, it cannot be achieved overnight. If this is to be your goal, then the first step is to build a portfolio of income-producing and appreciating assets such as a substantial portfolio of investment properties and shares. Once you have built a solid and substantial financial base then this can gradually allow you to shift your focus away from the need to work full time to generate an income and towards securing other revenue streams such as from a business.

WHAT IS YOUR PASSION?

As I previously noted, I had a reasonable idea of what my passion was and what my ideal day would be. But I also had a full-time job and an attractive monthly pay cheque as the Financial Controller of a listed mining company, which was difficult to walk away from. One of the reasons why it seems impossible to people that they might ever be able to go into business is because they think that they must quit their job and then immediately replace their income with business income practically overnight. It seems far too risky a notion, perhaps impossible to achieve, so they never take the chance and they never find out whether they could have been a business owner.

I suggest trying to think a little differently. Instead of worrying about whether a venture into the world of business might fail, instead consider how over time you can begin to replace your salary income with a business income gradually. I will refer to my own short story by way of an example. My wife and I were both lucky in one sense as we were both quite successful in our early careers and by the time we were in our mid-twenties we were both higher-rate taxpayers (you could consider this to be lucky or unlucky depending upon your perspective!). The problem was that neither of us felt great passion for our careers, so we decided to plan how we could do things a little differently.

Your salary will not make you wealthy, but business and investing can.

My wife had bought herself a house when she was only 21, and house prices around London skyrocketed during the UK housing boom of the

1990s, tripling in value very quickly. Real estate was something which she believed she had some experience in and had had some success with. Over the years we continued to add property after property to our portfolio in prime locations close to London and the centre of Sydney. While we were doing so we also committed everything to becoming the most educated and experienced share market investors that we could.

But even with a substantial portfolio of assets to our name and a large pool of equity, it was still very difficult to walk away from the security of our twin pay cheques. I knew that my passion and area of expertise was in the areas of finance and investment, but I was not yet sure how I could turn this into my day job. This is where the concept of 'modelling' can help. I found people who were already successful in the field I was interested in and to be blunt I modelled what had worked for them.

Find mentors who have achieved the goals you want to achieve.

One way in which it becomes possible to move away from full time work is to begin creating small sundry revenue streams for yourself. There are many ways in which you can do this. Investing in income-paying shares is one great strategy, but there are plenty of others.

Do something you are interested in – you will do it better.

Today's world is full of professionals who are too busy working to have time to mind their own business, and real estate buyer's agencies operate in a growing industry. Our business, AllenWargent was set up to help time-poor professionals and investment funds fulfil their financial goals through investing in quality, well-located real estate. Property and housing market economics are fields that I am passionate about and it gives me a real buzz to wake up every morning and receive emails from people who are achieving their financial goals and living their dreams through smart investment. It beats the living daylights out of waking up each morning with a large and resigned sigh in contemplation of another 60-hour week in the office!

ONE STEP AT A TIME

The goal of moving away from full time work can seem such a huge one that it may feel insurmountable. But, just as climbing Everest must start with establishing a base camp, the goal is one which can be achieved simply by taking one simple step at a time. Firstly, as previously detailed, it is important to begin building your financial base, a portfolio of assets which can continue to appreciate and pay you income whether you are working or not. This helps to take the pressure off your reliance on business success.

Then you can begin to consider in more detail what it is that you are truly passionate about and how you would live your ideal day if money were no object. You do not have to simply quit your day job and dive into business headlong, although of course plenty of people do. This could be a stressful approach and induce stress of a financial nature too. Instead, aim to think of how you can steadily build a profile which will allow you to generate income from your expertise. For most employees, trying to think of a steady transition from one state to another may be more achievable and realistic than taking a running jump from a well-paid role and starting a new business venture from scratch.

WHERE TO START OUT?

If you are currently employed but want to move in setting up your own business or being self-employed the task can seem daunting. I know, because I remember this clearly from my own experience. The thing to remember is that, just like anything else in life worth achieving, setting up a successful business is not something which happens overnight. Instead, it takes many hours of application and effort.

Always endeavour to remember the power of compounding growth. Start small, make small improvements and gradually increase your leverage over time. The problem facing too many people is that they believe that the only way in which they can ever be self-employed is to immediately replace their salary income with an equivalent level of business income, and the real world just does not work like that.

Start small and grow steadily.

In the early years of business distributable profits can be quite scarce which is precisely why I recommend building a portfolio of assets first which can continue to grow and compound for you before you go into business. Being a Chartered Accountant, I have often read business plans which begin with absurd projections for the first few years, making huge allowances for owner-manager salaries, support staff, company cars, and a raft of luxurious IT equipment, well-appointed offices, and more. If that is the type of business plan you want to take a crack at, then best of luck, but as a first-timer the odds are well and truly stacked against you!

In truth, it is possible to start businesses at the mid-tier level, but you might need a reasonably large fund of seed capital to achieve it, either through your own means or by raising funds from investors. I will assume here that if you have the financial intelligence to facilitate capital raisings from investors or fund the start-up of a larger enterprise from your own hip pocket, you are unlikely to be reading this book in the first place! When people come to me asking how they can get out of the rat race and start working for themselves I often ask them to consider writing a book or e-book about their passion or area of true expertise. First, I ask people to consider these questions:

- What is that you are passionate about?
- What do you know more about than anyone else?
- In what capacity or role can you add the greatest value to others?
- What would you be doing on a Monday morning with your time, if you could be doing anything you choose?

The considered answers to these questions should act as your guide.

'I think we're having fun. Our customers like our products and we're always trying to do better.' – *Steve Jobs*

STARTING OUT WITH A LITTLE

One of the reasons that in the modern era most people will always be employed rather than owning their own business is a misunderstanding of the funding requirements for a small business. If you begin to make a list of all the things you could need to start a business, the amount of seed capital you might require could be almost limitless – an office, staff, plant and equipment, a company car, a monthly marketing budget, and so on.

The flexibility afforded by starting small can be advantageous.

Starting out small in business has some tremendous advantages. A business which starts with capital funding is immediately under pressure to generate returns to repay loan interest and meet overhead. A business which starts out small can be allowed to evolve and be more flexible, and it can be acceptable to make some mistakes and to learn from what works and what does not along the way. Starting small with baby steps and over-servicing a few customers can be a great recipe for success, instead of trying to run before you can walk or leaping in at the deep end. If you can begin by providing an outstanding service to a few customers, they may then become repeat clients or refer you on to their friends and colleagues.

PHYSICAL PRODUCTS OR SERVICES?

One of the first major decisions you need to make is whether you are going to run a services business or one which provides a physical product. Over recent decades, developed countries have generally moved increasingly towards service industries to the extent that services now form the greatest part of economies (far larger than, for example, manufacturing or mining and resources).

Will you sell a physical product or a service?

My recommendation when starting out in business would be to find an established industry rather than trying to re-invent the wheel, and particularly, to find an industry which is growing. Then you can aim to win a market share of that growing industry. As it has been the services sector of the economy which has been growing over recent times, then this may be the ideal place to start.

Of course, this is largely down to personal preference and some people feel more inclined towards selling physical products. The thing about selling physical products is that you need stock or inventory. Stock ties up capital, you need a certain level of funds to get started and you will need to have somewhere to store your inventory. It is possible to overcome these challenges and if you are passionate about your product you will certainly find a way. Some start-up businesses use a just-in-time approach to orders or simply aim to acquire their stock after the point of sale. I am not saying that you should not go down this path, but you do need to be reasonably confident that you can make a success of a product line before spending thousands of dollars on buying inventory which you may not be able to shift.

Look for ways to solve other people's problems.

Think for a moment of how much industry today happens electronically. Once we had bookstores and record shops. Today people buy e-books and download their music from the internet. The internet has made the power of leverage available to those who have the ability and imagination to use in to their advantage. It is often said today that wealth is simply an idea, and I agree with this to a point. Creating a successful business is largely about how you can solve problems for people and add value to their lives, and the more you can improve people's lives, the more they will be prepared to pay you for your skills.

Take my path as an example, if for no other reason that it is the one I which am most familiar with. By profession I am a Chartered Accountant, a trade which lends itself ideally to a services style business. There are many ways in which I could have set up a business based around accounting. In the modern age, for example, there are start-up businesses which need accounting or book-keeping services but do not want to pay for a full-time staff member to carry out the work.

An accountant could therefore set up a business which executes accounting services for an hourly rate, and as the business expands it could bring in additional sub-contractors to process journals and reconciliations or perform more detailed accounting work. This is a good example of a services industry which helps time-poor people and start-up businesses today, and it can be a lucrative line of business for an entrepreneur.

For me, though, there would be just one small problem with setting up a book-keeping business: it would bore me to the back teeth! Remember, perhaps the most salient point of this book is to design a life that you are passionate about. In truth, I quite enjoyed book-keeping when I was a junior accounting clerk, but if I were to set up a services business providing a book-keeping service I'm sure that I would quickly become bored to tears.

To excel at something, you need to be passionate about it.

I am passionate, however, about investing, finance and the markets, studying demographics, and analysing the economy. This is not everyone's cup of tea, for sure, but I would be doing all these things whether I was paid for them or not. I knew that I had enough expertise to write high quality books and a daily blog on finance and investment, and I believed that I could improve the lives of others by helping them to invest successfully. The business we decided to set up was a property investment services business which helps investors to buy property as an investment successfully enough to outperform the market with their returns. This is a sizeable and growing industry in cities like Sydney and Brisbane in Australia, as time-poor professionals increasingly look to find experts to guide them through their property investment journey.

Look for established industries which are growing.

Educating the market about a new product may be a worthy goal but you will probably find it to be an uphill battle and will likely fail to translate your efforts into revenues which are fully reflective of your hard work. As noted above, you are likely to be more successful by slotting into an existing and growing industry, and through aiming to win a share of that industry. Find out what the best existing businesses in your field are doing and do it better.

The 80/20 Principle holds that you will likely source 80 per cent of your revenue from only 20 per cent of your clients, suggesting that the secret is to focus on finding those few good customers. And when you do find them, double down on them by trying to find more of the same types of customers, rather than spreading yourself too thin by trying to be all things to all people.

To summarise these key points:

- Fee-for-service businesses are generally easier to set up than those selling physical products
- You have a greater chance of success in an industry which you are genuinely passionate about
- Adapt your passion towards a business model which operates in an existing industry and is in a growth sector
- Aim to secure a share of this market!
- Find out what the best businesses in your field are doing and aim to do it much better than them – this concept is known as modelling

- Consider carefully who your ideal customer or client is, and then aim to find these customers
- To be truly successful in business you need to use your expertise to radically improve the quality of the lives of others

FUNDING YOUR BUSINESS

There is a popular notion that to start out in business, you need a substantial business loan of investment from business angels. Nothing could be further from the truth! In fact, taking out a business loan can be an extremely stressful course of action which adds pressure to a new venture which must provide the budding entrepreneur with an income upon which to live, but also has a new additional hurdle to overcome, that being the repayment of the interest and principal of the business loan.

The statistics show that a significant percentage of new businesses fail due a lack of cash flow, and a business loan merely adds to this risk. If you fail to repay the loan through the business, depending upon the terms of the loan and the structure of your business you may end up being personally liable to the bank or other source of funds. In truth, if you look at the actual statistics in terms of how new businesses are funded, the methods used are far more widely dispersed than you might imagine. Traditionally it was said that business ventures are funded by 'friends, fools and family' as much as they are by banks, but in the modern era there is a wide range of funding methods used.

Businesses can be started with relatively small levels of funding.

One of the outcomes of the financial crisis has been that in many instances debt has often been harder to source than it was previously. It was once not at all uncommon for entrepreneurs to take out a credit card liability with a finite interest free period and then to transfer the debt across to a new product with a similar facility at the end of the interest free term. Generally, that is harder to pull off today, which may of course be no bad thing!

An alternative to a business loan is to sacrifice some of the equity in your new venture. For example, you might relinquish a 25 per cent share in your new business in exchange for some early funding, whether it be from venture capitalists, business angels or simply a friend or family member.

While this can work, the payback down the track can of course be painful. Twenty-five per cent of a start-up business might not be worth too much in today's dollars, but a quarter of your business in a decade's time might be a hugely valuable investment and a painful sacrifice for you to make!

One of the more common complaints from since the financial crisis has been that banks have been lending far too much money for residential real estate and providing far too little funding for productive enterprise such as new business ventures. There is an element of truth in this – banks prefer lending against housing because even if the mortgage-holder defaults and disappears into the ether, the house and land is fixed in its place and cannot go anywhere! After all, most, though not all, properties are immobile. Lenders like this. You cannot easily disappear and take your house with you, and even if you could manage this, the land will still be there.

Banks are often understandably reticent to lend to new businesses at a competitive rate of interest without security.

The flip side to this is that a small business which has yet to prove itself and has no proven track record of making consistent and predictable profits. The business loan is likely to incur interest at a higher rate and be of a shorter term than a housing loan. Housing loans can be issued with uniquely favourable conditions: 25 year terms or even longer, low borrowing rates and small deposits, but business loans offer none of these benefits.

One trend that has been playing out in recent years is that new business owners have become increasingly wise to these factors, and instead of using a business loan which incurs a necessarily high rate of interest, they borrow against a property they own to fund their start-up needs in that way. Recall that I stated earlier in the book that a new attitude to debt can be a powerful tool if it is used wisely. I recommended that while investment debt for real estate can be an effective method of leveraging results, debt for luxury assets or credit card consumer debt makes compounding work in reverse and lead your personal finances into a negative spiral.

While arguably taking out a business loan is so-termed good debt because you can use it to leverage results and returns from your business, it is also the case that the greater the debt hurdle is for a new business, the greater the likelihood that the new venture will fail. I would rather see investment debt used sensibly for well-located real estate investments which will continue to bring income and capital growth in perpetuity than for funding a business.

In life and in investment it is often true that the clearest thinkers can see the most outstanding results. This is one of the reasons that I believe using debt for share market investment or business start-ups can often be as much of a hindrance as it is a help. Instead of concentrating on the basics of acquiring high quality investments which can be held on to forever, the leveraged share market investor frequently obsesses over whether annual and even monthly returns are exceeding the interest charge hurdle.

Using a moderate amount of debt to leverage share market returns can be OK, particularly where the interest rate charged is low (which typically means a line of credit against a house rather than a margin loan), but generally those with the simplest plans are often the most successful over time. Investment debt in the share market can cloud thinking processes. What is right for me, may not be right for you, of course. However, I do want you to consider whether you can set up a new business venture with no new debt. With an absolute bare minimum of seed capital. This may sound challenging but I can assure you it can be done, as we shall see!

DON'T GIVE UP THE DAY JOB!

As stated before, too often people think in black and white.

- 'How quickly can I retire?'
- 'When will I be financially free?'
- 'How long will it take me to launch a new business?'

It need not be so. In terms of financial freedom, I encourage people to think more in terms of a see-saw or counter-balance. When you start out in adulthood you may be 100 per cent dependent upon your salary income to survive and thrive. As you gradually begin to build a portfolio of assets you can slowly but surely become slightly less reliant upon your salary for building wealth, until eventually your investments begin to earn more than you can from your salary due to the snowballing effect. This takes patience, time and discipline, but eventually you surely will get there if you adhere to the task with gusto.

Why not try to think of your transition to self-employment in the same way? Some of the great business ventures have been started while the owners were still working in their day jobs. Clearly there is a delicate balance to be found here. It is not a smart idea to spend too much time focusing on a new business idea while you are being paid a salary if this detracts from your employment performance to the point where you are considered a drag. If you fail to add as much value to your current employer as you are being paid for, you may soon find yourself looking for a new job.

But this is not to say that you cannot sow the seeds of a small business idea while you are still in paid employment. Think once again of a see-saw or counter-balance. As your business idea begins to grow you can become steadily less reliant upon your job, and this is particularly so if you have a portfolio of assets working for you too. The fact is that starting out a new business is hard and cash flows can be tight in the early days. One of the ideas which can helpful, which I used myself, is to switch to becoming a contract employee who works short term contracts instead of full time.

Clearly you need to have a reasonably strong commitment to the idea that you can eventually become self-employed in your own right to do this, but undertaking short term contracts can help to keep dollars rolling in while you are busy establishing yourself in business. Indeed, for anyone interested in starting out in small business, it is vital to understand the importance of cash flow.

PREMISES: KEEP COSTS LOW

Years ago, I worked in the mining industry in Australia and being a Group Financial Controller was based at a Sydney head office. One of the things I noticed before the financial crisis was how many small mining exploration companies which had yet to generate a single dollar in revenues (let alone profits) had head offices located in prime locations such as Australia Square Tower on George Street. Often when you visited these offices or walked past the reception area, there would not be a single soul at home, except for a very bored looking receptionist intermittently clicking 'Refresh' on their Facebook page.

Just think of the wasted overhead! Hundreds of thousands of dollars which had been sourced from investors via share placements and other capital raisings being squandered on prime location offices which were rarely used, and that is even before we get on to the subject of executive remuneration for loss-making ventures!

Keep operating costs down to a bare minimum in the early days.

Office costs for small business can be relatively punitive, which is why you might consider working from home when you first start a new business. In the modern era, working from home is quite feasible, provided you have some space to use as an office and a strong internet connection. As you progress and your business gets up and running you may consider using serviced office space. Serviced offices can provide many of the benefits of renting a full office space including a telephone number, receptionist, a fax number and a street address which can be used to receive post as well as used as a registered office address, but at a fraction of the monthly expense.

FLEXIBLE STAFFING ARRANGEMENTS

Whilst working as a Financial Controller one of the most tedious tasks of each financial year was the annual budgeting process. It still makes me shudder a little just even thinking about the countless hours of back and forth between cost centre bosses and head office. On the positive side of the ledger, I did learn a lot about how to maintain a very close control on costs in a business environment. One important matter which continually struck me was just how high staff and employment costs can be in the modern age.

When budgeting for staff costs if you just drop in a figure for a staff member's basic gross salary you will get a nasty surprise come the end of the year, for the actual costs to the business are considerably higher. For example, there may be pension contributions to consider as well as bonuses, annual leave entitlements, long service leave entitlements, worker insurance costs, share option expense, and more.

Part-time staff working contracts for discrete pieces of work are becoming increasingly common.

In small business, you may not need to incentivise staff in the early days with share options or even bonuses, but there can nevertheless be significant ancillary costs of employing staff. When starting out in small business in the early days there may only be yourself and your spouse, or perhaps you and a business partner. When you require additional tasks completing it often makes sense to outsource or engage people on a freelance or contract basis. In some circumstances, you may be able to agree with a contractor that they perform work for which you only pay them once your customer has paid you, which makes a tremendous difference to the cash flow profile of a small business.

Getting people to invoice you for actual work done can be an effective means of controlling costs and ensuring that you do not pay excessive employee costs for which you are not receiving a commensurate value for the business. When we started out in our business we employed contractors to undertake standalone tranches of work, and it generally worked well. While taking on an employee introduces a range of additional challenges, such as for example what to do when the employee takes annual leave for holiday, paying a contractor for discrete projects can work well for all parties involved.

Outsourcing and contract work is becoming increasingly common and offers flexibility.

Another idea is to look for graduates or students who are seeking work as an internship for a few weeks or a couple of months. This is a good example of a win-win outcome as the intern can receive valuable training, experience and a reference for their CV, and you can benefit from their intelligence, enthusiasm and, in many instances, their superior and tech-savvy IT skills.

In the very early days of business you might be able to enlist some help from friends and family too, dependent upon your individual circumstances. If you go down this path, you still need to lay down a clear set of ground rules and may need to accept that others do not always share the same vision as you, particularly if you are not paying them a market rate for their time!

MARKETING AND PROMOTION

When marketing your business, you need to consider how you are going to stand out from the crowd. While it can be a good idea to model ideas that have worked for other successful businesses, ultimately your business needs to stand on its own two feet and offer a compelling reason for customers to choose your business ahead of the competition. The best approach is to begin by considering who your ideal customer is and work backwards from there.

Your culture is also your brand.

Be clear, direct and succinct. I have seen it said in business books that people can love your business, hate your business, or even sit on the fence, but they must always be crystal clear about what it is that you do! I believe that this is very true. By offering a specific description of what it is that your business does, your ideal clients know that you are to the 'go-to guys' in that sector or industry, while the customers which you do not want to attract will naturally be guided elsewhere.

WORD OF MOUTH MARKETING

The best source of business for a new venture is from your existing clients. Therefore, you should always aim to provide an exceptional service so that your existing clients come back to use you again and again. If you want to add value to your own life, first add value to others! Indeed, the key to building wealth and being successful is always to look to add more value than your charge every time.

When you have completed exceptional work for a client, aim to do two things. Firstly, ask them for a testimonial – hopefully if you have done great work for them, it will be a glowing one. And secondly, ask your clients to recommend your business to friends, work colleagues and family. While you should of course do this in a tactful manner and a way in which does not cause you to appear desperate, this is a legitimate marketing tool.

GOOGLE ADVERTISING

Advertisers can elect to bid for the Google keywords they want so that their sponsored adverts appear in the Google search engine results page. Google decides which adverts are displayed and in what positions based upon each user's maximum bid and quality store. This is a quick and easy way to generate leads in the early days of your small business.

SOCIAL MEDIA

Social media today is an important tool for expanding your networking reach. Some of the key networking sites which all new businesses should look to use in addition to leveraging existing social networks include:

- Facebook
- Twitter
- LinkedIn
- YouTube
- Your blog page
- Your business website
- And more …

A new business does not need to go overboard in terms of social media. You should not, for example, spend so much time on social media that you forget to concentrate on the core elements of your business! However, all new ventures should make use of the sites listed above and others which specifically relate to your chosen line of business. A key point on social media networking is that it should be done in a co-ordinated fashion.

In the social media world, you are what you share!

I enjoy using Twitter and use it regularly for keeping up to date with news and views, and I often share interesting findings from our chart packs. The great thing about Twitter is that while it is has now become a global phenomenon, it is still possible to connect with key people in your industry and interact with them on a one-to-one basis. On the other hand, you should always think three times before tweeting a comment and be very wary of making bold political statements or being openly critical or rude. It is frequently amazing how far some people let themselves go when the blood rushes to their head. Remember, the internet is written in ink!

All forms of leverage are a double-edged sword and must be used wisely.

Earlier in the book I noted that leverage is a double-edged sword. If you use debt to invest but buy poor or underperforming investments your losses will be magnified. And it is this way with social media. Articles and social media comments can go viral, which is both an exciting and terrifying concept at the same time. If you write a great article for the media which goes viral, for example, your profile can be raised a thousand-fold. However, becoming involved in an online slanging matching or argument and the negative publicity can be felt just as keenly.

Are you a boutique business operator or a supermarket?

The analogy I like to use is that while others businesses may be the Wal-Mart or K-Mart firms, we want to be a niche business which people will seek out for specialist service. Of course, if building a huge business is your goal then you can look to address all your enquiries and look to recruit staff to build your business empire! It all ultimately comes back to your goals. If your goal is to build a huge business then you need to put systems, procedures, and staff in place which can deal with a higher volume of clients and transactions. If, like me, your goal is to achieve a balance of work, play and travel then you may look to develop an outstanding niche or specialist business which clients will pay a premium to engage with.

For most business start-ups, you should look to co-ordinate social media in an organised fashion. Ideally you should link the Facebook, Twitter, and LinkedIn pages of your business so that your content is published once across each of these sites in and coherent manner. There are different approaches to what you should post and how often which tends to vary depending upon what line of business you are in. In time, you will find your own path on social media and discover what works and what does not.

Social media marketing should be lively, clever, compelling and co-ordinated.

Quality of content is more important than quantity. I like to update my blog daily which keeps readers checking in each day (or subscribers receive a free daily email), but it is far better to provide a punchy daily or weekly insight than it is to bombard readers with thousands or words of content per day. Less is more, and if you provide too much, few people will read it.

STRUCTURE AND COMPLIANCE

Broadly speaking business owners and self-employed persons have a choice of whether to operate as sole trader or partnership, or to set up a company within which to carry out their business. There are benefits and drawbacks to each structure. A company offers some level of flexibility in terms of distribution of profits (salary, director's fees, or dividends) and potentially asset protection. A self-employed person who operates a sole trader may appear to be like an employee, yet may still be able to claim legitimate deduction for expenses which are directly attributable to the business.

A company in its simplest terms is a set of legal and administrative documents which you trade and operate within, but there are significant implications for how this impacts the way in which you do business, invoice, and pay taxes. As a separate legal entity, a company can offer you some legal protection, although you may still require professional indemnity insurance to insure against you being sued personally.

Get the structure of your business right at the outset – this can prevent headaches later.

This is potentially a huge subject with myriad different angles which might be covered, and as such much of this topic remains outside the scope of this book. If you are unsure about the benefits of setting up a company and why you might choose to do so, speak to an accountant, particularly a professional who is familiar with company compliance as well as having a detailed understanding of corporation and personal taxes. While I of course encourage readers to always save money where possible, sometimes it is much more sensible to pay for expert advice, and this is one such case. If you are not familiar with company law and taxation implications, pay for an expert who is.

YOUR PRODUCTS

Think again of the 80/20 Principle and acknowledge the following key rule of business:

80 per cent of revenues and profits in your business are likely to come from 20 per cent of the products you offer.

What this means is that you should focus on having few products but ensure they are outstanding. For example, our business is in real estate – plenty of other real estate companies diversify into property management, investment strategy advice, vendor advocacy and other revenue streams, but thinking the 80/20 way I quickly realised that what our business can do better than others for customers is to achieve great results for them as investors through buying the right investment property to suit their financial goals.

Success leaves clues; double down on your successes.

Instead, recognise what is working well for you and double down on it. Where you have found there to be success in a certain product that you offer, instead of thinking of what other products you can provide, try to consider how you can maximise revenues from your existing successful product. How can you add value to more people with your successful product?

THE IMPORTANCE OF CASH FLOW IN SMALL BUSINESS

While I at times found working in the accountancy field something of a drag, I must say that the skill-set you learn as an accountant is irreplaceable. When young people today ask me about career choices, I tend to be wholeheartedly in favour of anyone who is considering getting a Chartered Accountancy qualification. Even if this not your true area of passion, the grounding that this qualification gives you can open so many doors for you to go on and achieve whatever you want to in business.

Accountants are often able to understand finance, how businesses run and company financial statements far better than others can – this is because they learn the basic principles of finance and book-keeping from the ground up. I recall that one of the most crucial things which we learned in the early days of accounting school was the importance of cash flow.

I am certainly not inclined to write a handbook of accounting terms here, but it is vital for a would-be business owner to understand a few key terms, including:

- **Revenue or turnover** – the value of your sales
- **Net profit before tax** – the net figure of what is left of your revenue after all costs except for tax charges
- **Net profit after tax** – should be self-explanatory after you have read the preceding bullet point!
- **Cash flow** – the actual cash which transacts in and out of your business

Casting my mind all the way back to accounting school, one of the first things we learned was how even an expanding business which is generating huge profits and ever greater revenues can still go bust. How so? The reason is that businesses do not become insolvent because they make profits or losses, they go under because they run out of cash. A growing business which is guilty of overtrading can find itself unable to pay its liabilities as they fall due because their cash flow profile is not right.

For example, if a company sells 1000 widgets for $10 each expecting to make $2 profit per widget, the business may appear to be generating a nice profit of $2000. But if customers refuse to pay for the finished product widgets for several months then the business can run into problems because it must pay for its new raw material inventory and other manufacturing costs up front. In the early days, the business may muddle through, but where the widget firm tries to expand quickly its up-front costs may fall due well before the receivables from customers roll in to balance the books. If no loan or bridging finance can be sought, the widget business goes bust … despite having no shortage of sales and profits recorded in the monthly accounts.

During the financial crisis, I witnessed the heart-breaking situation of friends losing their businesses because they had clients owing large balances which they were unable to pay. Tempting though it is to focus on sales and profits, there is absolutely no point in making a sale to a customer who is unable to pay. In fact, doing so is likely to send your business into a funk as well as theirs.

When business ventures fail, it is due to a lack of cash flow, not a lack of profit. Cash is king.

In my line of business, because I help clients to invest, it is relatively straightforward for me to ask potential customers how much cash they have available. After all, if I do not know the answer to that question, then I can hardly help them to achieve their investment goals. Most businesses do not have that luxury, but you do need to be certain that your customers are creditworthy because bad debtors can send business ventures to the wall. Be wary of customers who run up large debtor balances and do not be tempted to perform more work for them if there is even a small chance that they may never pay you. Equally, be wary of new customers who place very large orders. You need to be sure that they can and will pay you before you commit to making substantial sales.

Non-payment of outstanding customer balances are commonly a cause of a business venture failure.

It is not always possible, but the best way to improve the cash flow of a business is to get paid for your product or service in advance.

Can you get paid in advance?

Can you charge an engagement fee or take a customer deposit?

An engagement fee serves two purposes. Firstly, it provides some small compensation for time spent if a client decides to never purchase a property using your services. But more importantly, a client who is prepared to pay a small engagement fee, in my experience, is far more likely to be a serious buyer and not a tyre-kicker. Consider ways in which you can make these ideas work for your business too. It is not always achievable to have clients pay for your product or service dependent upon what line of work you are in, but the one thing is certain is that if you do not ask you will not get.

To be successful in business it is vital to understand the importance of cash flow. The primary financial statements of even the largest business include not only an income statement or profit and loss account (which details revenue, costs and profits or losses) and a statement of financial position or balance sheet (detailing assets and liabilities of the business), but also a cash flow statement which shows how funds have flowed in and out of the business over the reporting period.

INVOICING

When you set up a small business, it is a great idea to focus on what you are passionate about because this is what excites you and therefore you will excel at it. However, an entrepreneur must do more than what they are passionate about. In a small business or start-up venture you may need to be the research and development officer, the sales team, the marketing team, the distributions manager, the book-keeper, the accountant, and much more! Of course, you can choose to outsource areas of the business when you have the funds to do some of the tasks which you find tiresome or are administrative in nature. You may not have this luxury in the early days, however.

Billing on a timely basis is vital. You must always get paid for what you do.

One task which people seem to put off more than others is invoicing. And they should not! It is vital to the survival of a small business to ensure that you are paid promptly for what you do. Some entrepreneurs do not enjoy the process of invoicing because they do not like to ask their customers for money. This is the fastest route to failure and your business becoming insolvent. If you do work, you simply must get paid for it, and get paid for it on a timely basis.

One thing which is worth remembering is that if you invoice clients on a timely basis they are more likely to pay it on a timely basis too. If you put off the task for a few weeks or months simply because you don't feel like doing it, you can be sure that your client or customer will be less than motivated to pay the balance quickly too (and who can blame them, really?).

CHASE PAYMENTS!

If a customer owes you money, then you need to chase it – simple as that. In small business, it is common for clients to find all manner of ways to delay payment, but this simply serves to put more pressure on your own cash flows. In short, you either need to be mentally tough enough to chase up late payment of your invoices, or to engage someone else to do it for you.

BOOK-KEEPING, RECORD KEEPING, AND ACCOUNTS

Record keeping is potentially quite dull, but it is essential to do it right for a small business to be successful. Book-keeping is one of the tasks which can easily be outsourced by a start-up business, but I will suggest here that you might want to learn how to do this yourself, at least in the early days. As your business develops you will probably find that your time is better spent elsewhere, but in the early growth phase of your business there can surely be no better discipline than understanding where your business is spending or leaking money and how frequently it is getting paid.

Always maintain a separate bank account for your business.

All business owners should maintain a separate bank account from their personal finances to keep funds separate and to allow them to see how the business is truly performing. There is strong empirical evidence to suggest that entrepreneurs who keep a separate business account are more likely to consider funds within a business account part of the business, whereas those with co-mingled finances tend to view business funds as an extension of their own finances and treat those funds accordingly.

It also looks particularly amateurish to invoice customers using the details of a personal bank account. I recommend keeping a simple spreadsheet of your business bank account and categorising all forms of income and expenditure at the end of each month. This forms the basis of an income statement or profit and loss account, which is one of three key financial statements that should be prepared and reviewed regularly.

Income statement

- Revenue
- Costs and expenses
- Net profit before tax
- Tax
- Net profit after tax

You may not understand how taxes work such as corporation or company tax, or transactional taxes such as Goods and Services Tax (or VAT in Britain), and I do recommend that you learn. At the very least I suggest that you learn the book-keeping skills to keep a close track of what your business is doing in terms of its cash flow. If you are not sure what to do with relation to tax book a simple accrual based upon an estimate of what might be payable based upon a percentage of your profit. That way you should get no nasty surprises when your tax payment falls due at the end of the financial year.

BALANCE SHEET

The other financial statements include a statement of financial position or balance sheet, which details:

- Cash

- Receivables or debtors (i.e. outstanding invoices to be paid by customers)
- Payables or creditors (e.g. loans, supplier liabilities)
- Tax liabilities
- Equity in the business (e.g. share capital)
- Accumulated profits or losses

As the name implies, your balance sheet should balance in accordance with principles of double entry book-keeping. The total of your assets less the total of your liabilities should be equal to your equity, being the initial share capital and the total accumulated profits of the business. And, thirdly you should maintain a …

CASH FLOW STATEMENT

A statement of cash flows reconciles the opening cash balance of the period to the closing cash balance through analysing:

- Opening cash
- Operating revenue received from customers
- Operating expenses paid
- Taxes paid
- Investment cash flows (e.g. purchase of a new laptop or office equipment)
- Financing cash flows such as loans taken out or loan repayments
- Closing cash

For larger companies, there will be a host of other financial information which sits behind the primary financial statements in notes and points of disclosure, but for smaller and start-up businesses the above data covers the bulk of what is to be disclosed in a comprehensive set of accounts. This is where an accountant immediately has an in-built advantage in small business over those who lack financial literacy. It is imperative that you understand the cash flows of your business. Therefore, I recommend either learning the appropriate basic book-keeping skills to prepare the above data or engaging a book-keeper who can spend a few hours each month preparing at the very least the three financial statements listed above. You should also maintain detailed listing or sub-ledgers of:

- Customers or debtors who have still to pay you
- Invoices which you have raised and those which still need to be raised
- Client enquiries and leads to follow up
- Contact details of existing clients

While this may be one of the more tedious parts of being in business, it is imperative to be well organised so that you know which customers to contact and when. Remember that your existing customers can represent repeat business, or when you do great quality work for them, your existing clients can be your strongest points of referral for new leads.

ATTRACTING AND RETAINING THE RIGHT CUSTOMERS

Ask anyone who is experienced in business and they will tell you that one of the key rules of success is to learn what your customer wants and then to exceed their expectations every time.

If you want to be successful in any field, aim to add more value than you are paid for every time.

This is largely about getting your product and the customer service right. Who are your ideal customers? The 80/20 Principle also tells you that:

80 per cent of your company's profits are likely to come from 20 per cent of your customers.

What this means, of course, is that it is important to focus on finding those key customers which will provide most of your revenue streams and profits. Perhaps you do not need to worry too much about the smaller customers? Of course, I acknowledge here that running a successful business is all about reputation, and therefore you should never provide bad service to a customer – it may be better to provide no service at all than a sub-standard one.

Even more than this the 80/20 Principle holds that when you find customers who have been profitable for you, double down on your success. Take a step back and think: how can I find even more customers like these? And don't forget repeat sales! If you are short on leads, customers and sales never forget to go back to your biggest and best clients to see if you can do more business for them. This is certainly true in real estate where customers who have received an outstanding service come back to invest with our company a second and third time, but it is surprisingly often the case in other industries too.

DIFFICULT CUSTOMERS

Unfortunately, the 80/20 Principle also holds that:

80 per cent of your complaints are also likely come from 20 per cent of your customers … and probably not the same 20 per cent of customers which are generating your profits!

There are essentially two ways to resolve customer complaints. Firstly, identify the root causes of complaints, since most of them are likely to come from a minority of problems, and aim to solve or eliminate these issues. Alternatively, considering jettisoning the customers that are causing your headaches, since something in the process is not working correctly, either for you or for them.

The solution is either to trim the bottom – to get rid of those customers that are providing most of your headaches and comparatively little of your revenue – or to find the 20 per cent of problems that are causing 80 per cent of the complaints and eliminate those problems! The answer depends upon the type of business you are in the process of building, but either way you will find that business is far more pleasurable and successful both for you and your clients if you can eliminate the root causes of customer complaints.

DEALING WITH DIFFERENT PEOPLE

One of the most difficult skills for an entrepreneur to master is the ability to interact successfully with a wide range of people. I suspect the reason that I did this reasonably well was that when I was growing up my family moved around a lot, and so I went to four different schools in very different parts of the country. People certainly spoke very differently when I went to selective grammar school and generally came from well-to-do backgrounds, which was unfamiliar to me from when I had previously gone to school at a comprehensive in a less than flash part of town.

Perhaps by necessity I became something of a chameleon and found that I became able to mix comfortably with people from a wide range of different backgrounds. This can be an invaluable skill to have in your armoury as an entrepreneur because a successful business owner needs to be able to work with all different types of people. In an international business like ours, we work with people from countries all over the world too, particularly from Europe, Asia, Australasia and America.

Entrepreneurs need strong and versatile people skills.

How can you work with such a wide range of people successfully without upsetting them or saying the wrong thing? The answer is that you need to be able to quickly establish other people's values to establish a sound relationship with them. People become upset when you unintentionally clash with their rules for living, so you need to first establish and understand what their rules are. This may seem like a tough task, but once you are aware of this fact, successful relationships can more easily be formed on a common ground.

If you get this wrong and continually break or violate the rules and values of other people, they will quickly disengage and may begin to become upset and perhaps resentful. Even if they do not communicate this to you verbally, you may begin to feel or sense their negative vibes. The key to building successful relationships in business and in life is through clarity of communication. Let others know your own rules and values and therefore they can easily meet them, while you can encourage them to be similarly open to presenting their own rules and values. This way you can build trust and work towards win-win outcomes.

BREAKING DOWN INTO SMALL TARGETS

How can it be possible for someone starting out to possibly imagine building a business which they enjoy running without creating undue stress, yet allows money to flow to them? It may not seem at the outset as though such an outcome could ever be achieved. The secret, as you have no doubt guessed from the paragraph header, is to start small and to compound your business – slowly but surely building your expertise and knowledge, leveraging your networks, spreading your profile through word of mouth and client testimonials.

If you are planning to build a business which sells physical products, aim to start small with products that do not require large sums of cash outlay up front or in advance. You will need to find products which can command a reasonably high margin between the costs and the sales price leading to an acceptably high profit on each sale you make.

Look for high profit margins on your products.

If you start out by planning to emulate Microsoft, you will likely fail. Larger businesses have huge advantages and economies of scale allowing them to crush competition through superior branding, advertising and research and development techniques. So how can small business ever compete with larger firms? Through focus, expertise and delivering an outstanding bespoke service. A small, niche business can offer customers a superior experience which the right customers will pay handsomely for. If you were to set yourself a target of increasing the turnover of your business, here are some of the ways in which that could be achieved:

- Mailshot previous clients to ask of they are interested in repeat business
- Give incentives to existing customers to use your service or buy your product again
- Ask existing clients whether they may have any referrals
- Run a short advertising campaign in a trade magazine
- Follow up all previous enquiries that have been made to your business
- Get yourself in the media through sheer persistence!
- Smile and dial – make 100 phone calls to target clients (it may not be easy to do, but it can work well)
- Offer to speak for free at events or at businesses or trade organisations
- Attend networking events or use affiliate marketing
- Frequent social media sites
- Contribute to chat forums
- Find out what larger businesses are doing to win clients – and do it better than them
- And much more …

I have barely begun to consider here of the many possible ways in which you could look to generate new leads. Of course, revenue does not come for free – you then must deliver the service or product! But even just quickly brainstorming some of the methods which could be used to generate new leads makes me realise just how few of them I have ever pursued to the greatest of their potential.

ACTING BIG

While most businesses start out small, it is generally not a great idea to communicate to your clients that you are a tin pot operation, even if that is what you are when you start out. The first point of interaction with your business for many of your customers will be your website. If your website looks cheap, prospective customers will assume that you are cheap. It can of course be patently obvious when you look at the contact details page for a small business when they are pretending to be something that they are not. For example, when there are 23 email addresses including for sales, marketing, promotion, support, information, accounts, media … and so on. If the business has only been in existence for a week, you would hardly be fooling anyone that all these emails are not going to be feeding into one chap's email account.

However, you do not want your business website to be directing queries to amateur-looking email accounts either. As previously noted when we set up our business, in the early days we simply had our own email accounts and a handful of enquiry email accounts on the company website which fed back to us. This represents plenty of accounts for a start-up venture.

When you are starting out in business you may be working from home, but home telephone numbers on a website are generally not a good idea. Potentially you could include your mobile number, although personally I am not convinced that this looks too flash either. One solution in the early days is to use serviced offices which come with a receptionist service included. This way you have a landline number and if you are out of the office then the receptionist can easily forward the call through to your mobile phone.

SERVICED OFFICES

Serviced offices will become increasingly common hubs for small businesses in the future. The basic concept is that you pay a moderate monthly fee for shared office space with common areas, business lounges and work stations where you can base yourself and undertake your work. I found this to be a great solution in the early days of our business and the costs need not be too prohibitive. The idea of working from home may sound appealing but I never much liked the idea – I like to get out and about and there are too many distractions at home anyway, such as satellite television.

A serviced office package should include your business having a unique telephone number which the reception recognises when incoming calls are received – the receptionist therefore knows to answer with your business name. This is infinitely more professional than you needing to answer your phone while driving or standing in the lunchtime sandwich queue. The receptionist can then take a message or forward the call to your work station or to your mobile phone.

If you have clients who want to come in to your office for a meeting, then there may be an additional charge to book a meeting room space. Serviced offices are a great solution for fledgling businesses because they do not cost the earth but they do offer you a range of very useful and professional services.

TENACITY

I was not sure where to put this section of the book, but it does need to be written somewhere so I will simply drop it in here.

If you want to be successful in business, you must be tenacious.

If you are unable to display tenacity in business or self-employment, you will certainly fail to maximise your potential. This may seem a harsh assessment, but it is nevertheless a true statement. In the paid workforce, you can delegate, seek support from colleagues, or if things get tough at work you can simply change jobs. A start-up business venture affords few such luxuries.

It is a truth that in small business you will have good days and bad days when you are fed up and feel like you have had enough. And you will have days when you have arguments, frustrations, disappointments and miserable outcomes. There will be great successes too and days when your heart bursts with pride or excitement! However, as I have already said in this book, it is how you deal with the times of adversity which will ultimately determine the level of your success. Some people do not cope well with the tough times and dark days and their business will inevitably fold.

It is an unfortunate fact that when you decide to chase your dreams and embark upon the road less travelled there will be those who try to hold you back, criticise you or tell you that are doing the wrong thing. This is certainly the case when it comes to investing, and the same is true when it comes to starting out in business.

There will be good days and bad days – it is how you respond to the tough times that counts.

Friends, family and your peer group may be uncomfortable with the idea of you reaching for the stars or taking a different path, partly because it causes them to question their own beliefs and preconceptions and sometimes out of a genuine concern for your wellbeing. Generally, people are far more comfortable with you taking the same well-trodden path as them, and often are more comfortable with the idea of you being a moderate under-performer than a great success.

Think back to how people have reacted in the past towards you being thrifty and saving to achieve a goal – was it often vaguely disapproving, as though you are being something of a spoil-sport? But if you decide to spend hard on a luxury holiday or a big weekend on the town? Why not? Live for today! You are only young once! You need to understand why people react this way – it is generally for their own benefit than it is for yours.

Another thing which you need to be ready for if you do any form of media work is adverse reaction which can range from mild disagreement, to strong criticism to outright abuse or even worse! My advice is to be ready for it, because if you have an online presence you will experience some of the above reactions, and the level of intensity can be ratcheted up the further up the success ladder you move.

To succeed in business, you will need the mental strength to overcome negative feedback.

Some people say: 'If you don't like it, get out of the game' or 'if you cannot stand the heat, get out of the kitchen'. While this is to some extent true, I have found that it does not necessarily help you to cope with negative online feedback very well. Firstly, you need to understand that online comments and feedback are nothing more than simply words on a computer screen. It can feel personal, but when you stop to consider the sad keyboard warrior types who feel the need to abuse people from behind the anonymity of a computer screen, there is little to fear or even concern yourself with at all. The most useful advice I can give you in relation to this, is that each time it happens to you it seems progressively less significant or important.

OTHER BAD DAYS AND GENUINE MISTAKES

When you are self-employed and responsible for all aspects of your business, you must accept that some days you will not get things exactly right which can lead you to feel disappointment, hurt, embarrassment, or end up taking good-natured or bad-natured criticism. Always aim to over-service customers and add more value than you charge for rather than ever risk under-delivering.

Raising your personal profile also comes with many additional pressures. Some people have a fear of public speaking, while others are terrified of appearing on the radio or television or in news print. If you provide online content, you can expect that some people will not like your views and will tell you so. Learning to deal with criticism and mistakes are part and parcel of having a public or media profile.

Learn to accept worst-case scenarios and move beyond your limiting thought patterns.

On some particularly dark days even these mood-changing choices may not feel like they are working. Ultimately to experience ongoing success in business and in life you need to bring this all back to the Pleasure-Pain Principle. You need to link massive pain to the notion of letting negative thoughts and feelings or the criticism of others stopping for from achieving your goals. One simple but effective thought which I kept coming back to was this one basic mantra.

'I will <u>not</u> let this stop me from achieving my goals of being successful in business. Not today and not ever!'

This sounds so very simple, but I found that it has worked for me over the years. Even on the toughest days, decide to learn the lessons and messages that negative outcomes and emotions are sending you and resolve to come back stronger than ever before. Are you going to let small-minded criticism or negative emotions and feelings hold you back from achieving your goals? I will answer that question for you – no, you most sure as heck are not!

GETTING SUPPORT

Setting up a small business can be a surprisingly lonely affair at times! While you may spend much of your time out networking or talking to clients, engaging the services of others or outsourcing – all of which involve some form of human contact – being in business can be an all-encompassing experience and difficult to switch off from.

It is likely, if not close to a certainty, that you will have days when you feel low and wonder whether you are doing the right thing, particularly when you are first starting out in business. I have already discussed earlier in the book that one thing you can do is write for yourself a long list of ways in which you can change your mood when you are feeling low or disheartened. Break the pattern! Go for a walk, or do something different! Some moral support can also be invaluable. Having someone to bounce ideas off or get a second opinion from is priceless.

Surround yourself with like minds and positive, supportive people.

Starting out in business can be extremely testing for anyone and having another person to bounce ideas off or provide another perspective can be priceless. The hours involved in small business can be testing, and many business owners find it very difficult to switch off from work even after they have arrived home from the office. If you do not have a partner or friend to offer you moral support, find some from elsewhere.

Why not join an entrepreneurs group or find a kindred spirit who you can share ideas and problems with? The good news is that when your business goes through lean patches – and it surely will – your failures and mistakes are unlikely to be plastered all over the popular media. Nevertheless, the impact of challenging times can feel just as lonely or even draining at times and at these times a sympathetic ear or some moral support can be so valuable.

INVESTING IN YOURSELF VERSUS INVESTING IN YOUR BUSINESS

It is said that investing in yourself is the best investment you can make, for the positive effects can compound and flow on to your business, relationships, health and happiness. Yet small business owners are often so focused on business operations that they neglect to invest in their biggest asset of all — themselves! Let us take a short look at the principles of investment and how they can be applied to investing in both your business and yourself.

ASSESS YOUR BUSINESS COSTS AND RISKS

Small business owners should think critically about each dollar spent and whether it is working optimally for their business. The balance of investment in your business or yourself to some extent comes back to why you set up your business in the first instance. Was it to follow your passion? To create financial security for yourself through recurring income? Or to build a business which could be sold as a turnkey operation? We will consider here a little about your investment options.

1. Investing in your business

There are other forms of investment in your business besides a bank loan or an equity injection. They include a promotional campaign, a new business equipment or a new staff member. In each case, the key consideration for a small business owner should always be the acceptable risk-adjusted return on your dollars invested. Some types of expenditure or investment may appear to be discretionary, and in these instances, you must make a reasonable assessment of the likely benefits or return on the investment (ROI). If you plan to spend $1000 on an advertisement campaign, the promotion and exposure for your business or brand must add more than $1000 to the bottom line, with an acceptable margin of safety above the cost of capital.

Other forms of investment are mandatory. As an author, I might deem an investment in a laptop as a necessity since I cannot readily write further books without one! In all cases, stick to the fundamental business principle: every dollar invested must deliver an acceptable risk-adjusted return.

2. Investing in yourself

With today's busy lifestyles, too often folk neglect to invest in themselves. Your human capital can be defined as your skills, knowledge and experience, or the sum value of your capacities. A purely academic economist would advise that human capital is a measurement of the skill set of an employee or business owner — the more skills and experience you get under your belt, the greater your earnings capacity or potential. Always remember that as an entrepreneur or small business owner, the greatest asset of all for your business can be your own talent. Investment in yourself can take multiple guises and usually involves some sort of cost, be it a financial cost such as payment to attend a business course or a time cost.

SIX WAYS TO INVEST IN YOURSELF

You may have decided to invest in yourself, but what does that mean? Here are six ways in which you can invest in yourself:

1. Invest in your health

Exercise and good nutrition may involve some time cost, but without wellbeing, only suboptimal results can ever be achieved. The greatest wealth, as the traditional saying goes, is health. Exercising has the great knock-on impact of improving both your physical and your mental health.

2. Grow your skill set

Take courses to improve your skills, particularly in the areas you perceive are your weakest suits. If you detest the idea of public speaking, consider joining a public speaking group. Or find a small business mentor and take a course. While this can sometimes involve a cash cost, a quality business course should generate a return on investment well in excess of the initial cash outlay.

3. Hire help

Hiring help such as a bookkeeper, an administrative staff member or a cleaner may come with a financial cost, but the principle of opportunity cost holds that these may be funds well spent if they free up time for you to focus on more important or productive matters.

4. Choose mentors

One of the greatest shortcuts to success — both in small business and in life — can involve identifying mentors who have already successfully accomplished what you want to achieve, and then resolve to learn from what has worked for them and what has not. Model those who have succeeded, and follow their path. Better still, why not decide to improve upon their path?

5. Read to learn

As Harry S. Truman famously said: 'Not all readers are leaders, but all leaders are readers'. When engrossed in day-to-day travails, it is frequently difficult to see the wood for the trees or acknowledge the bigger picture. This can be particularly so during the early growth phases of a small business, where the business owner can be covering a wide range of roles. Stepping away from the detail of your business to read about new ideas and strategies can be a highly effective blueprint. There are so many wonderful resources written by brilliant business people that it would be a shame if you didn't set some time aside for them.

6. Make time

In an ideal world, we'd all resolve to invest in ourselves, yet many business owners don't because they don't have time. Still, we all have 24 hours in a day and seven days in a week, so we all have the same amount of time! What we mean is that we have other priorities!

HOW TO INVEST IN YOURSELF CONSISTENTLY

Firstly, at the start of each day write a list of bullet points of what you want to achieve, and tick them off as you go. This alone should make your day more effective. Secondly, just for one day, keep a time diary of how you spend each hour of the day. Take a careful note of the time expended on activities of a low yield, such as checking for new emails or idly perusing social media. Through efficiency and focus you should be able to make time to invest in both your business and in your most valued asset: yourself!

The rewards for someone who can transition successfully from the workforce are immeasurable. You can be totally free from a boss or the requirement to work set hours, and be a true master of your own destiny. What a wonderful place that can be! Of course, little in life that is genuinely worth having comes easily, so achieving this goal will require enthusiasm and tenacity. All I can say to you here is, it is worth the effort a thousand times over.

GO FOR YOUR LIFE

In the end, there are two ways to go about building a business. Firstly, the 'top down' approach involves designing a business plan and ideas and then putting them into practice. The 'bottom up' approach is more one of trial and error, seeing what works and what doesn't, and then changing course accordingly.

I recommend that to build a successful business you should aim to use a combination of the two approaches. Firstly, find an established and growing industry that you are passionate about improving, and find out what works for businesses in that sector so that you can model and then improve upon their best ideas. As a small business at the outset you can be nimble and offer a more personalised service. Then, use trial and error to improve and refine your business model as you go. Always aim to learn from your failures as much as your successes. Success leaves clues, and so do failures. Through a process of trial and error, you can gradually grow your business into a powerhouse to be reckoned with.

Chapter 11 Summary

- Making your vacation your vocation is an admirable and exciting goal.
- Consider what you are passionate about. Can you make this your business?
- You can start small in business, perhaps on a part time basis and without the need for significant start-up capital.
- Look for established industries that are growing, and observe carefully what the successful businesses are doing well.
- Businesses either sell products or services – the services economy is growing fast in developed countries.
- In small business, as in all business, cash flow is king!
- There will be down days and tough times, so finding moral support helps.
- Never, ever give up!

CHAPTER 12
THE
HOME
STRAIGHT

WHY OWN A HOME?

There are a couple of key considerations in with regards to this key question. Firstly, it makes sense to plan to own an unencumbered home, because then you no longer must pay rent. If the home that you live in happens to go up in value, then that's great for you too. There is another aspect to consider here, and that is whether you should also invest in property as an asset class for building wealth.

Whether property is for you or not will probably be intuitive. Some people love property – I know that I do – and others don't feel it is for them. This is a key consideration because, to be blunt, whether you think real estate is a good investment is very likely to shape your results. Why? Because people who believe that property is a good investment are prepared to undertake the right research to ensure that they buy the right property which they can hold on to without worry in perpetuity. Location, location, location as they old mantra goes.

People who are not in tune with property as an investment spend too much time sweating over whether prices will rise or fall, and when the market sinks into a stick patch – which happens regularly through market cycles since these always repeat – they panic and sell at the most inopportune moment, being the bottom of the market cycle.

A PLACE TO CALL HOME

Whether to strive to buy a home as young as you can is a very personal choice. For generations past it was widely accepted that the smart thing to do would be to buy a house as young as you could afford to do so, and then to trade up the housing ladder from there over time. This strategy generally served folk well, particularly through the days of higher inflation and rising household leverage which pushed house prices higher.

Today the decision is not quite so clear cut for younger people. In part this is because house prices are higher today than they once were, and the deposit gap can be challenging. Furthermore, while in decades past it was common to work in one career and often even for only one employer, today most of us can expect to work for several employers and possibly even in several careers. In turn this means that many of us expect to relocate several times – if not many times – through our working lifetimes.

One of the things about property is that the transaction costs of buying and selling are high, and if you move too often the costs can start to drag you back financially. It is at least worth considering whether you are better off renting in the early part of your career while you build a portfolio of investments. A word of warning, though. It is no use renting if you are not going to save the difference! One of the benefits of home ownership is that it can act as a form of forced saving.

AN UNENCUMBERED DWELLING

Despite what I have discussed above ultimately it is likely to be beneficial for most people to own an unencumbered home at some point in their lives, for the simple reason that this means you will not have any rent to pay. In financial terminology, it is said that owning a home saved you 'imputed rent'. One of the problems with renting forever is that in desirable locations rental amounts payable tend to rise over time. It's compounding again, but this time it's working against you. For this reason, the strategy that I deployed, and which you might want to consider if you are not already a homeowner, is to rent while you are younger and then buy a home suitable for your purposes when you reach a position of financial freedom.

Adopting this approach means that you avoid the risk of spending heavily on somewhere to live only to have to sell in due course because you need to relocate for work. It also means that if you can buy your home once and do so for cash, you do not need to take any mortgage debt which is not tax deductible – 'bad debt'. Of course, there is more than one way to skin a cat, and you can use a combination of strategies. The so-called best practice of buying the most expensive house you can possibly afford and then locking yourself into 25 years of mortgage repayments to plough your way through the debt repayments may not be the smartest thing to do. Down that route lies no freedom!

REAL WORLD

In the real world, the cornerstone of personal finances for most people in countries like Australia or the United Kingdom, where home ownership rates are high, is the family home or place of residence. In other words, most people are in one of these categories:

- (i) living mortgage-free in a home;
- (ii) paying down the mortgage on a home; or
- (iii) saving a deposit for a home.

The practical tips detailed above suggest that regardless of which category you are in, having a forced saving or investment strategy is a sound idea.

a) Mortgage free

If you are in the fortunate position of being in this category, it might be useful to continue making payments as though you still do have a mortgage into a separately allocated investment account. After all, you have already proven that you can spare that amount per month! You might also consider using some of the equity in your home to borrow to invest in a sensible manner. Using gearing to invest is a powerful means of accelerating returns, but should only ever be done moderately and sensibly, and obviously individual circumstances and risk appetites differ so consult a financial advisor where appropriate.

b) Paying off a mortgage

Think back again to the practical points listed above. Can you accelerate repayments on your mortgage debt? Can you make repayments fortnightly instead of monthly? Mortgage debt does not get treated so favourably for tax purposes in Australia or the UK, so paying down the mortgage more quickly is a strategy that works well for many.

c) Not a homeowner

If you live in a big capital city, it's likely that we'll see more people over time in this category, which leads to a decision to be made as to whether you even aim for home ownership at all in the first instance. Although admittedly my wife and I have lived in some of our properties over the years, generally I've been a renter because I realised I could accelerate my returns much faster by renting a smaller property and hammering the investments while I was younger. This strategy can work miracles if you can adhere to the principles of forced saving and re-investing gains.

However, you should caution against listening too much to those advising you to sit back casually and wait for an inevitable property correction. In cities like London and Sydney, that has generally over time turned out to be poor advice. It's far better to be proactive rather than reactive, whether your goal is home ownership or not. There's no one size fits all when it comes to personal finance, but obviously if you're not planning to be a homeowner, you'd want to avoid spending the remainder of your income, so implementing an automated saving and investment strategy is likely to be a great idea.

OTHER CONSIDERATIONS

One of the reasons that I wasn't keen on buying a home when I was younger is that I hate paying too much in the way of tax, and if you are going to move house frequently then you will inevitably be slugged with plenty of stamp duty and other transaction costs. By now it should be clear that I'm not that keen on the idea of paying too much tax or the inefficiencies of buying and selling property.

In fact, although my wife and I have lived in several of our properties for a period before letting them out as investment properties, neither of us has ever sold a property, having learned the valuable lesson of buy and hold. That said, the principal place of residence can have one benefit from a taxation perspective, the home generally being exempt from capital gains tax.

Chapter 12 Summary

- Renting when you are younger can make sense, and even help to accelerate your plan.
- Ultimately a coherent retirement strategy should plan for an unencumbered dwelling.
- Stamp duties and transaction costs act as a disincentive to move house too frequently.
- Home ownership can have the benefit of a capital gains tax exemption.

CHAPTER 13
WINNING!

YOUR NEW MONEY MANTRAS

The early part of this book focussed on deleting some of your old beliefs about money, and installing some powerful new money mantras that should form the basis of your plan to win your own race. As a reminder, here are your new money mantras.

Money mantra #1: I will make compound growth work for me and not against me!

Money mantra #2: I cannot earn my way to financial freedom from a salary. I will need to invest!

Money mantra #3: I will not waste money needlessly on capital gains taxes!

Money mantra #4: Buy and hold investing is generally more efficient than trading.

Money mantra #5: I will eradicate all bad debt, permanently!

Money mantra #6: I will acquire assets, not liabilities!

Money mantra #7: Think three times before spending money needlessly.

Money mantra #8: I will eventually find a way to save at least 20 per cent of my income!

Money mantra #9: Once dumb money recognises its limitation it is no longer dumb.

Money mantra #10: The most powerful force you can use is compound interest.

If you can learn to focus on these ten money mantras and worry less about what your peers are up to, then you will automatically be on the way to achieving better financial results.

WINNING THE RACE

We are nearly at the end of the book. Remember, with your new plan you are going to accelerate to the finish and not limp over the line! I didn't want to write about my own story too much in the early part of the book. After all, my journey has been fascinating for me, but you might not find it so enthralling!

Looking back over the journey I have experienced to date, what strikes me most is how the combination of leverage and compound growth in both business and investing can begin to see your results take on a life of their own. From very humble beginnings, I began to see results that I could barely have dreamed over only a matter of years before. Compound growth tables are interesting in a theoretical way, but when you begin to see how these principles used in practice can make a dramatic difference to your life, and to your family's future, there is a huge amount of satisfaction to be gained from this.

I noted earlier in the book that once you 'get' compound growth, you will wish you had started saving and investing sooner. This may seem disheartening at first. Don't be disheartened! I've come to understand that you should be grateful for the past, and everything it has taught you, and optimistic about the future. Life is all about the journey, not just about a certain destination! Moreover, don't begrudge others their success. There is plenty to go around, and don't forget that those who receive a bigger head start from their parents or an inheritance will never be able to achieve the same sense of satisfaction as someone that ticks off their life goals one by one, from the ground up.

FREEDOM!

Although this is ostensibly a book about money and investing, it's about designing the life you want to lead and then putting in place a framework that can allow you to achieve what you want. Through spending less than you earn and investing in a portfolio of quality assets that you can hold onto for the very long term you can begin to get compound growth working in your favour so that eventually you will be less reliant on your pay cheque. Then over time you can begin to think about making your vacation your vocation, which is to say becoming self-employed or starting a small business in a field that you are truly passionate about.

Financial freedom is a worthy goal. Can you imagine having no further anxieties or concerns about your personal finances? Can you imagine waking up each morning excited at the prospect of doing what you are passionate about? These are surely things to aspire to! In saying that, I do believe that it is important that you have a higher purpose for your investing goals rather than simply building wealth for the sake of so doing.

If you lack a vision or higher purpose of how you can make a difference with your new-found wealth then one day you may wake up and find that you have achieved your financial goals, and what happens then? Only you determine the answer to that question, but it may be that you find that your success feels somehow hollow. This book is no soapbox for the merits of tithing or charitable giving, only to note that true wealth is about more than the number of dollars in your bank account, and finding a means of contribution is indeed a worthy goal.

Thank you for reading this book. I hope that you found it interesting, motivational and enlightening! If you enjoyed the read, don't forget to leave a testimonial wherever you came across it. Now it's over to you. Start by setting yourself some inspiring and thrilling goals, and start the snowball rolling. By using time as your friend, you can and will win your own race!

What next?

- If you are interested in learning more about finance, economics, and the markets. I recommend checking out my daily blog at **http://petewargent.blogspot.com**

- Please contact me via my blog page to let me know how you are getting on!

REFERENCES

Chapter 1 – Running your own race

1 – *The Dirtiest Race in History: Ben Johnson, Carl Lewis and the 1988 Olympic 100m Final*, Richard Moore (Bloomsbury, London, 2012)

2 – ibid.

Chapter 2 – Financial fitness

1 – Parliament of Australia, aph.gov.au

2 – ibid.

Chapter 4 – Warming up

1 – *Awaken the Giant Within: How to Take Immediate Control of Your Mental, Emotional, Physical and Financial Destiny!* Tony Robbins (Simon & Schuster, New York, 1991)

2 – ibid.

3 – ibid.

4 – *Take a Financial Leap: The 3 golden rules for financial and life success*, Pete Wargent (Big Sky, Sydney, 2015)

5 – *Trading for a Living: Psychology, Trading Tactics, Money Management*, Dr. Alexander Elder (John Wiley & Sons, USA, 1993)

6 – ibid.

7 – ibid

Chapter 5 – On your marks

1 – *The Warren Buffett Portfolio: Mastering the Power of the Focus Investment Strategy*, Robert G. Hagstrom (John Wiley & Sons, USA, 1999)

Chapter 6 – Get set: Asset allocation

1 – *Outliers: The Story of Success*, Malcolm Gladwell (Hachette, New York, 2008)

2 – ibid.

3 – ibid.

4 – *The Warren Buffett Portfolio: Mastering the Power of the Focus*

Investment Strategy, Robert G. Hagstrom
(John Wiley & Sons, USA, 1999)

5 – *Jason Zweig, Commentary in The Intelligent Investor: The Definitive Book on Value Investing* (Revised Edition), Benjamin Graham, (Harper Collins, New York, 2003)

6 – ibid.

7 – ibid.

8 – '3 main lessons of psychology' – Dan Ariely, danariely.com, March 5, 2008

9 – ibid.

10 – *Predictably Irrational: The Hidden Forces That Shape Our Decisions*, Dan Ariely (Harper Collins, New York, 2010)

11 – *Get a Financial Grip: a simple plan for financial freedom*, Pete Wargent (Big Sky, Sydney, 2012)

Chapter 7 – Go! Time to invest

1 – *Get a Financial Grip: a simple plan for financial freedom*, Pete Wargent (Big Sky, Sydney, 2012)

2 – *The Intelligent Investor: The Definitive Book on Value Investing* (Revised Edition), Benjamin Graham, (Harper Collins, New York, 2003)

3 – ibid.

4 – *Motivated Money: Invested well? Compared to what?*, Peter Thornhill, (Motivated Money, Sydney, 2003)

5 – ibid.

Chapter 8 – Profitable property investment

1 – Office for National Statistics, ons.gov.uk

2 – Australian Bureau of Statistics, abs.gov.au

3 – Reserve Bank of Australia, rba.gov.au

4 – *Economics, Planning and Housing*, Michael Oxley, (Palgrave McMillan, UK, 2004)

Chapter 9 – Control the controllables

1 – *The 80/20 Principle: The Secret to Success by Achieving More with Less*, Richard Koch (Nicholas Brealey, 1999)

2 – ibid.

3 – Michaelyardney.com

4 – *Out of My Comfort Zone: The Autobiography*, Steve Waugh, (Penguin, Australia, 2005)

5 – *Black Box Thinking: Why Most People Never Learn from Their Mistakes - But Some Do*, Matthew Syed (Penguin, New York, 2015)

Chapter 10 – Accelerate: Pedal to the metal!

1 – *Think and Grow Rich*, Napoleon Hill (Skyhorse Publishing, 2016)

2 – *Who Moved My Cheese?*, Spencer Johnson M.D., (Penguin, New York, 1998)

3 – *Economics, Planning and Housing*, Michael Oxley, (Palgrave McMillan, UK, 2004)

GLOSSARY OF TERMS

Asset protection – a type of planning designed to protect assets from claims by creditors, such as lawsuits or other claims.

Bad debt – in business a bad debt is a receivable which cannot be recovered from a customer or another debtor. Today the term bad debt is also used to describe consumer or personal debt which is taken out for purposes other than investment i.e. debt which does not generate investment returns.

Bid-rent theory – a geographical economic theory which holds that greater competition for land closer to the centre of a city will result in higher land rents in inner locations.

Blue chip – investments of the highest quality such as a quality, reliable company with strong and consistent earnings. In residential real estate, this may refer to dwellings in premium suburbs in prime locations.

Brokerage fee – a fee charged by an agent to facilitate transactions between buyers and sellers.

Bull trap – a false signal which appears to show that a declining trend has reversed when in fact it is only a blip or interruption in a continuing downtrend.

Business angels – angel investors tend to be affluent or high net-worth individuals who provide funding for small businesses or start-up ventures often in the form of convertible debt or a share of the equity of the business.

Buy and hold – strategy of buying assets with the intention of retaining them for the long term which works on the theory that despite volatility the long-term trend in markets is upwards.

Buyer's agent – a real estate advocate or agent who works solely on the behalf of the buyer.

Capital gains tax – a form of tax which is levied on the sale on profit of an asset or property net of legitimate deductions.

Capital growth – the increase in market value of an asset of portfolio of assets over time.

Central bank – the national bank which provides financial and banking services for the government of a country and its commercial banking system. The central bank is also responsible for implementing monetary policy, issuing the currency and financial stability.

Compound growth – the year-on-year growth rate of an asset or investment over time. Where a consistent growth rate is achieved, gains will snowball over time.

Counter-cyclical investing – an investment strategy which aims to profit from the business cycle by buying when sentiment is at a low ebb and assets cheap.

Defined benefit scheme – a pension scheme where the employer determines the final benefit to be paid based upon age, seniority, earnings and years of service.

Defined contribution scheme – pension scheme whereby the employer and employee make regular contributions, with the final pension balance to be determined by investment returns net of costs as opposed to a pre-determined benefit.

Dividends – a sum of money paid regularly by a company to its shareholders out of its profits.

Dividend re-investment plan or DRP – a scheme which allows participants to re-invest their cash dividends through acquiring further shares in the company at each dividend date.

Dividend yield – a dividend expressed as a percentage of the prevailing share price.

Dollar cost averaging, or averaging – an investment strategy whereby the investor places a fixed dollar amount into a given investment on at regular intervals (e.g. monthly) regardless of what is occurring in the financial markets.

Economic moat – a competitive advantage of a business or company which is difficult for competitors to copy or emulate. Economic moats can take the form of a powerful brand or a niche technology, for example.

Entrepreneur – one who sets up a business venture with the aim of generating a profit.

Equity – may have several definitions, including the value of shares in a company, or the funds in a business contributed by the owners plus retained earnings or profits (also known as shareholders' equity). A real estate investor refers to equity as the value of a property asset less mortgage debt against the asset.

Equities – securities such as stocks and shares which carry no fixed interest.

Focus investing – a strategy which aims not to diversify too widely instead focusing on a few individual stocks or investments.

High frequency trading (HFT) – high speed computerised trading systems or platforms which use powerful computers and algorithms to execute a high volume of orders.

Human capital – the total of skills, knowledge and experience for an individual or an organisation.

Index funds – a type of fund designed to mimic the performance of a stock market index.

Inflation – a general increase in prices and corresponding fall in the value of a currency.

Inflation hedge – investment in hard assets with intrinsic value such as oil or natural resources. Can sometimes apply to certain real estate investments dependent upon type and location.

Kaizen – Japanese business philosophy of continuous improvements in business practices and personal efficiency.

Leverage – the use of borrowed capital or funds for the purposes of some form of investment with the expectation that the returns will exceed the interest payable.

Listed investment companies or LICs – a closed end investment scheme in Australia. Investors can buy shares in LICs which in turn hold investments in a range of other companies and trusts.

Liquidity – the availability of liquid or tradable assets in a market or company.

Management expense ratio (MER) – a measurement of what it costs a listed investment company or fund to operate, calculated by dividing annual costs by the value of assets under management.

Net worth – the value of total assets less total liabilities. Sometimes also referred to as net wealth.

Opportunity cost – the loss of other alternatives when one choice or strategy is made or taken.

Overtrading – engaging in or taking on more business than can be sustained by the resources available.

Pareto's Law – a principle which notes unequal distribution between inputs and outputs. For many phenomena 80 per cent or more of the outputs are accounted for by 20 per cent or fewer of the inputs.

Price-Earnings ratio or PE ratio – an equity valuation multiple calculated as price per share divided by earnings per share.

Yield – a percentage measurement of income from an investment calculated as the current annual income divided by the capital value.

Yield trap – investment strategy deficiency caused by a failure to understand the difference between the importance of yield (a spot figure calculate as a percentage terms) and ongoing income.

Zulu principle – the concept that it is possible to become an expert in a specific field relatively quickly through focusing on one area of expertise.

ALSO BY THE AUTHOR

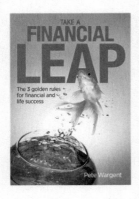

Get a Financial Grip: a simple plan for financial freedom (Big Sky, Sydney, 2012).

Rated in the Top 10 Finance books of 2012 by Money Magazine and Dymocks.

'Pete Wargent gives you a simple plan for achieving financial freedom at any age' – Chris Gray, author and TV presenter of Your *Money Your Call* and Channel 10's *The Renovators.*

Four Green Houses and a Red Hotel: new strategies for creating wealth through property (Big Sky, Sydney, 2013).

'Writing a book which is new and interesting yet relevant to our changing times is a tough gig. But Pete Wargent, one of Australia's finest young financial commentators, achieves this in his book, sharing a wealth of information. I have been investing for over 40 years and read nearly every book on property ever written, yet still learned new concepts in this book.' – Michael Yardney, Amazon #1 best-selling author and Australia's leading expert in wealth creation through property.

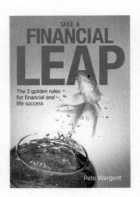

Take a Financial Leap: The 3 golden rules for financial and life success (Big Sky, Sydney, 2015).

'A blueprint for escaping the rat race and achieving financial freedom … by someone who's actually managed to do it!' – Michael Yardney, Amazon #1 best-selling author and Australia's leading expert in wealth creation through property.